PEACEKEEPERS AT WAR

Peacekeepers at War

A Marine's Account
of the Beirut Catastrophe

MICHAEL PETIT

faber and faber
BOSTON • LONDON

Published by
FABER and FABER, INC.
50 Cross Street
Winchester, MA 01890

Printed in the United States of America

LIBRARY OF CONGRESS CATALOGING IN PUBLICATION DATA
Petit, Michael
PEACEKEEPERS AT WAR.
1. Beirut—History.   2. Bombings—Lebanon—Beirut.
3. United States, Marine Corps—History.
4. Beirut International Airport.
5. Lebanon—History—1975-   6. Petit, Michael.
7. United States. Marine Corps—Biography. I. Title.
DS87.P485   1986   956.92   85-27517
ISBN 0-571-12545-X

Design and typography by Jim Cook
SANTA BARBARA, CALIFORNIA
Printing and binding by Edwards Brothers, Inc.
ANN ARBOR, MICHIGAN

To the Marines
who lost their lives in Lebanon

And we are here as on a darkling plain
Swept with confused alarms of struggle and flight,
Where ignorant armies clash by night.

—MATTHEW ARNOLD

CONTENTS

Acknowledgments

THIS IS A deeply personal book. The three years I spent in the Marine Corps were among the most difficult, bitter, and frustrating years of my life. They were also among the most exciting and rewarding. I began to write this book as a catharsis to purge the feelings of irrevocable loss and to come to terms with the haunting memories of an exact moment of time in my life—6:23 A.M., Sunday, 23 October 1983. But as the work began to grow, I realized a more important purpose: to disclose the story of the Marines in Lebanon so that their sacrifice will never be forgotten.

Although some characters are composites, the Marines in this account are real; they swear and sweat and cry. Some of their names have been changed to honor and protect their privacy and families, but the events presented are, to the best of my knowledge, true. No single Marine was in the position to completely understand the complexities of the United States' involvement in Lebanon, and as daily tragedies in that war-torn nation continue, it grows increasingly unlikely that anyone will ever be able to entirely identify the motives behind the conflict.

There are several Marines with whom I served in Lebanon that I would like to thank for sharing their memories of Beirut with me. All friends I will never forget, they are Lance Corporal Thomas Armstrong, Corporal Dennis Comfort, Corporal Daniel Conrad, Sergeant Kevin Dewey, Corporal Harry Freeman, Lance Corporal Kevin Funderburk, Corporal David Green, Corporal Mathew Lacey, and Corporal Bradley Ulick.

Several other friends offered their encouragement during the writing of the manuscript: Katherene Boe, David and Carolyn Geiser, David Gilliland, and Joseph Landkamer.

I would like to thank Louise Richardson, my editor, for her generous help, thoughtfulness, and patience.

My heartfelt appreciation goes to Ronald Kitts for his help with the maps.

I owe a special debt of gratitude to Alexander Blackburn, professor of English at the University of Colorado at Colorado Springs and editor of *Writers' Forum,* for his invaluable help and advice in preparing the manuscript for publication.

I especially want to thank Tamar E. Abrams. She was there from the beginning, and without her encouragement and support, I would have stopped writing half a dozen times.

Finally, I want to thank my parents. Their love helped me through the dark days of Lebanon.

—Michael Petit
Colorado Springs, Colorado
October 1985

I
Beginnings: The Thoreau Theory

1

A T TWENTY-TWO minutes past six on a still Sunday morning in October 1983, a Mercedes truck with a yellow railed bed and a gray cab entered a parking lot two hundred meters south of the four-story Battalion Landing Team headquarters at Beirut International Airport. The truck was a commercial model with no markings. Its civilian Lebanese license plate number was 508292.

The vehicle circled the parking lot twice, accelerated to a breakneck speed, and stormed through a concertina wire barrier. It then raced between two sandbagged sentry posts, went through an open gate in an iron fence, and crashed through the sergeant of the guard's fortified guardhouse. The driver, a martyr for his Muslim cause, was observed to be smiling as he sped to his death. Mounting a single step at the front of the building, the truck rocketed to the center of the first-floor lobby and detonated.

Two hundred and forty-one American lives were lost in the explosion.

In the basement of a building fifty meters to the north, I lay awake on my cot beneath a tent of green mosquito netting. The texture of that moment will remain with me always: the soft, methodical breathing of those sleeping around me; a beam of early morning sunlight sparkling with dust motes slanting into the room from the doorway; the smell of dank air.

I've always thought that in the moments before a disaster I would feel a precognition, a sense of dread or foreboding that would prepare me for cataclysm. Actually, the feeling was of laziness and pleasantness. Sundays were usually relaxing days highlighted by a picnic and a spirited game of volleyball. This Sunday would be spent digging the broken bodies of comrades from beneath tons of rubble.

In a split second my mood went from complacency to trepidation. The explosion was tremendous. Deafening, the deep rumble shook the building to its foundation and catapulted me from my cot. The air was full of choking dust that made it almost impossible to see and breathe.

"What the hell happened?" someone shouted.

"Is everyone okay?"

"The building must have taken a direct hit!" Although artillery barrages directed toward Marine positions had become commonplace in the previous months, none of the explosions had ever been this loud and violent.

I scrambled to my feet, grabbed clothes, and furiously dressed. A gut-wrenching knot of fear cramped my belly. I pulled on my boots, stuffing in the laces rather than waste the precious seconds it would take to tie them. Throwing on the flak jacket and helmet I wore everywhere, I snatched my M-16 rifle and ran into the larger room next to mine. In the gloom I could see Marines, friends with whom I had lived in close quarters and grown to know during the past six months, frantically dressing and shouting to one another. Some were already running up the basement stairs to their posts.

My mind went on automatic. I raced up the two flights to ground level knowing only that I had to get to my assigned position, the Bravo command post. The long passageway leading to the exit that faced the Battalion Landing Team building was dense with smoke. The ceiling had collapsed, and going that way was impossible. I spun around the corner and dashed for another exit. Shards of glass crunched under my boots as I stepped through a broken window. I ran east as fast as I could toward the secondary command post.

Communicators were setting up equipment and establishing their nets inside. I climbed down the long metal ladder that gained access to the basement. Confusion reigned as more personnel arrived; no one knew what had happened.

"All the buildings got hit simultaneously," someone speculated. "Our building, the BLT, the MSSG." But that didn't sound possible; there had been only one explosion.

Someone else suggested that an artillery round had hit the Battalion Landing Team building. "I saw it," he said. "The top floor is gone."

After several minutes of infuriatingly useless conjecture, one of the communicators passed the word that a car bomb had blown up at the BLT. That the building had been completely destroyed and so many killed was unfathomable.

"We need shotguns!" a voice from street level called down. Whenever our jeeps drove into the city or to one of the line companies at the perimeter of Beirut International Airport, one or two Marines rode along as a show of strength and as protection from snipers.

"I'll go!" I volunteered. I had to know what was happening. Being blind in the basement was torture.

I scampered up the ladder behind two other Marines and squeezed through the small window at the top. A chest-high sandbag wall protected the entrance to the command post, and as I ran around it I could see there was room for only two shotguns in the jeep.

"Where are you going?" I yelled.

"Alpha Company," the driver answered as the jeep sped away. "To reinforce the line."

Alpha was the rifle company guarding the nearby Lebanese University library. Strategically situated on a hill overlooking the village Hey es Sellom, the company received incoming sniper rounds and rocket-propelled grenade attacks almost daily. If we're being pulled and sent to the perimeter as reinforcements, I thought, things are turning to shit fast.

I rested my forearms on the sandbag wall. The sky was blue, and white clouds floated placidly by. It was too beautiful a day to think about death; but I was scared of dying.

The staff sergeant in charge of the enlisted troops climbed the ladder from the basement. He was worried. We were used to being shot at, but nothing like this had ever happened. I told him about the reinforcements and asked if I could run to the BLT and see what had happened. "I'll come straight back," I pleaded.

He nodded assent. The "steel pot" on my head jostled as I ran toward the Battalion Landing Team building. My camouflage flak jacket was constricting, making it difficult to breathe, and sweat trickled down my armpits and back. I sprinted around the corner of the main command post and past the diesel generators that provided our power. A long row of dogwood concealed my view of the BLT headquarters. Fist-sized clumps of concrete littered the ground.

I stopped running when I saw the line of cots with the twisted bodies of Marines piled upon them. The seminude men were partially covered with ponchos and bloodied blankets. Arms and legs dangled grotesquely. We've got to get them medical attention, was my first frantic thought. It did not occur to me they were dead.

I rounded the bushes and saw the carnage for the first time; the four-story Battalion Landing Team building had been reduced to a smoldering heap of rubble no more than fifteen feet high. I couldn't believe what I was seeing. Cedar trees on the hill overlooking the building were broken and stripped of greenery. The heavy, acrid smell of explosives hung in the air. The ground was covered with pieces of building, and a gray pallor of dust lay over everything like a shroud. Boots, seabags, scraps of paper, running shoes, torn sleeping bags, parts of uniforms, and shredded mosquito netting were strewn everywhere. Jeeps had been crushed and tossed about like children's toys. The plywood outhouses twenty meters from the building were splintered, and macabre streamers of toilet paper fluttered from the trees.

Everywhere I looked I saw bodies sprawled in gruesome positions. One Marine, still in his sleeping bag, hung from a tree. The decapitated body of another was under a jeep, his arms twisted at an impossible angle. The legs of yet another jutted from beneath a huge slab of concrete. The screams of agony from those still living seared like a red-hot knife. I stared at the building feeling helpless and numb.

That was the most devastating moment of my life.

         ✺   ✺   ✺

> Ready to fight,
> Ready to kill!
> Ready to die,
> But never will!

I screamed the chant at the top of my lungs along with the other boot camp recruits in my platoon. It was 1982, and I was standing at the position of attention next to a metal bunk bed the drill instructors wanted me to call a "rack." Standing there in boxer shorts and a T-shirt, thumping my chest like a crazed Tarzan, I felt ridiculous.

Senior Drill Instructor Staff Sergeant Auden stood at one end of the long squad bay, his face stern, biceps bulging like thighs, and uniform immaculate. I waited for his next command in the nightly ritual. My boots, running shoes, and shower shoes were precisely lined up underneath my rack, and my neatly folded uniform was ready, so I could jump into it instantly in the morning.

"Prepare to mount," the senior drill instructor bellowed in a clipped military tone.

"Prepare to mount, aye, aye, sir!" we shouted as one voice.

"Ready. Mount!"

We flew into our racks, knowing if we weren't fast enough we'd be jumping in and out of them again and again. As I lay on top of my green wool blanket at the position of attention, arms pinned to my sides and feet at a forty-five degree angle, I had a moment to reflect.

Everyone in boot camp had a good reason for being there, except me. The big, goofy-looking kid from Ohio had graduated from welding school and couldn't find a job. He was in the Marine Corps for the work experience. The guy who slept in the rack beneath mine had signed up in a patriotic fervor. Better dead than red, he was there to defend truth, justice, and the American way. The seventeen-year-old high school dropout, three racks down, had joined because, he said, after some reflection, "I don't have nothin' better to do." Even his reason seemed better than mine.

Most of the recruits were fresh out of high school. I had graduated eight years earlier, gone to college, and moved on to jobs in the big, wide world. Joining the Marines was something you did at eighteen, not twenty-five, and I was embarrassed that my family and friends would discover this blot on my life. I enlisted without conferring with anyone and wrote home only after I had arrived at the Marine Corps Recruit Depot at Parris Island, South Carolina.

Never having been a physically active person, I wondered why I was doing pushups until I couldn't do any more, situps until my muscles begged for mercy, and running until I threw up.

"Excuses are like assholes," our drill instructors were fond of telling us. "Everyone has one, and they all stink." It would have been easy to find an excuse to quit, but one reason I had joined the Marine Corps was to undergo a trial by fire. I have always had the naive notion that in order to become a mature male, it's necessary to experience a rite of passage. Tribal males have it easy. At thirteen they journey into the jungle as boys, hunt and slaughter a wild boar, and return as men. We have no equivalent in our society. Too much had been given to me, and I needed to earn a place within myself. I thought boot camp would be that rite of passage, but little did I know the rite was a year and a half in my future.

And so I forced myself to climb ropes and forge over walls on the obstacle course, slash and jab at the hanging dummies on the bayonet course, and crawl through muck on the infiltration course. This is what I wanted, I had to keep reminding myself.

Staff Sergeant Auden turned off the overhead fluorescents one bank at a time. In the distance the haunting strain of taps began to play. As if on cue, we paid homage to one of the Corps' heros by shouting, "Good night, Chesty Puller, wherever you are!" After a basso profundo hum, we launched into the "Marine Corps Hymn."

> From the Halls of Montezuma,
> To the shores of Tripoli.
> We will fight our country's battles,
> In the air, on land and sea.
> First to fight for right and freedom,
> And to keep our honor clean.
> We are proud to claim the title
> United States Marine.

In the dying echo of the song, the reasons I had joined no longer seemed to matter. For that moment at least, I couldn't help but feel proud to call myself "Marine."

The senior drill instructor thundered, "Ad-just," drawing out the first syllable. Only then was I allowed to break the position of attention and slide under the covers. Sleep came quickly, and at five o'clock the next morning I was screamed awake for another long day of learning what it meant to be a Marine.

🌿   🌿   🌿

The Marine Corps was not my first choice for a rite of passage. Two weeks before enlisting I had gone to the south of France with intentions of joining the French Foreign Legion. Many youths in America, at one time or another, have had a fantasy of joining the Legion; most outgrow it about the time they stop playing Cowboys and Indians.

I, however, still maintained a romantic idea of what joining would be like, no doubt from having seen Gary Cooper in *Beau Geste* one too many times. I wasn't running from anything: no lost loves, debts of honor, or tragic happenstance—traditional reasons for joining the French Foreign Legion. I simply thought it would be wonderful to sit astride a camel on Saharan sands and wear a dashing uniform while watching the sun slowly sink in Technicolor splendor.

Another image of the Legion appealed to me as well, one of ruthless fighters who feel the adrenaline of combat surging through their veins—men living on the edge while experiencing life to the full. I was big on living life to the full back then. I wanted to cram as much as possible into the years allotted me, and I developed a philosophy of maximum participation I called the "Thoreau Theory."

Over a century before Jack Kerouac founded the Beat Generation and Timothy Leary advised the world to "turn on, tune in, and drop out," Henry David Thoreau moved into the woods to live simply and to simply live. Such behavior was considered radical, and few contemporaries understood why Thoreau had seemingly abandoned society. Likewise, two years later when he returned from his cabin at Walden Pond, he was met with misunderstanding. As an explanation, Thoreau wrote, "I left the woods for as good a reason as I went there. Perhaps, it seemed to me that I had several more lives to live, and could not spare any more time for that one."

I seized upon Thoreau's idea of "several lives to live" and adopted it as my creed. Life is too short, and spending all of it doing the same thing, being the same person, was repugnant. Perhaps I wanted to live a life found only in B-movies, but I wanted to savor everything the planet had to offer. I wanted a life of adventure and excitement. I wanted to contemplate the universe while atop the Himalayas in Nepal, smuggle coca leaves from Bolivia and arms into Afghanistan, study primitive tribes in New Guinea, and traverse the continental divide on horseback while living off the land.

Being a soldier of fortune, a French Foreign Legionnaire, was one of the lives I wanted to live. I knew it would be tough, but that fit into my idea of undergoing a trial by fire. I didn't want, however, to be a legionnaire for the rest of my life. Even the most exciting of lives becomes jaded with repetition, and I didn't want to spend too much time being any one thing. I figured two years as a ruthless killer for hire was about right. Then it would be on to the next life, the next adventure.

The Thoreau Theory sounded good while working mundane jobs in the United States. But standing in front of the French Foreign Legion outpost in Marseilles, France, on 23 January 1982 at ten o'clock in the morning was an entirely different matter.

I wasn't disappointed I had traveled to Marseilles. Located in southeastern France, the port city makes up the western most boundary of the Côte d'Azur, the French Riviera. Marseilles, unlike many of the cities along the Mediterranean, is not a resort town but a working city of shipping and industry. It may lack the elegance of Monte Carlo and the beauty of the palm-lined boulevards of Nice, but the city more than makes up for any void with a magnificent ambience.

I was staying in the gut of Marseilles in a cheap hotel near the train station. My room was barely large enough for the sagging bed, and the sink in the corner had gone on strike years before. A bare light bulb dangled from the ceiling on a wire. The communal toilet was in a cubbyhole down the hall, and to take a shower I had to trudge down the street and pay six francs.

But in the early mornings I could stand by the open window of my room and smell the aroma of baking bread. Old men congregated daily in a nearby park to play *pétanque*, an unruly bowling game that caused a lot of shouting. Along the waterfront in the evening, prostitutes staked out corners to separate sailors from their money, while dimly lit nightclubs played sultry music. I was soaking up atmosphere and everything seemed new. Even the clamor of traffic drummed a fresh beat. Marseilles more than fulfilled all of my expectations as a gateway to adventure.

Finding the Legion outpost in a city of millions wasn't easy. Maps aren't made with the potential mercenary in mind, and after hiking miles without luck, I was forced to use the tourist information office. I had been trying to avoid tourist spots. The sound of an American accent would be enough to send me scurrying in the opposite direction. Tour buses teeming with Bermuda shorts and cameras ruined the mood of adventure.

I was trying to play it incognito like a spy on a secret mission. I didn't want to be spotted as a tourist, and I didn't want anyone, not even a stranger, to know my legion plans. I was convinced they would think I was insane.

With reluctance I entered the tourist information office. It was packed, and I waded through people to get to the counter. The clerk, a young girl with a page-boy haircut, didn't speak English. I pulled a grubby piece of paper from my pocket on which the French words for "foreign legion" were printed. She couldn't read them. I yanked my trusty French/English dictionary from my back pocket, pointed at the word *légion* and then quickly thumbed to the word for foreign, *étranger.* I felt as though I were wearing a neon sign that shouted my plans, imagining every eye in the place on me. The girl still didn't understand.

"Idiot," I mumbled under my breath. That she understood and gave me a piercing look.

I pointed a little more emphatically at the words in the dictionary and at my map thinking that might help. No such luck. The clerk finally turned to another girl in the office and spoke at length in French. I had a horrifying picture of the two asking everyone in the office to explain what I was trying to find out. Then all would have a good laugh at the crazy American tourist who wanted to join the French Foreign Legion. Fortunately, the second girl managed to interpret my wild gesticulations and circled the outpost's location with a red pen.

"*Merci,*" I gasped as I rushed for the door. I couldn't get out of the office fast enough. I headed for the area the girl had indicated on the map. The Legion outpost was nearby on the western side of the city close to the Vieux Port, the old port. The large, rectangular-shaped anchorage was filled with sailboats and trawlers, and fishermen stood on the quay crying the virtues of their catches. High on the hill to the south stood the Notre Dame de la Garde, a tower crowned by a thirty-foot gilded statue of the Virgin Mary.

The Legion outpost was on Boulevard Charles Livon at Fort Saint Nicolas, a jumble of buildings surrounded by a parapet. A simple wrought-iron sign over a gate announced *Légion Etrangère.* I must have paced back and forth half a dozen times before I finally mustered the courage to enter.

The place seemed deserted. Then two legionnaires exited one of the buildings and strutted past me and out the gate. Their tan uniforms were neatly pressed; each wore a white kepi, the typical French military hat with a horizontal visor and a round, flat top, perched smartly on his head.

I took a deep breath, thinking, here goes, and strode into the building. I turned left down a hallway and entered a dimly lit office. A legionnaire sergeant noted my presence with suspicion. Unlike the athletic legionnaires I had seen outside, a portentous belly hung over his belt.

"I want to join the Legion," I said.

He rattled off sentences in French. I was at a loss.

"Enlist," I said.

"*Un moment.*" He left the room.

The office was decorated with pictures of legionnaires. Some were sitting in jeeps with exotic weapons cradled in their arms. Others wore paratrooper gear. One young legionnaire was crawling through mud with a snarl on his face.

A map on an easel showed legion outposts throughout the world. French Polynesia in the Pacific, Guiana in South America, and the island of Corsica in the Mediterranean were marked with red. I can definitely have a life of adventure, I concluded.

The sergeant returned to the office and handed me a thin binder. Inside were descriptions of the Legion in five languages. I read the English section while the sergeant dug paperwork from his desk. My eyes opened wide when I saw the words "five years." Enlistment was for a minimum of five years. French citizenship would be mine after successful completion, but five years seemed a terribly long time.

The Legion would give me more than a new lifestyle. I would be required to give them all my personal identification. My passport, driver's license, wallet, even my clothes, would be taken. I would be given a *nom de guerre*, a pseudonym that in French means "war name." I would be giving up my identity. After initial processing, no one would ask my real name or why I had joined the Legion. I could literally become a different person and live another life.

What a great way to learn French, I thought. I'll have it pounded into my head for the next five years. Giving up everything to join the French Foreign Legion was wildly romantic. The idea of becoming a different person appealed to me, but I wondered if the reason was because I didn't like myself. Perhaps I was running away from something—me.

A little voice in the back of my head began to murmur "This is crazy!"

The legionnaire's attitude was perfunctory. He looked bored and didn't care whether I signed away the next five years of my life or not. I took the contract he offered. It was written in French, and I didn't understand a single word. He handed me a pen. I almost signed in a sudden surge of "go for it" but hesitated.

"I think about it more. I come back later," I said in a combination of French, English, and hand gestures.

The sergeant shrugged a *c'est la vie.* I think he knew I wouldn't be back.

I left the office and stepped outside into the bright Mediterranean sun. I had chickened out, pure and simple. Even at the very moment I made the decision not to join I knew I would always regret it. Nothing could ever compare to the romanticism and adventure. Joining was something I knew I would have been able to look back upon from a twenty-year perspective and always be happy I had had the experience.

As I walked back to my hotel through the narrow streets of Marseilles I wondered what I should do with the rest of my life. I still felt the need to undergo a trial by fire by doing something tough. I hadn't discounted the Thoreau Theory, and I still wanted to experience the military as one of my multiple lives.

The United States Marine Corps flashed into my mind. Not as tough as the Legion and certainly not as romantic, they were always looking for a few good men. I wasn't sure if I fit in that category, but I felt certain they would accept me.

Joining the Marine Corps was so ordinary though. I was giving up adventure for the mundane, excitement for the commonplace, and the chance to experience combat in the French Foreign Legion for the tedium of the desk job I was sure awaited me in the Marine Corps. Little did I know I was very much wrong on all counts.

I walked into the Air France office on Rue de la Liberation and bought a plane ticket to New York. The following night I was in a taxi riding through the cold, dark streets of Manhattan.

🏵   🏵   🏵

"Sit down and make yourself comfortable," the recruiter said. He shook my hand with warmth and zeal. "The Marine Corps has some great job opportunities to offer."

I was in America, the land of prepackaged hard sell. The Marine recruiter was a young, ardent sergeant obviously committed to the product he was selling. He extolled the great things the Corps could do for me and told me of the excellent employment opportunities once I got out.

I tried to interrupt his spiel with "Where do I sign?" but he was determined to convince me to enlist. I didn't want to explain I wasn't looking for training and that money and benefits weren't the reasons I had crossed the Atlantic to join. The Thoreau Theory suddenly seemed an odd rationale, and I knew he'd never understand it.

Finally realizing he had a live one on the hook, the recruiter took piles of paperwork from a file cabinet. I completed form after form in triplicate. The Marine Corps wanted to know every detail of my life, and I was grilled about everything from illicit drug use to the birth dates of my parents.

Once I finished the initial screening to the recruiter's satisfaction, he sent me to the Armed Forces Enlistment Station for more. I took batteries of intelligence and aptitude tests. I walked like a duck in my underwear along with fifty other men in front of a bored doctor. I was fingerprinted and photographed. I swore several times that I was neither a homosexual nor a communist.

Late in the afternoon of the third day, I stood with a group of earnest young men and women before an American flag. Like all the American fighting men who had come before us, from the greatest generals in World War I to the lowliest grunts in Vietnam, we raised our right hands and repeated the oath for which so many have died.

> I do solemnly swear that I will support and defend the Constitution of the United States against all enemies, foreign and domestic; that I will bear true faith and allegiance to the same; and that I will obey the orders of the President of the United States and the orders of the officers appointed over me, according to regulations and the Uniform Code of Military Justice. So help me God.

The irrevocable step had been taken. I was on my way to adventure.

2

*Y*OU ARRIVE IN *darkness. They plan it so confusion and the feeling of alienation are at a peak. Disoriented by a long bus ride, you are lost, not knowing which way lies the civilian world and freedom. You cross a causeway surrounded by swamp. Surrealistic trees draped with Spanish moss flash by in the headlights, and you fear you have entered a nightmare.*

The bus passes the first squat building, turns right, then left, then right; you are quickly lost in the ensuing maze. Voices mutter, "We're here! Wake up!" and you begin to feel the anticipation and fear of having arrived at the unknown. The bus squeals to a stop in front of a wooden two-story building. A sergeant in uniform steps on the bus and tells you to move quickly but orderly to the yellow footprints painted on the street. You scamper out and join milling passengers who finally sort themselves into long ranks. The bus roars away, and the last bit of the familiar has vanished with it. You have arrived in a place where you are no longer in charge of yourself, a place where your destiny is in the hands of others. You are at boot camp, Parris Island, South Carolina.

         ✿   ✿   ✿

"The first thing you will learn here at Parris Island is to do what you are told, when you are told, and as quickly as you can. Is that understood?" A gruff drill instructor stood before me, feet spread wide, hands on his hips. He spoke the well-practiced speech rapidly.

"Yes, sir," a few recruits said.

"The first and last word out of your mouth is 'sir.' Is that understood?"

"Sir, yes, sir."

"What?"

"Sir, yes, sir!" we shouted.

"You are no longer slimy civilians able to wear your communist blue jeans and hippie hair. You are now subject to the military judicial system, which means, among other things, that you can be tried by military courts-martial. Is that understood?"

"Sir, yes, sir!"

"You are required to obey all lawful orders and perform all assigned duties without question. Is that understood?"

"Sir, yes, sir!"

"Good. Now you can join *my* Marine Corps." I thought it odd of the drill instructor to claim the Marine Corps was his, but I soon learned that everything did belong to him—including me.

The drill instructor ordered us to move quickly inside the receiving barracks. We trotted single file through a doorway over which a sign read, "Through this portal pass prospects for the world's finest fighting force."

Neat rows of old-fashioned wooden school desks filled most of the long room. We began to sit.

"Who told you to sit?" the drill instructor demanded. "Get on your feet!" I scrambled to my feet with the others, watching the drill instructor intently.

"Get your eyes off me," he commanded. "You will look directly ahead at all times. Is that understood?"

"Sir, yes, sir!"

"Sit!"

We sat en masse.

Processing began. While clerks behind a long metal table took care of paperwork, I was instructed to write my platoon number on myself so I couldn't forget it. I scrawled a big 3009 on the back of my left hand with a black magic marker.

I addressed a government envelope to my parents and enclosed the message the drill instructor had dictated. "I have safely arrived at Parris Island and will write to you soon. Your son." I could imagine my parent's dismay when they received it. My mother, I knew, would cry. Her southern sensibility shocked, she wouldn't be able to understand why I had joined. My father would be hurt because I hadn't come to him before making the decision.

I listed the serial numbers of my bills and traveler's checks on a form and placed the money in a blue nylon bag, which I was ordered to carry on my shoulder like a purse. The drill instructor screeched "Hurry up!" after each command. Anyone making a mistake or falling behind was threatened with vague promises of death and dismemberment. I wanted to explain that if he would only stop yelling I could do everything a little more efficiently, but looking into the drill instructor's harsh and impatient eyes, I decided that wouldn't be a very good idea.

One by one, we were ordered to stand before the metal table and were unceremoniously searched by one of several drill instructors. Magazines, candy, cigarettes—all considered contraband—were thrown into a brightly polished trash can. One drill instructor roared when he found a package of condoms. "You won't be needing these, recruit!" he bellowed.

The drill instructor eyed my passport and traveler's checks with scorn as I stood before him. "Where did you think you were going?" he demanded. "Las Vegas?"

I started to speak.

"Shut up!" he thundered. "Get it and go!" I scooped up my possessions and fled to my seat.

The check-in procedure took much of the night. Except for one brief interval when I was allowed to place my head on the desk I didn't sleep.

At first light, we filed into a back room to have our heads shaved. Hair was the last mark of our individuality, and as the civilians in line before me emerged from the room tentatively touching their newly bald heads, they had become recruits indistinguishable from one another. Gone was the cockiness with which some had entered. A seemingly tough kid sidled past me with tears in his eyes.

The barber buzzed my head like shearing wool from sheep. As my hair fell to the floor the last shreds of my humanity fell with it; I felt humiliated and violated. Thoreau, I thought, I hope you appreciate this.

After a mess-hall breakfast, we were marched to uniform issue. I stripped off my civilian clothes along with the other recruits, rolled them into a tight bundle and placed them on a wooden counter partitioned into sections. Armed with a bar of soap and wearing the shower shoes they had issued me, I entered a large room with fifty shower nozzles attached to overhead pipes. A large ring hung from each.

A stocky Marine wearing a camouflage uniform entered the room. "My name is Sergeant Miller, and I'm one mean son of a bitch." He slammed the two-by-four he was carrying against the wall. "Is that understood?"

"Sir, yes, sir!" echoed from the walls.

"You will do nothing until you are told to do so. Is that understood?"

"Sir, yes, sir!"

"Screw up and you'll get the broad side of this!" The splintering sound of wood smashed against brick made me jump. "Is that understood?"

"Sir, yes, sir!" I shouted for all I was worth.

"Hang your towel from the pipe." I removed the towel from around my waist and draped it over the pipe.

"Grab the ring." I grasped the ring. "Pull."

Cold water gushed on my head and made me gasp.

"Stop. Soap your head."

I ran the bar of soap over my head and face and washed the bristles of my scalp with my free hand.

"Stop. Pull." Soap stung my eyes as I rinsed.

"Stop. Soap your chest." Miller took us through the shower one body part at a time, grinning luridly. I was convinced he was a sadist. He finally ordered us to towel off and line up for uniform issue.

I was given four sets of camouflage utility uniforms, four hats, two pairs of black leather boots, green socks, a webbed belt with a brass buckle, boxer shorts, and T-shirts. I stuffed everything into a seabag and went back to the wooden counter to dress in my new clothes. Miller strode across the counter top, banging the two-by-four to punctuate his yells admonishing us to hurry. I flinched each time he slammed the board against the counter, thinking he might whack me if I didn't move faster.

During the following days the processing continued. I took more intelligence and aptitude tests and went to medical for a battery of vaccinations. I shoved my civilian clothes into a paper grocery sack and deposited it in a warehouse for safekeeping. I named my next of kin on life insurance forms in case I dropped dead and again answered the same questions I had already answered at the recruiting station.

I slowly learned what would be required of me once my platoon was picked up by the drill instructors who would actually train us. The Marine Corps has its own language. Much of it is derived from naval traditions, and I began to master its vocabulary. A mop was no longer a mop but a *swab*. The wall became a *bulkhead*, the floor a *deck*, and stairs were *ladders*. The bathroom was a *head*, and the hats we wore were *covers*. Candy, which we never saw, let alone ate, was *pogy bait*. And I quickly learned never to call a drill instructor a "DI." That stood for "dumb idiot" and would bring a sharp rebuke.

Initial indoctrination complete, I loaded my seabag onto a flatbed truck and marched behind it to another part of the island to meet my drill instructors. Training would finally begin in earnest.

"Move! Move! Move!" the three drill instructors screamed as we unloaded sea bags from the truck. I had arrived at H Company, Third Recruit Training Battalion, and from that moment until the moment I left several months later, my every action was carefully orchestrated.

The drill instructors ran us ragged as we clamored up the stairs to our third deck squad bay. Our names were read from a roster, and we were assigned a rack and a number. I was to be known as "48." I dumped my gear into an olive-drab footlocker, which was aligned on a yellow line painted on the deck. I would spend many hours standing with my heels on that same line at the position of attention. I clamped a combination lock on my footlocker and, on order, slid it under my rack.

"Zero!" one of the drill instructors shouted. He was an exceptionally muscular man with a demeanor that glared orneriness. I looked around not knowing what he wanted. "When you hear the word 'zero' you are to immediately stop what you are doing and say, 'Freeze, private, freeze.' Is that understood?"

"Sir, yes, sir."

"Zero!"

"Freeze, private, freeze."

"Zero!"

"Freeze, private, freeze." We shouted the words again and again until they were burned into our brains.

The drill instructor then made us sit in something he benignly called a "school circle," which was to us a torture chamber. The entire platoon was jammed, unable to move, into as small a space as possible at one end of the squad bay. He introduced himself as Senior Drill Instructor Staff Sergeant Auden. The other two Marines were Drill Instructor Sergeants Clark and Bivitalski. They were to be our gods for the next twelve weeks.

Boot camp was like a tent gathering of religious zealots. The chorus of "sir, yes, sir" after the drill instructors' every utterance was like an affirmation of the faithful. We screamed "Hurrah!" in answer to motivation checks and were told we were part of the few who, if deemed worthy, could earn the hard-won titles Leatherneck, Devil Dog, and Marine.

We spoke in the third person. Referring to ourselves as "the private," we never addressed a drill instructor as "you."

"I am not a 'you,' " he would bellow. "A 'ewe' is a female sheep. Do you want to fuck me, private?"

I made the mistake only once.

Before speaking to a drill instructor, even to use the toilet, we had to ask permission.

"Sir, the private requests permission to speak, sir!" A gangly recruit stood trembling before Sergeant Bivitalski. With a sadistic smirk pasted on his face, Bivitalski took particular delight in toying with us.

"What do you want, private?"

"Sir, the private requests permission to make a head call, sir!"

"No!"

"Sir, the private requests permission to make an emergency head call, sir!"

"Emergency is it? No! Go away!"

"Go away, aye, aye, sir!"

The recruit shouted, "Left, right," as he stepped back. "Good morning, sir!" He executed an about face and tried to hold it until the entire platoon was allowed to make a head call an hour later. He wasn't successful. Bivitalski named him "Pisser" and was out to get him after that. Pisser left the platoon a week later in tears, recycled to the beginning of training in a new platoon and with new drill instructors.

Discipline was the drill instructor's creed; everything boiled down to that one word. Staff Sergeant Auden took himself very seriously, and anyone who smiled or found something humorous in one of the many rituals we performed was in big trouble. Auden was teaching skills necessary for us to survive in combat, and he never let us forget it.

The psychological pressure was tremendous. Marine Corps theory is that before a man can be built, the identity he brought with him must first be destroyed. Physical incentives were added to the formula to break us, and when we showed a lack of discipline we found ourselves in the so-called rose garden doing pushups, situps, and jumping jacks in rapid succession. Hot and sweaty, we were ordered to roll in the soft sand or throw it into the air until we were covered with dirt. The experience was humiliating.

Like lumps of clay, we were carefully shaped by the drill instructors into clones of the perfect Marine. We were to be fit, well-disciplined automatons who immediately and unquestioningly obeyed all orders. Nothing short of that was acceptable.

Not everyone was able to handle the molding process well. One recruit purposely put his head through a plate-glass window. Another threatened to kill himself.

"Go ahead, chicken," Sergeant Clark taunted. "Just don't get blood everywhere."

A kid named Rivera refused to do anything. While suicide threats and even self-inflicted injuries might be expected, the drill instructors couldn't understand someone refusing to play the game at all.

Rivera was yelled at unmercifully, but he only sustained a broader grin. One day Rivera was gone like the other misfits, but his unresponsive behavior was further degraded. The senior drill instructor conducted a special burial ceremony in his "honor." Rivera's footlocker was slowly carried down the length of the squad bay by four recruits while Auden sang a haunting funeral march. M-16 rifles loaded with blanks were fired nine times. "Too bad the shots weren't in Rivera," Auden proclaimed.

I hated what they were doing to me. At times I felt remote, like an observer of events I couldn't control. My mind was a blank as I watched myself react without feeling. I knew when I joined the Marine Corps I would be forced to change, but confronted with the person I was becoming, I rebelled against the idea.

Yet, slowly, so imperceptibly I didn't notice, I began to respond to the training. I started to shout "Hurrah!" with fervor. As my physical stamina increased, I actually began to enjoy the long formation runs as we sang:

> Mothers of America send us your sons,
> So we can do the job that you haven't done.
> Teach them discipline,
> Teach them courtesy,
> Teach them respect now,
> That's the Marine Corps way!

Even being yelled at and humiliated was no longer the ordeal it once was. I was being remade into the Marine Corps image.

When graduation finally came, I was proud of my accomplishment. Joining the Marine Corps was the toughest thing I had ever done, and I felt I had endured and survived my sought-after trial by fire. Being called a Marine for the first time by the commanding general of Parris Island made me stand a bit taller. I didn't know it at the time and would have told anyone they were insane for suggesting it, but boot camp would prove to be the best part of belonging to the Corps.

After graduation, I received orders from Headquarters Marine Corps in Washington, D.C., which assigned me to Parris Island for duty. I had enlisted with no guarantees, preferring to let fate decide what job I would have and where I would go. I had made a crucial error during the testing procedures by demonstrating my typing skills, and I was sent to the Recruit Administration Center to work as a clerk. There would be no adventure for me I thought: no far off lands, no assaulting beaches from landing craft, no rappelling combat-ready from helicopters.

Instead, I became one of the people doing paperwork, as bus after bus pulled up in the middle of the night ejecting potential Marines. I saw the me that had arrived at Parris Island mirrored in their frightened faces. I saw the me I had become in the recruits who neared the completion of boot camp, marching proudly in formation, all snap and polish, unhesitatingly obeying every command.

Parris Island is a three-year duty station, and I would be there for my entire enlistment. I was bitterly disappointed. Several months into boredom and frustration, I noted with interest that U.S. Marines had been sent to help evacuate Palestine Liberation Organization (PLO) fighters from Lebanon. The front page of the local newspaper carried a picture of a Marine speaking with a French Foreign Legionnaire.

That legionnaire could be me, I kept thinking as I chastised myself for not having followed my original plans. I was stuck in the desk job I had predicted when I was in Marseilles, instead of living a life of adventure. I had no one to blame but myself.

How startling true for me the maxim is that you should never wish for something unless you truly want it because that wish might come true. I unexpectedly received orders directing me to join the 24th Marine Amphibious Unit. Three months later, a year and two months after joining the Marine Corps, I was on board a United States warship advancing full speed ahead toward Beirut, Lebanon.

II
Rules of Engagement

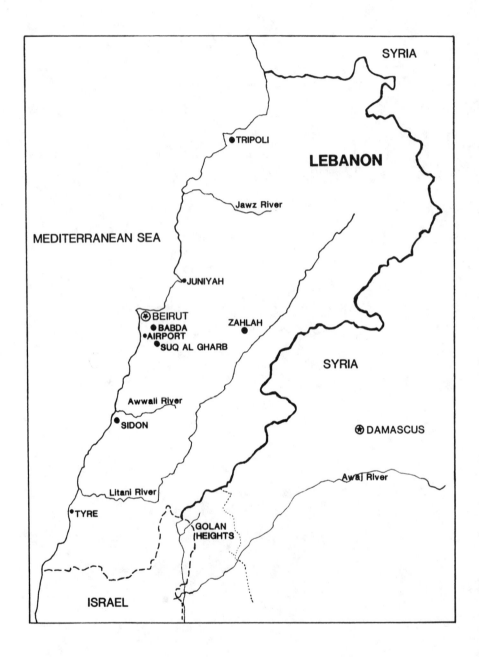

SYRIA

●TRIPOLI

LEBANON

Jawz River

MEDITERRANEAN SEA

●JUNIYAH

⊛BEIRUT
● BABDA
●AIRPORT
●SUQ AL GHARB

ZAHLAH
●

SYRIA

Awwali River

●SIDON

⊛ DAMASCUS

Awaj River

Litani River

●TYRE

GOLAN
HEIGHTS

ISRAEL

3

A MARINE AMPHIBIOUS UNIT (MAU) is the smallest and most responsive of the Marine Corps' Marine Air Ground Task Forces (MAGTF) and has four components: a command element (to which I was assigned), a ground combat element, an aviation combat element, and a combat service support element. Our mission was to assume responsibility as the United States Contingent of the Multinational Peacekeeping Forces in Beirut, Lebanon. Under the command of the Navy's Sixth Fleet in the Mediterranean, we were the muscle behind U.S. foreign policy in the Middle East.

The ground combat element is the heart of a MAU, and the Battalion Landing Team 1/8 (1st Battalion, 8th Marines; the BLT) was attached to us. Most of the eight hundred men in the unit were grunts, the underappreciated combat Marines on the front lines and in foxholes. They were divided into four companies—Alpha, Bravo, Charlie, and Weapons—and were reinforced by tanks, artillery, combat engineers, amphibian assault vehicles, and reconnaissance personnel. The remainder of the Marines in the BLT belonged to Headquarters and Service Company and provided the combat troops with communications, motor transport, supply, and administrative support.

The Marine Medium Helicopter Squadron (HMM) 162 was the aviation combat element of the 24th MAU. Marines in aviation are known as "wingers" and are often thought of as falling below Marine standards, especially by the ground element. Frequently denounced as belonging to some other Marine Corps, wingers are viewed as less disciplined than the grunts. They wear their hair a bit longer, never put polish on their boots because of the fire hazard around helicopters, and usually wear greasy coveralls instead of squared-away uniforms. Flight mechanics, however, spend long hours keeping the helicopters in flying shape, and rather than being less disciplined than the ground troops, they simply have less time for games.

The MAU Service Support Group (MSSG) 24 was our combat service support element. They were tasked with supply maintenance,

motor transport, medical and dental services, and military police
support. But everyone thought their sole reason for existence and only
worthwhile job was to make sure we received mail from home.

Marines have been continually deployed in the Mediterranean since
1947, with units rotating about every six months. MAUs usually train
much of the time by practicing amphibious assaults with troops of the
various nations lining the Mediterranean in order to improve combat
readiness. The Marines are embarked aboard three to five U.S. Navy
vessels known as an Amphibious Ready Group. This ARG, or MARG
as the one in the Mediterranean is called, joins with a MAU to form an
Amphibious Task Force. Between training operations, the Marines and
sailors of the force make frequent port calls to emphasize U.S.
commitments to the region.

My deployment, however, was to be different. We weren't going to
the Mediterranean for training but for the real thing. The Marine
Corps' mission is to be on call for "such duties as the president may
direct," and we were directed to secure positions near Beirut International Airport, maintain a presence in support of the Lebanese
Armed Forces, and provide a stabilizing influence for the government
of Lebanon.

Sending a peacekeeping force to Lebanon was not a new idea.
Marines first waded ashore on 15 July 1958 on orders from President
Dwight D. Eisenhower. Religious strife divided Lebanon, threatening
to precipitate a bloodbath between Muslims and Christians. Lebanese
President Camille Chamoun requested the presence of U.S. troops
because of internal chaos and threats of foreign aggression. Syrian
infiltrators were entering Lebanon and aiding the rebel cause with men
and material. A coup in nearby Iraq sparked U.S. fears that anti-
communist Lebanon would soon fall, and Marines, historically charac-
terized as "The First to Fight," once again found themselves on
foreign soil. The U.S. intervention permitted the Lebanese to form a
new government that included representatives from each of the major
political parties. Peace was temporarily restored, and the last American
troops left the country on 25 October 1958, three months after arriving.

History repeats itself with subtle variations. Twenty-four years later
the Marines were back, ostensibly for the same reasons as in '58.
Lebanon was again a country at war with itself.

Lebanon is smaller than the state of Connecticut, covering an area

120 miles from north to south and 20 to 55 miles from east to west. The country consists of four regions extending eastward from the coast: the Mediterranean lowlands; the Lebanon Mountains, also known as the Chouf; a fertile valley called El Bekaa; and the Anti-Lebanon Mountains. Syria borders the north and east, Israel the south. Christianized in the fourth century A.D., the population remains, in contrast with most Arab nations, almost fifty percent Christian. Arab Muslims conquered Lebanon in the seventh century but never fully Islamized it, and the mountains became a sanctuary for persecuted Christian and Muslim sects as well as political dissidents.

Modern Lebanon is a mosaic of religions: Maronites, Greek Orthodox, Catholic Melchites, Gregorians, Jacobites, Nestorians, and Protestants are among the Christian sects; non-Christians include Shiite, Sunni, Druze, and Jews. Recognizing this volatile mixture, the National Constitution of 1926 required that the allocation of government jobs and appointments be based on religion. The National Covenant, an unwritten gentleman's agreement worked out by Christian and Muslim leaders in 1943, established the practice of selecting a Maronite president, a Sunni premier, and a Shiite speaker of parliament.

Lebanon was granted independence from France during World War II, and since that time Lebanese life and politics have been dominated by the rivalry between the Christian and Muslim communities. The problem was aggravated by the influx of thousands of Palestinian refugees displaced by Israel's declaration of sovereignty in 1948 and by the Six Day War in '67. Southern Lebanon became a base for PLO guerrilla operations against Israel. Israel retaliated with commando raids. When the Christian-dominated Lebanese government sought to restrict PLO activity, the Palestinians, who until then remained neutral in the conflict between Christians and Muslims, sided decisively with the sons of Islam. Civil war erupted.

Beirut, the capital of Lebanon, was a shining star in a region dominated by authoritarian and militaristic regimes. The city was a banking center for the Arab world's fabulous oil wealth and a shelter for intellectual and cultural freedom. The beautiful sand beaches and wide boulevards lined with shops and hotels made the city a popular attraction for Western tourists. Nineteen months of civil war, however, left the Lebanese economy shattered and the "Paris of the Middle

East" in ruins. Fifty thousand were dead and another three hundred thousand destitute.

The civil war officially ended on 15 November 1976 with the entry of an eight-thousand-man Arab peacekeeping force. Yet, for the next six years, Lebanon remained a battleground. Hostilities between the PLO and Israel continued, and on 6 June 1982 Israel launched a major offensive against the Palestinian fighters entrenched in the villages of Lebanon. Despite a cease-fire arranged by U.S. special envoy Philip Habib, Lebanon teetered precariously on the brink of further disasters. The situation the 32d Marine Amphibious Unit, commanded by Colonel James Mead, found upon entering Lebanon on 25 August 1982 necessitated executing a previously negotiated PLO withdrawal. While I was busy processing recruits on Parris Island and longing for excitement, President Ronald Reagan told the Marines:

> You are about to embark on a mission of great importance to our nation and the free world....You are tasked to be once again what Marines have been for more than two hundred years—peacemakers....I expect that you will perform with the traditional esprit and discipline for which the Marine Corps is renowned.

The Marines left twenty-one days later, on 10 September, after a successful evacuation of PLO fighters and returned to normal duties in the Mediterranean.

The respite from Lebanon was brief; the government soon requested that the Marines return to establish order as part of a multinational force that ultimately included British, French, and Italian troops. Lebanese President-elect Bashir Gemeyal had been assassinated by a car bomb and was quickly succeeded by his older brother, Amin. In the ensuing chaos, Israeli forces took control of West Beirut to prevent a regrouping of the PLO. The following day, Lebanese Christian militiamen entered the Sabra and Shatila Palestinian refugee camps south of the city and massacred hundreds of civilians, including women and children, to avenge the death of their president. The Lebanese Armed Forces (LAF) were clearly unable to maintain control of Beirut and the surrounding countryside. Marines of the 32d MAU once again landed in Lebanon on 29 September 1982, beginning an ill-fated expedition that was not to end until a year and a half later.

The Marines were welcomed warmly by the populace. The major

threat the Marines faced was from accidental detonation of over one hundred thousand pieces of unexploded ordnance around the airport. On 30 September, the Corps grieved over the first fatality of the peacekeeping mission; Corporal David Reagan was killed while clearing a minefield.

The 32d MAU was relieved on 29 October by the 24th Marine Amphibious Unit, commanded by Colonel Thomas M. Stokes, Jr. He reported:

> This is really no different than it's been for the past 207 years. Whenever there is a crisis, one of the quickest ways to stop it is to send in the U.S. Marines. We helped restore order and discipline back on the old sailing ships in 1775, and that's precisely what we'll do in Beirut.

Three days later on the first of November, a three-hundred-pound car bomb was remotely detonated on a highway over which the Marines received supplies from the ships offshore. The event signaled that the Marines were not in as much control as they had thought. Restoring order would not be a simple task. The terrorist attempt was an amateurish failure, but I was not amused when I received orders to join the 24th MAU when the unit returned from Lebanon and accompany it on its trip back.

At this time, Marines began training the Lebanese Army through the U.S. Office of Military Cooperation. It was hoped that Lebanon could establish a viable military entity capable of assuming the security responsibilities for Beirut and eventually for all of Lebanon. Radical Muslim sects began to perceive that the American role was no longer one of inactive presence but one of active assistance. Joint patrols with the Lebanese Armed Forces were conducted, which only served to emphasize those perceptions.

Israeli-American relations in Lebanon were extraordinarily tense. U.S. policy, at the request of the Lebanese government, was to prohibit the movement of armed personnel other than members of the Multinational Force or Lebanese Army through Marine positions at the airport. Some Israeli officials accused the United States of using the Marines as a buffer for Palestinian guerrillas.

On five separate occasions in January, Israeli Defense Force patrols attempted to cross Marine checkpoints. Each time the patrols were denied entry to the American area of operations.

The confrontations came to a head on 2 February at nine o'clock in the morning. Marine Captain Charles B. Johnson halted a column of three Israeli tanks headed directly toward his position at the Lebanese University library and denied them access. He asked to speak to the senior Israeli officer. A lieutenant colonel emerged from the lead tank and stated he was going to proceed despite the captain's refusal. The tanks began to move forward toward U.S. positions. Johnson, his .45 pistol loaded and at the ready position, jumped atop the tank and told the officer to stop. After speaking to a higher authority by radio, the Israeli lieutenant colonel backed down and ordered his tanks to depart.

The Marines at Parris Island cheered the man who had stopped a tank single-handedly and wore their Captain Johnson "If you come through it will be over my dead body!" T-shirts with pride. The U.S. increased pressure on Israel to pull out of Lebanon, and as I said my good-byes to South Carolina, I wondered if maybe someday I'd be a hero too.

The 24th MAU sailed for home on 14 February, relieved by the 22d MAU, again commanded by Colonel Mead. The Marines of the 22d MAU participated in a rescue operation during a severe blizzard in the mountains east of Beirut during late February, rescuing Muslims and Christians alike. Despite this, some Muslim factions thought they detected a subtle shift in U.S. policy from a pro-Lebanese attitude to one pro-Christian.

The French came under fire later that month when several jogging soldiers were sprayed by automatic gunfire. Two soldiers were injured in the incident. In another attack, a grenade was tossed into a French jeep patrolling West Beirut. Another soldier was wounded.

In March, a twelve-man Marine patrol was surprised by a grenade thrown from a building in a community north of the airport. Five Marines received minor wounds, and defensive measures, such as varying patrol routes and times, were begun. The Marines also began carrying loaded magazines in their weapons, although they were not allowed to chamber a round.

I reported, as my orders directed, to Headquarters, 24th Marine Amphibious Unit at Camp Lejeune, North Carolina, in late February to meet the advance party returning from Lebanon. A few days later the entire unit arrived with tales of action in Beirut. The newcomers like myself listened with wide-eyed anticipation to the war stories of the "mau-maus" (Marines who had already completed a deployment, or float).

I was assigned to the S-3 operations section, and although I was still behind a desk typing and filing, I knew adventure was at long last in my future.

Reporting to a new unit is like starting a new job in the civilian world. Anxious to make a good impression, one tends to go overboard trying to please, and boot camp training only makes it worse. I had had little contact with officers in my job at Parris Island, and the drill instructors in boot camp taught us to fear them. MAU headquarters was loaded with top-ranking officers, and I was in awe of all the brass. The other junior enlisted Marines teased that I was a "boot" and smelled of new uniform issue.

From the moment I met up with the advance party, I was lectured about the man I would work for in the operations office, Gunnery Sergeant Thorn. "You're going to get dogged," the advance party clerk warned. "He had Elroy and Dodson working on the green machine twenty-four hours a day." The green machine was a field computer used for word processing and equipment management. "He's a real son of a bitch, but you'll find that out for yourself."

I didn't have any problem identifying Gunny Thorn when he stepped off the chartered Trailways bus that brought the unit in from the ship. He was the one who shouted an obscenity every fourth word in a deep, gravelly voice. His face was craggy, and he had a nose hooked like a beak.

"Petit," he said when I introduced myself, "I'm just like a goddamn rose. I look mighty pretty, but I've got sharp thorns. You fuck up and I'll sting the shit out of you." Gunny Thorn was a hard-drinking, hard-living cuss; the quintessential Marine.

A MAU typically has three months' turnaround time to get ready for the next float. That's just enough time to unpack, resupply, pack up, and be on the water again. The work pace is hectic as new personnel check in to replace the old, and the entire operations office, with the exception of Gunny Thorn, was new.

My co-worker, a black lance corporal from Philadelphia named Alan Mandenheart, arrived at the unit a month after me. Gunny

Thorn got my name right about half the time, calling me everything from Petlik to Petard, but he could never remember Mandenheart's name and called him Mudfart. The first words out of Gunny's mouth when Mandenheart joined the unit were "Mudfart, I'm just like a goddamn rose." Gunny gave everyone that same speech.

Mandenheart got stung by the Thorn right away. Having just come off a float with the BLT, Mandenheart wanted nothing to do with ships. "I've already done my pump!" he protested. But the rule was we could be assigned to two deployments in a row, and no amount of protest could get Mandenheart out of the orders Headquarters Marine Corps, in its infinite wisdom, had assigned him. In the meantime, the Thorn was pissed as Mandenheart tried one excuse then another to get out of the MAU.

Gunny stuck Mandenheart with all the shit details. I felt sorry for ol' Mudfart as he painted the section's supply boxes olive drab for the second time, but at least it was him getting dogged and not me.

Major George Converse was the new officer in charge of operations. Bald except for a couple of long hairs on top, which he carefully cultivated, he was supposed to take care of Mandenheart and me when the Thorn gave us a hard time. I don't think the major knew we had assigned him that extra responsibility. Mandenheart and I had taken seriously the departing S-3 clerk's words of wisdom. "When you have trouble with the Thorn," he had advised, "and you will have trouble, just go to your 'Dad.' Don't forget he outranks Gunny Thorn."

Major Converse was easygoing and atypical of Marine officers. Mandenheart and I couldn't have asked for a better "Dad," and I knew I wouldn't have any trouble talking with Major Converse, even though I was a bit in awe of the gold oak leaves he wore. Mandenheart and I liked to pretend we were on a first name basis with the major and called him George, but not to his face.

Preparations for the float continued through March. Gunny Thorn, true to the rumors about him, was a hard man to work for. He not only dogged Mandenheart but began to dog me. I typed more reports than I had ever typed in my life, and it seemed I was constantly on the green machine. I followed news about Lebanon less closely even though we were scheduled to leave within two months. Finding a few minutes of spare time was enough to worry about.

☙ ☙ ☙

"At least fifty-seven are known dead, seventeen of whom are Americans."
I sprang from the rack where I had been sleeping and ran to the
television set at the far end of the barracks. "A Marine security guard
was pulled from the wreckage," the announcer was saying, "his body
wrapped in a tattered American flag. Marines saluted their fallen
comrade as he was taken from the site in a Red Cross ambulance."

I watched in horror as bodies were pulled from the ruins of the
American Embassy in Beirut. It was 18 April 1983, and a van bomb
loaded with explosives had collapsed the front of the seven-story building as easily as toppling a house of cards. The United States was
emerging as the prime target for those who opposed the role of the
Multinational Force in Lebanon, but I couldn't understand why they
were so anxious to maim and destroy to make that point.

"Those people really mean business," someone said, and I couldn't
help but agree. I felt unsteady knowing that I was leaving for a war-
torn country where I was hated simply because I was an American.
The realization struck me that going to Lebanon might not be good for
my health, or my continued existence.

The Islamic Jihad Organization, an obscure pro-Iranian group of
Shiite Muslims loyal to Ayatullah Khomeini, took credit for the
explosion. No one had ever heard of them, but the group was to gain a
great deal of notoriety in the following months.

My fear over the embassy bombing slowly lessened as the story
faded from the evening news. No terrible tragedies occurred in
Lebanon during the few weeks we had remaining in the States, and as
preparations to leave rose to a feverish pitch, I dismissed the worry
from my mind. Nothing like that can ever happen to me, I thought.

The final week before leaving on a six and a half month deployment
is a mad dash of packing. I filled two sea bags and a backpack with
personal gear; at work we crammed wooden "mount-out" boxes with
office supplies and manuals. No one bothered to tell me that I'd be
carrying everything up steep ladders on the ship, and I gave no thought
to how much extraneous junk I was taking.

The enlisted troops of the MAU were awakened before dawn—zero
dark thirty in Marine Corps language—on embarkation day. I was

ready for World War III, wearing flak jacket, helmet, gas mask, cartridge belt, and combat harness on which hung two canteens filled with water, a first-aid kit, and magazines for the M-16 rifle slung over my shoulder. I posed for pictures outside the MAU headquarters building with the eight-inch K-bar knife I had bought at a surplus store clenched between my teeth. It was fun playing G.I. Joe, and I felt like John Wayne in the movies.

An hour-long bus ride took us to Morehead City where the ship was docked. The ship was a gray monster towering above the pier, dwarfing us. Hundreds of Marines and pallets of gear were arrayed on the dock waiting to be loaded. We got off the bus and joined the other units.

"It's hurry-up-and-wait time," Corporal Hadley said. "Marine Corps Order 3845.3C, subsection 82, paragraph 23-1 states that Marines will be up and ready five hours before they have to be somewhere, so they can wait eight hours, because whatever they're supposed to do will be delayed at least three hours." Hadley had been in the Marine Corps four years and was on his second float. As far as Marine Corps life went he was an old salt. His father was a retired master sergeant, and the only way Hadley managed to keep from overdosing on the Corps was to maintain a fatalistic dry wit.

We sat on the dock for hours before we were given the order to move on board. Hours after that we had finally carried the last of the heavy mount-out boxes and sea bags into the dark bowels of the ship.

The ship set sail for open sea late that night. I watched the twinkling points of light on shore disappear in the distance, waving goodbye to the United States and to another chapter of my life. I thought about Thomas Wolfe, hoping he was wrong and that you can go home again, but knowing he was right. Whatever might happen, I knew when I returned I would be changed, and home would never again be the same.

But I had already made my choice and couldn't back out. For now, at least, I was on board the USS *Iwo Jima*, home for the next seventeen days.

4

THE SCREECH of the amplified boatswain's whistle startled me awake.

"Reveille, reveille," a voice over a loudspeaker announced. "Heave out and trice up. The smoking lamp is lit throughout the ship in all authorized spaces. Now reveille."

"Get up, get up!" Sergeant Layland good-naturedly shouted. "It's another beautiful Marine Corps morning where every day's a holiday and every meal's a feast!" Waking up is bad enough, was my first thought, but why do they have to be so obnoxious doing it?

The whistle blasted another shrill note. "Breakfast for the crew and embarked Marines."

I rolled groggily out of a rack that was barely wider than my shoulders, my back aching. The rack, inches above the deck, consisted of a thin, foam mattress on a piece of canvas lashed into an aluminum frame. Body weight caused the canvas to sag. The racks were stacked four high with only a foot and a half of space between each, and the bottom of the rack above mine hung in my face.

"What the hell does 'trice up' mean?" someone asked.

I jockeyed for space in the narrow aisle between racks with the other enlisted troops of the MAU. We waltzed around one another putting on trousers and shirts. Saying "excuse me" was an exercise in futility. An elbow in the face was followed by the close encounter with a knee to the groin. I felt like I was in the scene from *A Night at the Opera* with the Marx brothers where Groucho hides dozens of people in his small stateroom only to have them all come tumbling out when a steward unwittingly opens the door.

I sat on the floor to put on my boots, and howls of protest erupted as I blocked the aisle.

"Can't you do that somewhere else?" the Marine who slept across the aisle demanded.

I looked around and shrugged my shoulders. There wasn't anywhere to go. The large berthing area was filled with a hundred or more

Marines dressing and making their racks. The only extra space was in the "lounge," a table along the far wall that had a television set on one end. A dozen Marines sucking on their first cigarette of the morning were crowded around it.

"Get that rack triced up," Sergeant Layland said to me. "You've got morning clean up." Layland wore a smirk of superiority that expressed his joy at giving orders and handing out dirty jobs.

Giving and accepting orders in the Marine Corps is known as chain of command, and it extends from the commandant of the Marine Corps, a four-star general, right down to new recruits. I was "strictly charged with rendering obedience" to orders from Layland, but because I was a boot, I could get away with almost anything short of directly disobeying or telling him to shove it. I could always plead ignorance if challenged.

Layland worked in the communications section of the MAU so he wasn't in my direct chain of command. Nevertheless, he was bossy and tried to take control of my life as well as the lives of everyone else, ensuring we were up immediately after reveille, that our racks were made, towels hung neatly, and the berthing area was cleaned. I resented his intrusions, feeling I had survived long enough without a mother hen and didn't need one now.

Not knowing how to trice up a rack, I asked two of the seasoned Marines to show me what to do. They pushed up on the rack's metal frame, and the four-high stack folded upwards like an accordion. A long hook, which hung from the ceiling, held the racks in place, and there was a little more space in the aisle, but not much.

I opened the small locker near my rack and took out my shaving kit. The locker was only a foot square by about a foot and a half long, and into the small space I crammed the items I'd need on a daily basis. The rest of my gear, still packed in sea bags, had been tossed into a cage with a hundred other bags and immediately lost. Finding it (somehow mine was always on the bottom of the stack) was at least an hour-long job.

The MAU headquarters berthing area, which we shared with Marines from some of the other subordinate units, was in the deep recesses of the ship, and as I climbed the flight of steep stairs to the head I could hear the crash of water against the hull. The head was a tiny room with two toilets, a urinal, three showers, and one sink. I shaved as best I could; there was no plug in the basin, and the water shut itself off each time I let go of the faucet.

I went back to the berthing area, jammed my shaving kit into my locker, and swept and swabbed the deck as Sergeant Layland had ordered. Then I headed towards the mess deck for breakfast and was confronted with another unpleasant fact of shipboard life—standing in line. The line for chow seemed to run forever. I followed the endless row of grumbling Marines through narrow passageways and finally traced it up a flight of stairs to the hangar deck.

The hangar deck was an enormous area as wide and almost as long as the ship. A dozen CH-46 Sea Knight and four CH-53 Sea Stallion helicopters were housed in the hangar, and two missile-equipped AH-1T Cobra helicopters were lashed to the deck with thick chains. An elevator on each side of the ship was designed to raise and lower the helicopters to the flight deck above, and through one of the huge metal doors I could see the sea swiftly sliding by. The chow line meandered among the helicopters and ran the length of the hangar deck. I took my place at the end.

Lines were a fact of life on board *Iwo Jima* and couldn't be avoided. There were lines to get into and out of the chow hall, lines to purchase toilet articles in the ship's store, and lines to get into the small library to read. There were even lines to use the head. I carried a paperback to wile away the inevitable waits, but eavesdropping on gossip from home or speculating on the reliability of the latest rumor was much more enjoyable.

The outrageousness of rumors aboard a ship in the middle of the ocean increases in direct proportion to the ship's distance from land. Rumor, or scuttlebutt as it's known on the high seas, is the life's blood of Marines and sailors and the only thing that makes the boring days at sea tolerable. The rumor making the rounds my first morning on ship was that the *Iwo*, the first of a new class of ships designed specifically to operate helicopters, had listed badly and sunk immediately after its launching in 1960. The ship had been raised, but the only modification made was changing the hull number from LPH-1 to LPH-2. I felt certain the talk was just a rumor, but seeing only water in every direction did nothing to boost my confidence.

The line for breakfast moved surprisingly fast. Soon I was at the serving window, and a Marine assigned to mess duty plopped a scoop of greenish rehydrated eggs on my metal tray. Greasy, half-cooked bacon, slightly burned potatoes, and a large scoop of unidentifiable mush followed. The meal was topped off by a few slices of lukewarm toast. The food wasn't home cooked, but it was plentiful and more than enough to eat.

🎖 🎖 🎖

The days on ship passed quickly as we settled into a monotonous routine. Work began each day at 7:30 with a whistle blast over the ship's intercom, the 1-MC. "Commence ship's work," the boatswain would announce. "Muster on station. All sections submit muster reports to the personnel office by 0815 hours."

I was kept busy in the operations section filing and typing messages. I slowly began to learn about the structure of the military command system, which was both complex and confusing. In the United States the MAU was under the command of the Fleet Marine Force, Atlantic (FMFLant), but while making the transatlantic crossing we were under the command of the U.S. Second Fleet and known as Task Force 23.5. As soon as we entered the Mediterranean, however, we came under the command of the U.S. Sixth Fleet and were known as Task Force 62.9. Our designation changed once again when we arrived in Lebanon; the MAU became Task Force 62, while the Amphibious Ready Group became TF 61. I didn't pretend to understand why our command structure changed so frequently. I merely hoped those at the top knew what was going on and who was in charge.

Somewhere in the middle of the Atlantic we were given a briefing on the situation in Lebanon by the MAU's intelligence section. Staff Sergeant Garcia, a portly man who was fun-loving and witty, lectured us on the different uniforms of the various factions we might encounter while in Beirut. There was a morass of different groups, each heavily armed, each bent on destroying the others, and each convinced that its God was on its side. I wondered who in their right mind would sell weapons to fanatics like those.

It was clear from the questions asked that the other Marines in the MAU were as confused by the complexity of the Lebanese situation as was I.

"Why did the Israelis move into Lebanon?"

"Why do the Christians and Muslims hate each other?"

"Who are the Phalangists?"

"What does the PSP want?"

Staff Sergeant Garcia answered questions plainly and honestly—sometimes with "I don't know"—but he was usually able to clarify the complicated situation.

"The Phalangist Party," he explained, "is the major Christian party and is made up of about fifty thousand members, mostly Maronite Christians. They want a strengthening of the Lebanese system by social means, and they get many of their weapons from Israel, which perceives them as less radical and therefore less of a threat than the Muslim sects.

"The PSP is the Progressive Socialist Party and is a leftist Muslim organization headed by Walid Jumblatt. It's made up of Druze, a Muslim offshoot founded in the eleventh century by Muhammed ibn-Ism'ailal-Daraziy. The Druze are demanding a bigger share of power in the Christian-dominated Lebanese government. A lot of their support comes from Syria.

"Another major party is the Syrian Social Nationalist Party, and they support pan-Syrian nationalism. And, of course, there's the PLO, the Israelis, the Syrians, the Sunni, the Shiite, and a dozen other minor factions demanding attention and complicating matters. Add to that Russian advisors in Syria, the French, Italians, British, and us in Lebanon, and you get an idea of the lit powder keg we're sitting on."

"I have a question," Lance Corporal Chase, one of the radio operators, said. Heavyset with dark hair, Chase looked a little like young Hemingway. He was always coming up with off-the-wall ideas and had quickly earned the nickname "Space Chase."

"Go ahead," Staff Sergeant Garcia said.

"Is it going to be possible for us to invest in Lebanon?" he deadpanned. "Don't they have a lot of oil or something?"

Loud guffaws met his question. "Get out of here, Chase," someone said.

"Seriously, I think we could make a lot of money. Maybe we could get a fund together or something."

Staff Sergeant Garcia ignored Chase's comment and the ruckus died down.

"I don't understand what we're doing in Lebanon in the first place," one of the corporals said.

"Our goal is to help Lebanon maintain its sovereignty," Garcia answered. "Right now the LAF, the Lebanese Armed Forces, have control only of the city of Beirut. With us securing Beirut International Airport, it frees the army to spread its influence to the outlying areas and eventually to all of Lebanon."

Gunny Thorn began to pass out blue, wallet-sized Rules of Engagement cards, which the operations section had prepared.

"These are your goddamned ROE cards," he croaked. "Read them and memorize them and don't fuckin' lose them."

Rules of Engagement are guidelines under which U.S. troops operate during peacetime. Written under the direction of the Department of Defense, the ten rules outlined what we could and could not do in certain situations and delineated our orders while in Lebanon. The card read:

GUIDELINES FOR ROE

1. When on post, mobile or foot patrol, keep loaded magazine in weapon, bolt closed, weapon on safe, no round in the chamber.
2. Do not chamber a round unless told to do so by a commissioned officer unless you must act in immediate self-defense where deadly force is authorized.
3. Keep ammo for crew-served weapons readily available but not loaded. Weapon is on safe.
4. Call local forces to assist in self-defense effort.
5. Use only minimum degree of force to accomplish any mission.
6. Stop the use of force when it is no longer needed to accomplish the mission.
7. If you receive effective hostile fire, direct your fire at the source. If possible, use friendly snipers.
8. Respect civilian property; do not attack it unless absolutely necessary to protect friendly forces.
9. Protect civilians from harm.
10. Respect and protect recognized medical agencies, such as Red Cross and Red Crescent.

Some of the Marines were outraged.

"How are we supposed to protect civilians from harm? It sounds to me like there aren't any civilians over there."

"I don't know about you, but if someone shoots at me, I'm going to shoot back whether I've got permission or not."

"The hell with minimum force. I'm going to give them everything I've got!"

"Shut your goddamn sucks," Gunny Thorn barked. Everyone stopped talking. "These rules are designed to keep you from going over there and shooting anything and everything that moves. Suppose you're on patrol and a sniper shoots at you from a fourth-floor window. What are you going to do? Spray the whole goddamn building with machine gun fire?"

"Damn right," someone said.

"Bullshit! I was sitting in the back of a jeep in downtown Beirut last float. A car was just passing us when I spotted a pistol in the back seat aimed right at me. I couldn't see who was holding it, and I almost shit my skivvy drawers. A second later a six-year-old kid popped up. I could have blown him away if I hadn't used a little restraint, and then where would I have been? Leavenworth for the next ten fucking years.

"The only time you return fire is when you have a clear shot at the bastard, and then make damn sure you aren't going to hit an innocent bystander. Just because you see a weapon is no reason to fire. Hell, every ten year old and up over there walks around with a fucking Uzi machine gun hanging from his shoulder."

"What about this situation?" Chase said. "Suppose you were in heavy traffic and someone threw a grenade into your jeep. You couldn't get rid of it without blowing up a car. What would you do then?"

"Son," Gunny said. "You'd be fucked."

Everyone laughed, but despite the undercurrent of excitement that long months of combat training might finally be put to actual use, it was clear from the intensity of the conversation that most of the troops were a little nervous about going to Lebanon.

❦   ❦   ❦

"This is a drill, this is a drill," the 1-MC intoned. "General Quarters, General Quarters. All hands man your battle stations. Set Condition Zebra throughout the ship. Dog down all watertight hatches and gun covers. Damage control petty officers make condition reports to damage control central. Now General Quarters."

Sailors dashed frantically to their battle stations. Heavy watertight doors throughout the ship clanged shut and were sealed. The Marines on board had been instructed to stay put during Navy drills, and I was trapped in the operations office.

A gong sounded. "T plus One," the boatswain announced. He gave the time in one-minute increments until he finally said, "Time plus ten. Condition Zebra set throughout the ship." That meant all watertight hatches were closed and the ship was ready for battle.

Constant drills were necessary not only to remind us we were headed for hostile waters but also to fine tune the skills of the crew and ensure the embarked Marines knew exactly what to do in an emergency. It was always a comfort to hear the words "this is a drill, this is a drill" before General Quarters was announced. Without those words it would have been panic time.

Fifteen minutes into General Quarters an alarm bell rang. "Fire. Fire. Fire. Class charlie fire in the after engine room, location five tack sixty-nine tack two tack charlie. Away the firecracker team, away." An out-of-control fire on a ship is every sailor's nightmare, and Navy fire fighting teams rush to the location given by the 1-MC as quickly as possible.

A short time later a Klaxon sounded, and the boatswain announced, "Prepare to abandon ship."

That was my signal to put on a life jacket and go immediately to the flight deck and report to my life raft station. It only took a couple of seconds to run up the short flight of stairs near the office and go outside.

The flight deck was a huge expanse painted with white lines and numbers; several helicopters ready for flight were chained to the deck near the bow. Marines milled about looking for their life raft stations. I found the MAU headquarters' area on the starboard side of the ship. Above us towered the ship's island, which housed the bridge, flight deck control, and radar.

The MAU's second in command, the executive officer, began calling our names from a roster.

Life rafts were stored in metal barrels along the sides of the ship and could be released either manually by pulling a line or automatically after the barrels reached a specified depth underwater. They were designed to inflate by themselves and contained rations and fresh water for forty people.

"Commence with destruction of classified materials," the 1-MC announced.

Corporal Hadley was standing near me. "How do we get into the life rafts?" I asked.

"You jump into the water, swim over to your raft, and climb in."

I looked over the railing. The flight deck was at least sixty feet above the water, and it was a very long way down.

"Abandon ship. Abandon ship," the captain announced. "The nearest point of land is 348 nautical miles, bearing 282 degrees north northwest." I shuddered to think the drill could have been real.

Our performance was critiqued once the abandon-ship drill was over and everyone had been accounted for. Problem areas in getting to the flight deck were noted for future reference, but having been through the experience once, I knew I would know exactly what to do if I had to actually abandon ship.

A short whistle blast sounded over the 1-MC. "Secure from General Quarters. Set Condition One-Alpha throughout the ship. Set the normal underway watch. On deck, watch section three."

                                💮   💮   💮

Evenings on board the *Iwo* were the times I missed home the most. There was nothing to do but lie in the rack and read or write letters. The lounge area was always jammed with Marines playing cards and watching month-old programs on closed-circuit television. Spades was the most popular card game, and whoops of laughter and the riffle of cards could be heard in the berthing area at all hours. There was no privacy on the ship and no place to go to simply be alone.

We had been issued small American flags so we could be identified as members of the U.S. Contingent to the Multinational Forces. I spent a couple of evenings sewing the flags on the left sleeves of my uniforms. Other Marines took time to spit shine their boots and iron their camouflage utility uniforms. Marines in boot camp are taught to keep their hair trimmed and their uniforms neat and squared away, and although some become less conscientious with time, maintaining a professional appearance is a source of pride for most Marines.

Promotions for enlisted Marines below the rank of sergeant are based on a "cutting score," which is computed by compiling the proficiency and conduct marks given to the individual by the Marine's officer in charge, adding in the total time spent in service and in rank, and awarding extra points for passing physical and military tests. My rank was lance corporal, and I was a "non-rate," which meant any unsavory job that came along would be mine. I loathed taking orders from corporals and sergeants five years younger than I and was desperate to get promoted. I played Marine quite well, keeping myself squared away, jumping when officers said jump, and "yes sirring" them to death.

Cutting scores are high, making it difficult to get promoted unless the Marine has been in a long time. A meritorious promotion system was set up for outstanding Marines who couldn't meet the cutting score, and I was nominated to appear before the promotion board and answer questions on military subjects. The months of diligence paid off, and I was selected for meritorious promotion to corporal.

Pomp and ceremony is an important aspect of the Marine Corps. Accomplishments are always presented to an individual before the entire unit, and an all-hands formation was held on the hangar deck shortly before our arrival in Lebanon for my promotion to corporal.

"Platoon, atten-hut!" Staff Sergeant Summers commanded. The enlisted troops of the MAU headquarters snapped to attention.

Summers was a tall, athletic black Marine who was in charge of all the little jobs that came up. The welfare of the troops was also his responsibility, and he was always on the hunt for workers to do the unit's manual labor.

He saluted the executive officer and reported, "Sir, headquarters platoon all present or accounted for."

The operations officer, Major Converse, called the separate formation of officers and staff noncommissioned officers to attention, saluted, and reported to the executive officer.

The executive officer executed an about-face, reported to Commanding Officer Colonel Geraghty, then took his place between the colonel and the top-ranking enlisted member of the MAU, the sergeant major.

"Person to receive award," the sergeant major thundered, "Center, march!"

I marched from behind the enlisted formation to a position four paces from the colonel, right-faced, and saluted. Colonel Geraghty returned my salute then began pinning corporal chevrons on my collar, as the adjutant, the officer responsible for the unit's correspondence, read from the promotion warrant that ordered me to "carefully and diligently discharge the duties of the grade to which appointed."

The colonel shook my hand and congratulated me. I saluted, left-faced, and marched back to my position behind the platoon.

"Stand at ease," Colonel Geraghty said. The unit relaxed its stance. "I've received a message from Commandant General Barrow that I'd like to share with you." He took a piece of paper from his pocket and read:

> For Colonel Geraghty and the men of 24 MAU. As you assume the responsibilities of the United States Contingent, Multinational Force, I am confident that you will meet every challenge in a superb fashion, representing both Country and Corps with the highest degree of excellence.
>
> Your task is not easy. You will frequently be challenged by demanding and potentially dangerous conditions that will tax the discipline and professionalism of each and every Marine.
>
> You have worked hard to prepare for this mission, and I have no doubt that you will continue to uphold the highest traditions of our Corps in the effort to bring peace to Lebanon.
>
> Good luck and Godspeed.

Colonel Geraghty put the sheet of paper back in his pocket. The executive officer stepped forward three paces and about-faced.

"Take charge and carry out the plan of the day," the colonel said.

The executive officer saluted. "Aye, aye, sir." He about-faced and ordered, "Platoon commanders, take charge of your platoon and carry out the plan of the day."

Major Converse and Staff Sergeant Summers saluted the executive officer smartly and acknowledged the order with, "Aye, aye, sir." Both about-faced toward their formations.

"Dismissed," Staff Sergeant Summers said. The formation began to break up, then he added, "Get him!"

Marines began to converge on me. New rank is always "pinned on" after every promotion, and all the enlisted troops who outranked me were eligible to take a turn. Two of the bigger guys grabbed my arms on either side before I could get away and held on tight. Their fists reared back and Whack! right in the biceps. They spun me a half turn and hit me again with their fists. They also used their knees to smack me in the thigh, pinning on my "blood stripes." I was pounded with fists and knees by Marine after Marine until I was too sore to move.

They finally stopped bludgeoning me, and my chevrons were officially pinned on. I had earned the right to wear the blood-red stripe on my dress uniform trousers, a tradition established in 1846 during the Mexican-American War when 90 percent of the Marine officers and noncommissioned officers became casualties during the successful assault of the fortress Chapultipec. I was still near the bottom of the Marine Corps hierarchy and still an Indian in a unit that was mostly chiefs, but now, at least, I could demand a little more respect as a corporal and a noncommissioned officer.

※   ※   ※

The atmosphere of the ship became charged with excitement as we neared the coast of Lebanon. Upon entering the Mediterranean on 21 May, an advance party had flown to Beirut to begin preparations for the change of command with the 22d MAU, already on peacekeeping duty. Shortly afterwards, on 25 May Colonel James Joy, the Sixth Fleet Marine Officer, arrived on board *Iwo Jima* to brief the MAU officers on operations in Beirut.

The changing of units ashore without losing the ability to respond to any contingency is a tricky bit of business called a relief-in-place. The Marines of the 24th MAU were to move ashore by helicopter and amphibious assault vehicles to temporarily supplement the Marines already in position. Once the new arrivals were briefed on procedures, the troops of the 22d MAU would withdraw to their own ships and sail back to the United States.

For the supply sections of both MAUs a relief-in-place is a time of hectic reconciliation of equipment rosters. Rather than bring all new equipment ashore during the relief-in-place, some items, such as tents, cots, water purification, and sanitation facilities, are left for the new unit's use. Each MAU, however, brings its own helicopters, weapons, ammunition, and assault craft ashore.

I began my preparations for going ashore by repacking my gear. I dug my sea bags from the cage and filled my ALICE pack (All-purpose Lightweight Individual Carrying Equipment pack) with the uniforms and personal items I'd need ashore. The MAU headquarter's supply section issued each of us twenty 5.56mm rounds for our rifles, and I filled one of my magazines with nervous anticipation, hoping I wouldn't have to kill more than twenty men on my first day in Lebanon.

D-Day, the day scheduled for the relief-in-place, was set to begin on 29 May at 0700 hours. We sailed past the Isle of Crete three days before the big day, and Colonel Geraghty flew by helicopter to Souda Bay for transfer to Beirut to coordinate the relief-in-place from shore. Most of MAU headquarters, myself included, would be flying into Beirut International Airport on the morning of the twenty-eighth. As the days before arrival dwindled to one, sleep became all but impossible.

The ship's routine became more maddening the final day; the tension and excitement was almost unbearable. I spent a morning that seemed frozen in time packing files and office supplies into the mount-out boxes we would carry ashore. The afternoon dragged on and on as I wrote a few letters home, thinking they might be my last for some time.

Dinner was the traditional meal Marines eat the night before an assault: steak and lobster. The mess hall line was exceptionally long, and it seemed every Marine and sailor aboard the *Iwo* had gone through twice before I had a turn.

"Dump all trash and garbage clear of the fantail," the 1-MC announced shortly after chow was over. I took two plastic bags filled with trash from the office and carried them through the hangar deck and outside to the fantail. Water churned behind the ship as it cruised at its sustained speed of twenty knots per hour, and I felt immense guilt as I tossed the two bags overboard, adding to the pollution of the Mediterranean. The bags floated into the distance and disappeared in the growing dusk. I watched as the stars emerged one by one, reminding me, as they always do, of mortality and of the grandness of the universe.

I went to the berthing area and spent the remainder of the evening checking my gear to make sure I wasn't leaving behind something important. I adjusted my flak jacket and helmet one last time and ensured my sleeping bag was tightly lashed to the bottom of my ALICE pack.

I went to the head and took a naval shower, leaving the water on only long enough to get wet. I soaped my body and spread shampoo on my hair, then turned on the water to rinse. I stood under the hot water a long time despite the restriction on using too much fresh water, feeling I deserved a long shower on my last night aboard ship.

After drying off, I went down the flight of stairs to the berthing area, put on a pair of shorts, and crawled into my rack.

At ten minutes before ten o'clock, a whistle blew over the 1-MC, and the boatswain made his nightly announcement: "Maintain silence about the decks for the chaplain's evening prayer," he intoned.

A hush descended upon the berthing area. The Marines sitting around the table in the lounge stopped playing cards and bowed their heads. Someone lowered the volume on the television set.

"Heavenly Father," the chaplain prayed. "As we complete our sail to foreign shores and assume our peacekeeping mission, we ask that you guide us in your ways of love and understanding. Look over our loved ones at home and protect us so that we may soon return to them. Help us remember your son's words 'Blessed are the peacemakers: for they shall be called the children of God.' In your name we pray. Amen."

"Amen," many of the Marines echoed. The television set jumped back to full blast, and cards for the marathon spade game were reshuffled.

At precisely 10:00 P.M. the boatswain proclaimed, "Taps, taps. Lights out. All hands turn in to your own bunks. The smoking lamp is out in all berthing spaces. Maintain silence about the decks. Now taps."

The overhead fluorescent-white lights went out, and red ones flickered on, bathing the berthing area in an eerie, hellish-red glow.

Tomorrow's the day, I thought, the culmination of what I've been wanting for so long. I just hope this is what I truly want.

I lay awake for a long time.

III
The 'Root

5

HELLO, ALBERT!" Ross hollered his favorite nickname for me as he climbed the stairs that led to flight deck debarkation. I was lined up in the passageway just outside the departure room with thirty other Marines from MAU headquarters, waiting for my helicopter ride into Beirut.

"How's it going, Big Guy?" I asked. Ross was six foot four, personable, and outgoing. He had earned the nickname "Big Guy," among others, not only because of his stature but also because he was always boasting about the gargantuan size of his male organ.

"Still yankin' it," he answered. Ross was a motion picture combat photographer and, like me, assigned to the operations section of the MAU. Laden like a pack mule with ALICE pack, .45 pistol, and photo gear, he had a little trouble navigating the steep stairs. The thick, black-framed military glasses he wore kept sliding down his nose, and his sandy blond hair was matted to his forehead.

Ross and I had become fast friends because of our mutual problem: Gunnery Sergeant Thorn. The Thorn kept a firm rein on everyone in the operations section, but his control of Ross and the other combat photographer, Staff Sergeant Tolbert, was positively dictatorial. Gunny wanted to know what *his* photographers were doing at every moment and constantly used his rank to remind them he was the boss. Ross had spent most of the transatlantic crossing hiding out in the ship's darkroom, emerging only for meals or to sneak into the berthing area shortly before taps. I didn't have a hiding place and had to spend most of my time in the office pretending to listen attentively as Gunny told me his life story.

"Ready to go ashore, Ross?" I asked.

"I'm ready to unleash this huge monster," he said, pointing at his groin.

I felt like Ross looked. The ship was hot and humid, and I was sweating profusely under my flak jacket. An M-16 rifle may weigh just 6.5 pounds, but carrying it on your shoulder for more than half an hour makes it feel closer to sixty-five pounds. I leaned against the wall and tried unsuccessfully to lift a bit of my ALICE pack's weight from my aching shoulders.

With Ross' arrival, most of the twelve-man operations section was assembled and ready to board our helicopter. I was assigned to stick number four, the fourth group flying to the beach, and had been waiting in the passageway almost an hour. I could hear the thunder of helicopters coming from the flight deck one level above, and as each bird landed and took off, I became more impatient to escape the ship's heat.

"Stick three!" someone in flight deck debark yelled. The line surged forward as Marines ahead of me began moving left into the departure room.

Gunny Thorn strode around the corner. "Petnik! Mudfart!" he growled at Mandenheart and me. "Get that goddamned mount-out box into debark control. Tolbert, you and Ross grab the other one."

Ross and Staff Sergeant Tolbert hauled one of the heavy mount-out boxes filled with office supplies and files into the departure room, while Mandenheart and I struggled with the second one. My M-16 immediately slipped from my shoulder into the crook of my arm, and the rifle butt kept banging against the side of the box as I walked backward.

As Mandenheart and I stacked the two boxes in the departure room, Gunny Thorn charged in carrying two huge rolls of acetate, a clear plastic that was used as overlays to mark checkpoints and troop positions on tactical maps. "Goddamn shit," Gunny mumbled to no one in particular.

Combat Cargo was the Marine division on USS *Iwo Jima* responsible for the flight deck debarkation room and getting us to the aircraft safely. Its members were easily identifiable by the white jerseys they wore. Jobs on the flight deck are categorized by the color shirt worn, and during flight operations, with helicopters landing and taking off every few minutes, Marines and sailors gallop about in orderly confusion in purple, brown, yellow, and white shirts.

"Stick four!" the white-shirted Marine in the departure room yelled.

Mandenheart and I picked up our mount-out box and followed the white shirt and other Marines to the flight deck. I led the way up steep stairs, while Mandenheart bravely struggled with what had become the heavy end of the box. A sign outside the departure room had read WE ARE NOT PORTERS—CARRY YOUR OWN GEAR! SIGNED, THE WHITE SHIRTS, but one of the combat cargo Marines at the top of the stairs, seeing that I was about to drop the box on Mandenheart's head, helped me lug it up the last few steps.

The *Iwo* was capable of launching up to seven CH-46 helicopters simultaneously, but only two spots were active at that moment. Several U.S. Navy ships were in the distance as helicopters buzzed by overhead.

A white shirt led the line of Marines toward spot number five near the stern of the ship, making sure we stayed close to starboard and to the left of the white line painted on the flight deck. The roar of the helicopter was deafening as I approached. The white shirt leading us held up his right fist and waved his arm sharply to the right. Marines at the front of the line turned ninety degrees and headed straight for the rear ramp of the helicopter.

A wash of hot air, caustic with the smell of burning fuel, took my breath away as I moved past the blast of the helicopter's jet engine. Another white shirt stood at the rear ramp and directed me onto the aircraft. The ramp, despite its nonskid surface, was slick. I slid a half step back for each step forward and almost dropped my end of the mount-out box before I was finally able to set it down in the center aisle.

The helicopter crewman, his face invisible behind a dark visor, pointed at nylon seats that ran along the sides of the helicopter and motioned for me to sit. A Sea Knight helicopter has a payload capacity of seventeen troops plus all their gear, but as more and more Marines boarded carrying ALICE packs, sea bags, flight bags, map stands, mount-out, boxes, and garment bags, the helicopter seemed more than filled to maximum capacity.

I located my seat belt and fastened it around me as the crewman began handing out life vests and flimsy helmets made of plastic and canvas, called cranials. I took my camouflage helmet off, holding it between my knees, and put on the cranial. Built-in cups fit over my ears, and the deafening thorp-thorp-thorp sound of the helicopter's rotor blades became a loud echo.

The life vest was little more than a belt that went around the waist.

Mine wouldn't fit around both me and my ALICE pack, so I faked it by holding the gray pouch against my stomach. If we crash, I thought, that insignificant bit of inflatable rubber can't hold a flak jacket above water, let alone me.

With everyone crammed into place and belted to the seats, the helicopter's ramp slowly ascended, leaving a large open space through which I could still see the deck of the *Iwo*. The helicopter stood still for a moment then vibrated spasmodically.

I felt exhilarated as the helicopter slowly lifted and hung suspended a foot above the deck. Hovering for a moment, the helicopter moved sharply sideways, and the ship seemed to rush away. We began a steep ascent and banked abruptly to the left. I turned and looked through the round window behind me, seeing a surprisingly small *Iwo Jima* below and to the left.

"Goodbye, ship. Goodbye, safety," I mumbled to myself before facing forward.

We leveled off for the ten-minute flight to the beach, and I realized my teeth were clenched. Ross, sitting across the aisle from me, mouthed the word "smile" and took my picture.

I tried to look everywhere at once. The cockpit was full of complex controls, and from my vantage point, I watched as the pilot steered, gently maneuvering the cyclic control stick between his knees. The interior of the helicopter was a crazy patchwork of hydraulic lines and cables, and the sea, only 200 feet below, rushed by at he dizzying rate of 120 miles per hour.

We were practically over the beach before I saw the first sign of land. The deep blue of the Mediterranean turned azure, then green, then brown as shoals flashed by. Swimmers in the water and sunbathers on the beach were replaced by cars parked along a strip of highway; olive-drab tents pitched amid scrub and reddish sand gave way to the hangars and concrete runways of Beirut International Airport.

The helicopter began a disorienting 360 degree turn before landing. Blurry mountains and buildings streamed by in a circle, and a distant helicopter, briefly visible through the ramp opening, hung motionless like a fat, green bumblebee. Its defensive turn complete, the helicopter hovered above the runway before settling gently to the ground. I braced myself for a jolt that never came.

I unclicked my seat belt and began passing cranials and life jackets forward to the crewman. Upon the crewman's signal I stood and gathered my gear. A white shirt on the ground directed exiting Marines to the right. Mandenheart and I picked up our mount-out box and carefully walked down the ramp.

The momentous occasion had arrived—I was finally in Lebanon. I stepped off the ramp onto the runway apron. I felt electrified. This is adventure! I jubilantly thought. This is what makes life worth living!

Mandenheart and I carried the box to the edge of the runway. Stone houses and makeshift shanties across a dusty road and past a barbed-wire fence were only a hundred feet away. Children wearing tattered clothes had stopped playing to wave.

The helicopter revved its engines, lifted slowly, and headed back toward the sea. Its roar faded in the distance as swirls of red dust died at my feet. I was left standing in bright sunlight amid an unnerving quiet.

"Goddamn motherfuckers!" Gunny Thorn ranted, breaking the tension. "How the hell are we supposed to get this gear to the goddamn command post without a jeep?"

I took off my ALICE pack and sat on the mount-out box. Three minutes later, two jeeps towing trailers arrived.

"Gentlemen," one of the drivers said. "Welcome to the 'Root!"

I helped load gear, then jumped into one of the trailers and sat on a sea bag.

The trip to the CP, the command post, was a ride of less than five minutes. A mound of dirt ran along the side of the road near the runway, and a bored Marine standing guard on top saluted the jeep as it passed.

"That's Rock Base," the jeep driver said, pointing left to HMM 162's base of operations. Four or five olive-drab tents were pitched inside a barrier of concertina wire. A Trans Mediterranean Airlines jet on its belly, engineless and rife with bullet holes, was just outside the wire.

"You can see LZ [Landing Zone] Red where you landed from here," the driver continued. "And over there on the right is the Lebanese Army's boot camp." LAF troops wearing green, dusty uniforms ran in formation, singing a song in Arabic that sounded like a parody of those I had sung in boot camp.

The jeep drove past aircraft hangars where Lebanese nationals worked, then turned right and passed through a Lebanese-controlled checkpoint. Up a small hill, the jeep almost ran over a Marine sentry who stood outside a sandbag bunker. The sentry flagged us left through a wrought-iron gate and saluted nonchalantly. We turned right and squealed to a stop in the CP's parking lot.

"Still looks the same," someone said.

"Yeah, the same old hellhole."

"Stop the jabber and get the goddamn jeep unloaded," Gunny Thorn said.

The CP had been the airport's fire station. Six corrugated iron doors covered the bays where the fire trucks had been housed, and a few sandbags were piled around the front entrance of the building. Rusty bars covered glass windows on either side of the main door making the place look like a prison. A green, brown, and tan camouflage sign with yellow lettering over the door read:

COMMANDER U.S. FORCES ASHORE
BEIRUT, LEBANON
22 MAU
COLONEL JAMES MEAD
U.S. MARINE CORPS

Mandenheart and I carried the mount-out box into the CP and went back outside to unload our personal gear. I piled my junk under the trees on the far side of the parking lot.

"Where will we be sleeping?" I asked Gunny.

"Don't worry about that right now," he assured me. "We'll get you set up later." Gunny left and went into the CP.

Ross and I sat in the shade under a tree. Staff Sergeant Tolbert sauntered over and joined us.

"Shouldn't you guys be out taking pictures?" I asked.

"*He,*" Tolbert said venomously, "won't let us."

"We haven't been able to do our jobs yet," Ross said. "I've already missed footage because that so-called gunnery sergeant thinks he knows how to do my job better than me."

The three of us sat under the tree talking as morning slowly turned into afternoon. I was becoming hungry, but no one seemed concerned that we didn't have anything to eat. Hot meals wouldn't be served for several days until the Battalion Landing Team cooks had set up the field kitchen.

Tolbert volunteered to go on a foraging mission and headed to a tent pitched on the left side of the parking lot. He returned a few minutes later with three dark brown plastic packages and tossed one to me. "Have an MRE," he said.

I read the writing on the package aloud:

MEAL, READY-TO-EAT, INDIVIDUAL
MENU NO. 5
BEEF STEW
ACCESSORY PACKET A
CADILLAC PRODUCTS, INC.
STERLING HEIGHTS, MI 48077

"Cadillac Products," Ross said. "I've heard of them. They make dog food."

Tolbert snarled, tearing at the thick plastic of his MRE with his teeth.

I used my K-bar knife to slice through mine and dumped the contents on my lap. Inside was a plastic spoon wrapped in cellophane, a package of cocoa powder, crackers, peanut butter (fortified), de-hydrated fruit mix, and a thin, green cardboard box that claimed to have beef stew inside. Accessory Packet A turned out to be a package containing instant coffee, cream, sugar, salt, chewing gum, matches, and toilet paper.

The food was edible, though a bit dry, and I judged my first meal in Lebanon, and my first MRE, as not bad.

"I wonder where everyone is?" I asked. "I think somebody forgot about us."

"This is another perfect example of Marine Corps leadership," Ross said. "Whatever happened to taking care of your men first?"

"Does this mean you won't be reenlisting?" I asked.

"No, of course not! I love sitting here sweltering in the heat. In fact, I think I'll reenlist and throw more years of my life away!"

"Let's find a place to sleep tonight," I suggested. "If we wait for the Thorn, we'll be sitting under this tree next week."

Ross agreed, and we took a path around the right side of the CP, leaving Tolbert as gear watch. Three tents had been pitched directly behind the command post, and a radio antenna with a high-voltage sign on it towered above me on the right. Fire trucks, with their windows smashed out, were parked on a narrow dead-end street. The trucks were full of bullet holes.

A massive two-story building that had seen better days stood across the street. Its walls were scarred, bricks had fallen to the ground, and some of the rooms were open to the weather and filled with rubble and trash.

"Someone said something about us staying in the basement," Ross said.

We entered the building and turned left, following a long, dark passageway that went past empty rooms. In the large open area at the end of the corridor two Lebanese soldiers with black curly hair sat around a table eating lunch with an old man. The smell of garlic was strong enough to make my stomach turn. A sign on the wall informed me I was in what was once the CIVIL AERONAUTICS TRAINING AND SAFETY CENTRE. A double-glass doorway opened onto a sidewalk that led down a hill to a huge building.

"Is that an old hotel?" I asked Ross.

"I don't know. I think that's where the Battalion Landing Team is headquartered."

I nodded hello to the Lebanese, and Ross and I headed back the way we had come. A stairwell extending both up and down was at the opposite end of the building, and we went down into darkness.

"This place looks like a good hideout for Yasser Arafat," I said.

"You may not be far from wrong. Someone said this was once a PLO hospital."

Two flights down, we entered a large, windowless room. A red splotch on the entry wall looked like someone had been executed by firing squad. Marines were setting up cots using the feeble light emitted by bulbs dangling from the ceiling. The room smelled of stale air and bodies. Hand-drawn calendars counting down the days were etched on the walls, and someone had written WE GONE! in bright red letters above one. Rusty pipes that looked like sewer drains jutted from near the ceiling.

"Looks like this is the place," Ross said.

Ross and I toured the basement. It had four rooms, the largest of which, an elongated L-shape, could hold about forty men. A short corridor led to a small room where two cots were set up, and a dead-end corridor on the right held two more. A rubble-filled room with a hole in the ceiling to the outside was walled off by a piece of screen tacked to plywood. The last room in the basement was closed off by two wooden doors. I pushed them open with my foot. A single bulb hung from the ceiling, and although only one cot was set up, the room was large enough to hold at least six.

"I wonder what that says?" I mused, pointing to Arabic writing scrawled on the far wall.

"No doubt DEATH TO YANKEE PIGS." Ross joked.

"Let's get set up in here before someone else takes this spot. I don't want to be in the main room with everyone else if we can help it. We'll have a lot more privacy back here."

Ross and I retrieved our gear and took it to the basement. We appropriated two cots from the large room and set them up in the far corners of our new room. I unrolled my sleeping bag and spread it on one of the cots, staking out a claim.

"Be it ever so humble," Ross proclaimed as he plopped onto his cot, "And it's so very humble—there's no place like home."

          ❧   ❧   ❧

D-Day. For most people the word conjures up images of the Allies storming the beaches of Normandy, of wave after wave of heroic men battling for a hold on a few inches of blood-soaked soil. For me the word is synonymous with filling sandbags.

Staff Sergeant Summers snagged me early on D-Day morning after an MRE breakfast of ham slices washed down with water.

"How would you like to go to a party?" he asked.

"Do I have a choice?"

"No."

"In that case...I guess so. What kind of party is it?"

"A working party," he said mirthfully. "Filling sandbags."

So while helicopters swarmed overhead and amphibious tractors assaulted the beach carrying loads of combat-ready Marines to their positions ashore, I stood waist deep in a pit digging sand with a shovel.

Filling sandbags is a fine art. Care must be taken not to put too much sand in the bags or they will burst. Sandbags not full enough, however, won't stack properly, and walls made with them will collapse. I became an expert at putting the precise amount of sand in each bag.

The green burlap bags came in bundles of five hundred each and had to be turned right-side out in order to keep the seam on the inside. I took turns with my sandbag partner, Corporal Hadley, sometimes filling the bags and sometimes turning them inside out and holding them open for him to fill.

Six of us were on the working party, and we filled trailer after trailer with the heavy bags. We took turns driving the jeep across the road to the CP, where we helped another working party unload the bags, so they could build a wall along the front of the building. I was happy to be in the group filling the bags without supervision. Gunny Thorn had crowned himself sandbag czar, and each time I made a trip to the command post he was bitching about one thing or another.

The climate of Lebanon is similar to that of southern California, rarely exceeding eighty-five degrees in the summer. However, the humidity is high, and filling sandbags was hot, sweaty work. I took off my camouflage blouse and T-shirt and was soon covered with fine, red sand.

"Didn't 22 MAU do anything while they were here?" I asked. "There were hardly any sandbags at the CP before we started."

"24 MAU does all the work while 22 gets all the glory," Hadley said. "They left the place a mess, and we come in and straighten up."

"Yeah," Silone agreed. Silone was a pudgy kid with greasy, black hair and an acned face. Although he had lived in the U.S. most of his life, emigrating from Italy, he had never become a citizen and still carried a green card. His middle name must have been "hard time" because everyone gave him one, calling him "big, fat slob" when they were angry or shortening his last name to "Silly" when they felt like being nice. He was leaning against the jeep and chugging water from a canteen on another of his numerous breaks.

"Get to work, Silly!" Corporal Hadley ordered.

"Come on, Jeff. I can talk too."

"Talk and work!"

Silone reluctantly began to turn empty bags inside out. "Why do we have to turn these stupid bags inside out?" he asked. "So what if the seam shows?"

"Good question!" Corporal Beckford exclaimed. Beckford was a refugee from the sixties, though he was probably just out of diapers at the decade's end. A rebel bucking against the Marine Corps system, he was exceptionally well-read but obsessed with death and spiritualism. Many of the guys thought he spent much of his time on a different plane of existence and steered clear of him.

"I guess it shouldn't make that much of a difference," Hadley said.

"It doesn't make any difference!" Beckford insisted. "The purpose of sandbags is protection, and whether there's a rough seam on the outside or a smooth, finished one doesn't make one bit of difference to the incoming round."

"Let's fill the bags without turning them inside out," I suggested. "If they don't like it, what can they do? Fire us?"

We filled an entire trailer, about a hundred bags, with less than perfect sandbags that hadn't been turned inside out and drove to the CP.

"What kind of shit is this!" Gunny roared. "Take these goddamned bags back over there, dump out the sand, and fill them up right."

Everyone groaned. Hadley and I looked at each other and started smiling. I had to bite the inside of my cheek to keep from laughing out loud.

"I can't use half-assed bags to build this wall," Gunny ranted. "It'll look like shit."

Gunny's philosophy was that there's the right way to do things, the wrong way to do things, and the Gunny Thorn way to do things. And if the Gunny Thorn way wasn't the best or easiest, that was too bad because his way was how things were going to be done.

Gunny took one of the supposedly faulty bags and placed it on the top-most row of the wall. "Maybe we can hide the jagged seam if we put them back to back," he said. He took a second bag and placed it next to the first, stepping back for a good look like an artist examining a masterpiece. "Okay, I can use the damn things, but from now on fill them up the right way!"

I drove the jeep back to the sand pit towing an empty trailer.

"We should have known," Beckford said.

"Actually, I wish he would have made us empty out all the sand and refill the bags," I said. "It would have been so ludicrous that no one would believe it."

I filled sandbags with the others until early afternoon. We ate an

MRE lunch under the trees in front of the CP. The wall I had helped build was thigh-high and ran most of the length of the building.

"Not high enough," Gunny had said. I was dreading the thought of filling sandbags all afternoon, but there wasn't any way to duck out of the working party. Fortunately, Staff Sergeant Summers managed to round up more bodies, and an even dozen of us left for the sand mine after lunch.

Corporal Nevelson, a veteran mau-mau everyone called Nels, said he knew where we might have an easier time digging. He took us behind the building where the service support element of the MAU, the MSSG, was headquartered. Two wooden troughs had been abandoned next to a huge bluff of red sand, and we set up an assembly line to fill sandbags.

Beckford and Silone shoveled sand into the trough while Hadley pushed it down into the bag that I held open under the trough. I was on my knees, and my arms were covered with the sand that didn't make it into the bag. As each bag was filled, I set it aside for someone else to tie shut and load into the trailer. The setup went like clockwork, and we thought we were hot stuff for coming up with such a clever scheme.

I got tired of having sand dumped over me and asked Corporal Hadley to trade jobs with me.

"I don't know about that," he said. "My secondary MOS is filling sandbags." MOS stands for Military Occupational Speciality and is a four-digit number that denotes an individual's job. I was an 0151, an administrative clerk, while a 2531 was a radio communicator. Jobs in the intelligence field begin with 02, and an 0311 was a basic rifleman, a grunt.

"Come on, Jeff," I begged. "I've had enough OJT [on-the-job training] to fill a pretty mean sandbag."

"I don't know. You haven't even been to Scooper School! Then there's Shovel Drill and Bag Stacking Class. Are you sure you can handle it?"

"I'll give it my best shot." Hadley handed me his shovel, and I started pushing sand down the trough and into bags.

Within a few hours, we had filled more sandbags using the troughs than we had all morning long by digging with shovels alone. I felt good. All of us were on a shit detail and knew it, but we made the best of it by keeping up a playful banter.

Not everyone was willing to work hard, however. A Marine named Taylor had a surly attitude and acted as though sand wouldn't wash off. He hadn't loaded more than three sandbags on the trailer and wore a scowl no amount of joking would erase. Even lazy Silone was putting in his fair share of work.

Finally, Hadley, fed up with Taylor's haughtiness, confronted him. "Why don't you drop the attitude and start working?"

"Make me."

"I don't have to make you. I'm ordering you."

"It's not that bad," I said. "In fact its kind of fun wallowing around in sand, filling bags, and making jokes. If you'd help out maybe you'd find out it's not that hard."

"I am working," Taylor said belligerently.

"Just get out of here," Hadley said. "We don't want you."

Taylor raised his fists, ready to start slugging.

"Get out of here!" Beckford shouted. Everyone picked up the words like a chant.

"Get out of here! Get out of here!"

Taylor stalked away.

"So much for *semper fidelis*," Hadley quipped sarcastically.

The working party continued to shovel sand and fill bags until dusk. With the last of the sandbags loaded, the trailer's tires were almost flat and couldn't support another ounce. I walked behind the jeep with the others while Silone drove to the CP.

It was almost 7:00 P.M. before we finished building the wall. Sand covered every inch of my body. I had it in my hair and in my boots. A film of grit covered my teeth. Even my pockets were full of sand. All I could think of was Shower!

"You've got field day," Sergeant Layland immediately informed me when I stepped into the basement. He had a twinkle in his eyes and was barely able to suppress his joy at sticking me with basement cleanup.

"The showers close in ten minutes," I argued.

"I don't care."

"I'm covered with sand."

"As far as I'm concerned you're on cleanup. Go talk to your 'Dad.' "

I stomped back to the CP. I couldn't find Major Converse, but Gunny Thorn was outside the staff NCO tent.

"Go get a goddamned shower," he croaked after I had explained.

I practically skipped back to the basement to get my shower gear. Hadley and Silone had waited an extra minute for me, and the three of us walked the quarter mile to the field shower, taking a shortcut through the motor pool.

Heaven! I was in heaven as the shower's hot water gushed over me. It was musty inside the tent, and the pipes clanged rhythmically as the diesel engine pumped heated water through them. But even the loud chuff-chuff sound of the engine and its occasional belch of blue smoke was not enough to take away the sheer luxury of feeling clean again.

"Three more minutes!" the mechanic running the shower shouted.

I rinsed under the water for a final, glorious minute, then went through an open doorway into the dressing tent pitched alongside. I dried off and put on a clean pair of cutoff shorts and a T-shirt. Rolling my filthy uniform into a tight bundle, I stepped outside to wait for Hadley and Silone.

The air was deliciously cool. The sky was clear and dark with a peppering of stars above the mountains to the east. The wistful sound of a harmonica came from a nearby tent.

"It's a beautiful night," Hadley said when he saw me staring at the mountains.

"Look at that!" I shouted, pointing at a stream of glowing red points that arched across the mountain. "It looks like fireworks. Maybe a Roman candle."

"That's not fireworks," Hadley said. "Those are tracer rounds from small arms fire. They're up there fighting."

We took the long route back to the basement so we could stay on pavement and avoid walking through sand. I glanced repeatedly toward the mountains but saw only the twinkling of village lights. Whoever was up there fighting, I decided, had called it quits for the evening. Perhaps they had concluded it was too beautiful a night to kill or to be killed and that there would be time enough for dying. "We owe God a death," Shakespeare wrote, but I knew I wanted to wait until the last possible moment before I paid my bill.

6

B Y FOUR O'CLOCK on the afternoon of 29 May, Battalion Landing Team 1/8 had completed its turnover with outgoing BLT 2/6
and assumed responsibility for the defense of Beirut International
Airport. BLT 1/8's first mobile and foot patrols were conducted that
afternoon. A platoon was designated as American Embassy Security
and flown to the joint United States/United Kingdom Embassy in
West Beirut. Embassy facilities had been shared with the British since
the van bombing of the American Embassy in April, and the normal
detachment of a dozen Marine security guards was inadequate to
defend the building.

The relief-in-place was completed on 30 May, and the 24th Marine
Amphibious Unit officially assumed full responsibilities as the U.S.
Contingent of the Multinational Force at two o'clock Greenwich mean
time. I knew the transfer of command was official because Gunny
Thorn had Mandenheart and me scale the CP and turn over the sign
above the main entrance. The opposite side of the sign identified
Colonel Timothy Geraghty as the commander of U.S. Forces ashore in
Lebanon.

Mandenheart and I decided we were on the road to fame and
fortune. Two photographers present for the colonel's relief-in-place
press conference took our picture as we changed the sign, and after that
kind of exposure we figured a six-figure movie contract, or at least a
spot on the "Tonight Show," couldn't be far behind.

I watched the news conference with interest. Colonel Geraghty
stood behind a podium outside the CP wearing his flak jacket and
helmet. We had been ordered to wear war gear whenever outside, so
that any lurking newsmen could see the Marines were prepared for
anything.

One of the reporters asked the colonel to comment on the presence
of the Marines in Lebanon.

"I personally feel that the commitment the president made here is
the correct one," Colonel Geraghty answered. "The Multinational

Force is providing a stability that is crucial at this point in time. The progress that the government of Lebanon and the Lebanese Armed Forces have made—and it has been truly remarkable progress—could not have taken place without the peacekeeping forces."

"Are the Marines well-prepared, Colonel?"

"Commodore France and I had the distinct advantage of being able to prepare for our stay in Beirut very early in the game." Commodore Morgan France was the Navy officer in command of the ships offshore as well as the overall commander of U.S. forces in Lebanon. "We were able to train together extensively," the colonel continued. "Navy and Marines. The early preparations, and the early insistence that this would be a team effort, has paid off. It's working here the way it should work."

The reporters continued to ask questions. Colonel Geraghty answered vaguely, being careful to stay in line with official U.S. policy. I realized he was a consummate politician. The enlisted troops knew the colonel was bucking for a star, and being the on-site commander in Lebanon was a big chance for recognition and to advance his career. Colonel Mead had commanded the 32d and 22d MAUs in Lebanon. He was now a brigadier general.

Colonel Geraghty was an exceptionally handsome man. He looked like a commander. He had an easy smile of perfect white teeth and a touch of gray in his hair and around the temples that gave him a distinguished look. Well-educated, urbane, witty, he was easy to respect.

His military credentials were impeccable. He had served in Vietnam, leading numerous reconnaissance patrols in the I Corps, and had been awarded the Bronze Star with Combat V and the Vietnam Cross of Gallantry, among other decorations. He had spent eighteen months before joining the MAU as an assistant chief of staff, Second Marine Division. It was no wonder that the junior enlisted troops called him "Uncle Tim" when there was no chance of being overheard. If Major Converse was our "dad," then Colonel Geraghty was definitely his older brother and the leader of the family.

After the news conference, I took off my blouse and got to work setting up the operations office. A pallet of mount-out boxes that had been stored in the hold of the ship for the transatlantic crossing was brought ashore, and Mandenheart and I carried boxes full of publications and six months of office supplies into the CP. The operations office had been assigned to the front of bay number one. It took three of us to force open the rusty corrugated iron door so we could see outside.

I set up two field desks and stacked the mount-out boxes on their sides, so I could easily gain access to the hundreds of publications we kept on file. Gunny asked me what I thought of our work space. I told him I was surprised it was so spacious. "In fact, this is better than our office back in North Carolina!" If I had known how much time I was going to spend kept behind my desk, I wouldn't have been quite so excited.

Gunny gave me a long list of jobs he wanted done, then disappeared. He was good at that.

The S-4 logistics section of the MAU was housed in the bay next to operations. A smooth debarkation off the ship, one of the major responsibilities of the logistics section, was complete, and the clerks had little to do except act as dispatchers for the headquarter's five jeeps.

I poked my head around the wall that separated the two offices. "Skating out of work again, I see," I said.

Corporal Brown looked up from the letter he was writing. "Get out of here you brown-nosing bootlicker," he snarled.

"Faggot!" I shot back.

"Homosexual shithead!"

Greetings out of the way, I sat on a corner of the table Brown was using as a desk. "Gunny gave me a shitload of work, Ben," I said. "I don't even want to get started."

Ben propped his feet on the table and tilted his chair back. "You're a corporal now," he drawled. "Make Mudfart do it." Gunny Thorn's name for Mandenheart had obviously stuck.

"Mudfart can't," I said. "Gunny put him on a working party."

Ben shrugged. He was a good ol' boy, a little on the red-neck side, and always had a cigarette dangling from the corner of his mouth. Devoted to his wife, he wrote her every day. "Did you hear what happened out at Alpha Company?" he asked.

"No."

"One of our boys on sentry got a bit bored last night and shot two Lebanese soldiers clean through the legs with one round. Claims it was an accidental discharge."

"Is that possible?" I said.

"No way! The Marine had to have been aiming to get both soldiers. That boy's in trouble now. Wait 'til those reporters get ahold of this!"

" 'Ruthless Marine Shoots Innocent Lebanese Soldier.' I can see the headline now."

"I'm sure 'Uncle Tim' will come up with a pretty good explanation."

"Yeah. But I sure would like to be there when he gives it."

Ben and I laughed, but an explanation to the media wasn't forthcoming. They never picked up the story. The monthly report to Headquarters Marine Corps stated the incident was accidental, but Ben later told me the lance corporal who pulled the trigger had been sent back to the ship and was up for a summary court-martial.

⚜   ⚜   ⚜

The routine of being in Lebanon settled on me like a dark cloud. Excitement turned into the mundane in an agonizingly brief time. I read about the BLT's mobile and foot patrols, wishing I could go into the city.

Four to seven foot patrols were conducted in the area around Beirut International Airport, and two mobile patrols went into the city each day. The operations office received a map overlay of the routes a week in advance. Care was taken to make sure the number, route, and times of the patrols were varied and that a pattern was not established.

Many of the patrols were made with Lebanese Army personnel. A lieutenant from the LAF accompanied the mobile patrols, and a four-man fire team (a basic combat unit composed of a team leader, automatic rifleman, grenadier, and scout/rifleman) went on selected foot patrols. The patrols made position reports by radio to the Combat Operations Center (COC) in the BLT building. MAU headquarters had its own COC, which was responsible for maintaining control on a higher level.

There was absolutely no chance of me going on one of the BLT patrols. That wasn't my job, and Gunny liked to keep me in the office. I was his administrative clerk. When it was the operation section's turn to supply a man to ride shotgun on one of Colonel Geraghty's trips into the city, Gunny always blustered, "Mudfart can go, goddamnit. He's not doing anything."

We've only been here a short time, I reminded myself. I'll get a chance to see all the sites everyone else has already had a chance to visit—the Embassy, the Ministry of Defense, the Presidential Palace.

"Trash run!" Scaly stuck his head over the sandbag wall and shouted. "Who wants to go?"

"I'll go!" I jumped up, grabbed my helmet, flak jacket, and rifle. Gunny wasn't in the office, and it was my chance to get out.

Scaly was a quiet lance corporal of slight build who worked for Staff Sergeant Summers. He made a trash run to the nearby dump several times a week and needed someone to accompany him each time as a shotgun and to help dump trash from the trailer. His real name was Watson but everyone called him "Scaly" because he seldom took a shower.

The trash trailers were parked across the street from the CP, and Scaly backed a jeep into position. He jumped out and hooked up a trailer overflowing with trash. Scaly was a driver by MOS, and he burned rubber as he double clutched the jeep and raced out of the compound.

We turned left at the wrought-iron gate, and Scaly drove like a demon past the CP. MSSG headquarters, more sandbag than building, was to the right as we charged through the main gate. A large sandbag and plywood sentry post was in the middle of the road, and the Marine on duty waved us through. A blue sign above the guard shack announced:

TRANS MEDITERRANEAN AIRLINES
CIVIL AVIATION
43 BATTALION, LEBANESE ARMY
24 MARINE AMPHIBIOUS UNIT

Someone had planted a small Lebanese flag in the middle of the sandbags, and I slapped a magazine into my rifle as we passed.

Scaly veered right and merged with cars racing down a four-lane boulevard heading away from the airport. We wove through traffic and passed a joint Marine/Lebanese checkpoint. Our jeep was flagged straight through by a scruffy Lebanese soldier, but most of the civilian cars were stopped and given a cursory search.

A large mosque was on the right a quarter mile further down the road. It had been built by the PLO before their evacuation from Beirut, and rather than being ornate, its onion-shaped dome was made of austere concrete surrounded by wooden scaffolding. A tall minaret stood to one side, and loudspeakers mounted at its top blared Arabic, which was unintelligible to most of us.

Scaly turned left, whipping around the corner. He made an immediate right, raising a cloud of dust as we jounced down a dirt road. I could smell the stench of the dump long before I could see it.

A dozen kids spotted us and began running for the jeep as we approached. The fastest two jumped into the trailer while the jeep was still moving. They frantically dug through the trash, tossing out sheets of plastic and empty MRE boxes. The other kids ran beside the jeep shouting, "Hello, Joe!"

Scaly jerked to a stop. The trailer was a mound of kids digging for choice bits of uneaten MREs. We got out of the jeep.

"Get out of here!" Scaly screamed. He savagely pushed kids away to get to the trailer hitch. We each grabbed a corner of the trailer and flipped it over, spilling trash and kids everywhere.

I felt sorry for the children. They were filthy. Ulcerated sores oozing pus dotted the legs of one boy who couldn't have been more than eight. Another was missing a hand. His bright eyes gleamed as he salvaged an unopened package of cocoa powder from the heap.

Scaly and I righted the trailer, and as I reattached it to the hitch, Scaly strode to the jeep and produced an unopened MRE from behind the driver's seat. He held it high in his right hand. The kids knew what was required of them and gathered in a group. Scaly tossed the meal fifty yards in the opposite direction, and the children made a mad dash for the prize. An older boy got to it first. He smiled gleefully and clutched it to his chest like a child holding a gaily wrapped present on Christmas morning.

"I hate this place," Scaly said. "Let's get out of here."

We jumped into the jeep and sped back to the CP. The haunting faces of the children were frozen in my mind. This is why we're in Lebanon, I concluded—for the children.

Scaly put the empty trailer back in its spot and hooked up the next in line. We drove back to the dump to empty it.

I made four trips in all that morning. By the final load, I looked upon the scene with hardened eyes. I pushed the children away from the trailer as viciously as Scaly, screaming at them to get back. I wanted them to go away, and I hated them for making me hate myself.

I avoided trash runs after that and no longer felt as anxious to leave the safety of my desk.

7

I WAS DRUNK. Laura Branigan's earthy voice wailed from a cassette player on the shelf above the bar. Clint Eastwood, facing death in a spaghetti western on video tape, mouthed unheard words. Arabic and French subtitles flashed by at the bottom of the TV screen.

The bar was known as "Branigan's of Beirut." Marines from 24 MAU on the previous float had painted the name on the wall in large, red letters outlined with black and blue. A lightning bolt sliced through the middle, and neatly printed on a sheet of paper taped to the wall underneath was the word REVISITED.

"Give me another Almaza, Archie," I shouted.

Archie, driver by day, bartender by night, opened the crusty refrigerator and took out a lukewarm beer. He slid the green can down the bar toward me and marked a tick next to my name in a notebook. At fifty cents a pop, beer flowed like piss, even though each man was supposed to be limited to two a day.

I popped the top on the can and guzzled, hoping if I drank fast enough, I wouldn't have to taste the bitter Lebanese brew. I drained half the can; that was the only way I could get it down.

All the enlisted troops in MAU headquarters not on duty were either in the bar or standing outside in the cool evening air waiting for the movie to start. Silone was setting up the single projector on a table in the parking lot to show yet another B-movie, *Piranha!* The screen was a white square painted on the building across the street.

I had given up on the movies several nights before. An almost constant stream of jeeps and six-ton trucks passed the command post, washing out the picture and obliterating the sound. Other than writing letters home, reading or getting drunk, there was little to do in the evenings.

Ross strode into the bar.

"Long schlong!" Archie whooped. "What'll it be?"

"I ain't nothin' but a love machine," Ross began to sing. "Pull my thing and watch me sing!"

"Give him an Almaza on my tab," I said.

"Oh, no," Ross deadpanned. "I do not drink beer. We Marines prefer soda or juice. Alcohol dehydrates us."

Archie snickered. Ross was poking fun at an article published in the newspaper *USA Today*. The "journalist" had written that the Marines in Lebanon didn't drink beer because it dehydrated them. If we had been asked, the reporter would have discovered we were rationed because a drunken Marine on one of the line companies had shot up a ditch with an M-16.

Archie handed a beer to Big Guy who quickly proceeded to down it. Ross was a beer connoisseur, even brewing his own back in the States. He ran several miles each noon along the perimeter road that encircled the airport to keep from getting a beer gut, and he actually liked the taste of Almaza.

The Laura Branigan tape ended, and Archie popped in a heavy metal group. I beat a hasty retreat to the parking lot. Space Chase, half-looped, was leaning against the sandbag wall. A few Marines were sitting on top of the wall, while others had found a spot on the pavement or on one of the chairs purloined from the work spaces. Two enterprising Marines had yanked the bench seat from the back of a nearby jeep and were getting comfortable until one of the officers told them to put it back.

Not all of the Marines in the parking lot were assigned to MAU headquarters. Although each subordinate unit had its own club facility and showed a movie every night, coming to MAU headquarters was like making a trip downtown.

Colonel Geraghty walked past the spot where Chase and I stood, heading toward the main entrance of the CP. Chase, gregarious and ever mindful of an opportunity to make a few brownie points, said, "How are you this evening, sir?"

Colonel Geraghty stopped. Two Marines from another unit jumped to attention and saluted smartly. Chase and I didn't bother because we felt comfortable around "Uncle Tim." The enlisted troops of MAU headquarters had been instructed to salute only those who were ranked colonel and above since the headquarters area was always swarming with brass. I hated saluting officers anyway, feeling it was demeaning, and was thankful for the relaxed rules.

"Fine," the colonel answered. "How are you men tonight?"

"Great, sir!" Chase exclaimed.

"What's the movie?" the colonel asked.

"*Piranha!*, sir."

"What's it about?"

"It's a fish, sir."

"I know it's a fucking fish," the colonel said. "What's the movie about, Chase?"

Everyone within earshot roared. Chase turned crimson. "It's about a fish, sir," he stammered.

The colonel, smiling, shook his head and walked away.

"Way to go, Chase!" someone screamed, pounding him on the back.

"Lights!" Silone shouted. Someone turned off the flood lights that lit the parking lot and reel one of the movie began. I quit watching after a piranha, out of the water for hours, jumped across a room and attached itself to the jugular of one of its countless, unsuspecting victims.

I went to the operations office and found Mudfart writing letters and listening to a transistor radio.

"Yo, blood, what it be like?" I asked. Mudfart and I had a game going. He was teaching me how to be black.

Mudfart laughed and gave me a high five, slapping my hand.

"I've been practicing those moves you taught me," I said.

"Bet." *Bet* or *bet that*, as Mudfart had explained, meant "okay."

I waved my hand up and down and slid backward along the floor à la Michael Jackson. Mudfart just laughed.

"Yo," I said. "Let's put a quarter on the slab and get in the serious mix with some freaks!" (Let's meet some women!)

"By george, I think he's got it," Mudfart said in his best British accent.

"Are we going to get mail tonight?"

"Yeah, five thousand pounds. S-1 already went to pick it up."

We received mail several times a week. It was flown from JFK in New York, to Rome, and then straight into Beirut International. Usually in our hands by evening, mail was the highlight of the day.

S-1, the administrative section of the MAU, was in charge of mail call, and I didn't envy them their job. The clerks were bombarded with questions about mail all day long: "When are we going to get mail?" "Is the mail sorted yet?" "Why didn't I get any mail?"

The S-1 clerk sauntered wearily into the office with two red mail bags slung over his shoulders. He had just come from the main post office at MSSG. Three Marines trailed behind him like dogs following a bitch in heat.

Five thousand pounds of mail wasn't a lot for all the Marines on shore, and it only took a few minutes for the clerk to sort the packages and handful of letters for MAU headquarters. I picked up the operation section's short stack and anxiously thumbed through, finding only disappointment. No mail for me.

I tossed Mudfart his heavily perfumed letter and went to Branigan's to give Ross his package. Captain Kettering, the Fire Support Coordination Officer, was in the company grade quarters in the bay next to Branigan's. Kettering was a big bear of a man who kept his head shaved except for a dark patch on top. The style was called a "high-and-tight," and only Marines who were extremely gung-ho wore it. It seemed whenever Kettering received mail I didn't, and when I got a letter he did without.

"Looks like it's your turn for mail tonight, sir," I said, handing him a letter from his wife.

"Mail? We got mail? Did I get any mail?" Lieutenant Block chattered rapidly. "Where's the mail?" Block was a second lieutenant fresh out of The Basic School. Boyishly thin with reddish-brown hair, he was twenty-three but acted ten years younger. He liked to think he had been in Vietnam and was always talking about "Da Nang '69, The Rainy Season." He constantly fondled the butt of his .45 for reassurance, but most of the time he wandered around the compound talking to himself. He would approach a group of enlisted troops, stand arms akimbo, and manfully state: "How's it going, men?" No one ever answered. Bets had been placed on who would be the first to lose it. Lieutenant Block had won hands down.

"The mail's in S-1 . . . sir," I said. I cringed to have to call him "sir." Block raced out of the officer's quarters.

"Thanks for the letter, Corporal Petit," Kettering said.

I found Major Converse in the Staff NCOs and Officers Club and gave him his letter. The Officers Club was at the opposite end of the CP from Branigan's and a lot nicer. It had tables and chairs; we had wooden benches.

The officers and senior enlisted men were watching a video tape.

The tapes came from Habibi's Video in the Chouf, and one of the Arabic-speaking Marines from the Interrogator-Translator Team picked up a supply once a week on "intelligence gathering" trips. While the enlisted troops were prohibited from drinking hard liquor, the officers club served both mixed drinks and beer. We weren't allowed to watch just any video tape either. Colonel Geraghty had banned the film *Caligula* as too pornographic for the enlisted troops, and we had to resort to a secret showing in Branigan's after hours.

Major Converse thanked me for the letter. Several of the officers and staff NCOs who hadn't received anything eyed it covetously.

Silone had changed reels while I was delivering mail, and now the piranha were chewing on a ship. I headed for home.

Watching the Christians and Muslims slug it out in the mountains at night had become a popular spectator sport, and I decided to climb to the top of the Safety Center building before going to the basement. It was easy enough to get to the top. A flight of stairs took me to the second floor, and I was able to crawl out onto the lower roof through a missing wall. A ladder gained access to the upper roof and a panoramic view of the city and mountains.

A half dozen Marines stood outside passing around a pair of binoculars as they watched a firefight in the hills.

"See that building?" someone pointed out when it was my turn to look through the lenses.

I focused on the spot indicated. Every few minutes, a burst of tracer rounds would majestically soar from a third- or fourth-floor window and arc into an adjacent building. The volley of rounds was quickly returned, and everyone oohed and ahed as though they were watching a Fourth of July fireworks display.

It was easy to forget men were up there dying.

I handed the binoculars to the next Marine in line and went to the basement to hit the rack.

The United States Contingent of the Multinational Force was a separate political entity. The Marines maintained a friendly relationship with the other forces involved in the peacekeeping effort, but there wasn't a combined headquarters. None of the member forces reported

operationally to one another or to the Lebanese Armed Forces, and
since each had been asked to assist Lebanon on an individual basis,
each pursued an independent and bilateral relationship with the
government.

The British, French, Italian, and American contingents maintained
a central communications link at the Lebanese Presidential Palace in
Babda, a suburb of Beirut. Duty officers monitored radio nets and
provided liaison among the contingents as well as with the Lebanese
government. Colonel Geraghty attended a weekly coordination meeting held at the Ministry of Defense in the Chouf to discuss military,
political, and intelligence reports with his counterparts.

In addition, a Marine officer lived with each force to provide close
personal contact and to coordinate cross-training exercises. The officer
had to be fluent in the language of his assigned force, but it was difficult
to find Italian speakers. Although Silone spoke fluent Italian, he wasn't
qualified to do the job; he wasn't an officer.

Being liaison officer was a posh assignment, particularly in the
French camp. The French soldiers were allowed to go on liberty in the
city, each man had a wine ration, food was more sumptuously prepared, and they had something the Marines didn't—women in the
compound. A platoon of nurses was assigned to the French headquarters.

The French held occasional parties to which some of our officers were
invited. Early on the morning of 16 June, Major Converse informed me
I would be driving him to the French headquarters that evening.

I had just returned from a mess hall breakfast at the Battalion
Landing Team building. Hot meals had finally begun, and we had a
break from MREs twice a day. The food wasn't very good, meals
prepared for 1,200 never are, but at least it was a change from the
monotony of the same twelve prepackaged meals.

NCOs ate in style; we had our own dining hall. Two plywood and
mosquito-screened shacks had been built in front of the BLT. Rather
than wait in the long line for the main mess hall inside the building,
officers and staff NCOs had their shack, we had ours. For breakfast, a
cook would fry eggs to order on a portable grill, while the main mess
hall served greenish rehydrated eggs. I missed milk the most. Occasionally, lumpy and undrinkable dried milk was available, but most of
the time it was weak Kool-Aid, warm water, or nothing.

I awakened each morning at 6:00. Thankfully, reveille wasn't held in our basement berthing area, and we were allowed to get up on our own terms. The Combat Operations Center in the CP was manned twenty-four hours a day, and the radio operators on the night shift were allowed to sleep late.

MAU headquarters had a luxury that the subordinate units did without—running water. Two heads equipped with showers, toilets, and sinks were inside the CP. The smaller head was for field grade officers ranked major and above. The larger one was for staff NCOs and company grade officers. The junior enlisted troops were allowed inside the heads to clean them but never to use them.

We had access to a dilapidated head on the first floor of the Safety Center building, which we shared with a couple of Lebanese soldiers. It didn't have a shower, but three of its four sinks worked most of the time. The three toilets worked sporadically, at best. I used the head for shaving, peering into a cracked and dirty mirror mounted above the sinks. The Lebanese water was untreated and contained raw sewage. Braver souls than I brushed their teeth using it, but I always had a canteen of purified water at my disposal.

Outhouses were strategically placed about the compound. One was on the path to the BLT and another was near MAU headquarters. Both were a long way from the basement in an emergency.

A miasma of flies and stench hovered about "piss tubes," which were long pipes that jutted from the ground near the outhouses. The "shitters," as the outhouses were called, were three seaters with a plywood wall between each seat for a bit of privacy. Waste matter was collected in sawed-off, fifty-gallon barrels, and the weekly job to be avoided at all cost was changing the barrels and burning the fecal matter after mixing it with diesel fuel.

Marines not fortunate enough to be assigned to MAU headquarters had to shave outside with water obtained from "water bulls," which were mobile five-hundred-gallon tanks that were filled each day with purified water. A Marine would place his all-purpose helmet under the faucet, fill it with water, and use the steel pot as a shaving basin. MAU headquarter's water bull was stationed against the movie building and was chiefly used for drinking water.

We thought we were special because we had our own head and protected it zealously from the BLT Marines who lived down the hill.

A bright yellow sign outside our building warned THIS BLDG IS OFF LIMITS TO ALL BLT MARINES.

Most of my workday was spent handling message traffic. The number of messages received from dozens of government agencies such as the CIA, DIA, and Department of Defense was voluminous. It seemed that everyone in the world wanted to tell us something.

I picked up message traffic at 0700 each morning from the communications center behind the CP. I sorted through each message, highlighting its subject, then placed it on a read board. The board went into the Combat Operations Center, so the officers could take a look at it sometime during the day.

The messages were in a peculiar military code. They were from places like COMNAVSURFLANT, COMSIXTHFLT, CINCUSNAVEUR LONDON, USCINCEUR VAIHINGEN GERMANY, CMC, and FMFLANT. Some had been sent ZEN, some ZNY. We received SITREPS, OPREPS, INTELREPS, and OPORDERS. Keeping it all straight was confusing.

I removed old messages from the read board each morning. After separating the important ones for filing, I placed the rest in the burn bag. Most of the messages were marked Secret or Confidential and couldn't simply be thrown away. Several times each week I trudged to a barrel behind the CP with two grocery sacks full of papers. I would spend hours feeding the messages one sheet at a time into the flames until nothing but ashes remained. But no matter how thoroughly I burned, it seemed a few scraps of paper always survived.

"You've got to be more careful," Staff Sergeant Garcia would warn me, holding out a charred fragment of message. "This could get you into trouble. Remember OPSEC is the key."

OPSEC (Operational Security) was constantly drummed into our heads. "Loose lips sink ships," was a phrase I thought had gone out of use after World War II, but it was still an important motto being used by the Marine Corps in 1983.

Lunch time was free time. I quit work at precisely 1100 hours and didn't resume until 1300. Marines are allowed two hours for lunch so they can do physical training (PT), but I hardly ever spent my lunch time running. Instead, I became the Julia Child of MREs.

My ingredients were simple. No flambées or soufflés for me. I would mix the beans from one MRE with the meat sauce from another. *Voilà*, chili. Or, my *pièce de résistance*, a dehydrated beef patty boiled in water and served with cheese spread on crackers. An after-dinner drink was cocoa powder mixed with instant coffee and heated: *café au chocolat* in a canteen cup.

Mudfart and I saved items from our MREs in a box for later use. Most of the time it was full of ham and chicken loaf, the MRE that had won the Alpo award, but we also managed to save pineapple and maple cakes, chocolate brownies, crackers, and packages of peanut butter. We kept the packages of apple and grape jelly under lock and key, however. They were a scarce MRE item, and if we left them unguarded some unscrupulous individual would take them. Peanut butter and jelly on crackers made a great snack.

After lunch, I would put my nose back to the grindstone, sometimes. Gunny Thorn was never in the office, particularly in the afternoons. He was always in one of three places: the club watching a video tape, his tent sleeping, or telling his life story to one of the reporters who seemed to haunt the compound. Mudfart and I didn't object. The office ran more smoothly without the Thorn standing over our shoulder and barking orders.

Mudfart usually spent afternoons working on one of the signs Major Converse constantly dreamed up; signs plastered all over the CP identified everything. I filed messages.

Sometimes Mudfart would suddenly sniff the air like a crazed bloodhound. "Women!" he would shout.

We would both spring to our feet and rush to the sandbag wall, peering eagerly into the parking lot. Mudfart was never wrong. A woman, usually a reporter, was always standing outside the entrance to the CP.

"I can smell a woman within a hundred yards," Mudfart boasted.

The news "woman in the compound" spread rapidly, and Marines would poke their heads out doors and peek over the tops of sandbag walls to get a glimpse.

My work day ended at 4:30 P.M. I would head straight for the mess hall to get the evening meal out of the way. The showers ran from five o'clock to seven, and washing away the red dust that permeated the air and my skin was a necessity.

After a shower, the evening would stretch before me: another night of Branigan's, another night of hoping for mail, another night of B-movies, another night of boredom.

The sun was setting, silhouetting mosques and spiraling minarets against the sky, black on blood-red. An unearthly hymn echoed through the hushed city calling the faithful to prayer. Inside mosques and homes, followers of Muhammad solemnly faced Mecca and fell to their knees.

It was Islam's holiest month: Ramadan. The date, 16 June, marked the anniversary of the Battle of Badr, and it was only ten days before the celebration of Lailat al-Qadr, the night on which the *Koran* was sent down from heaven.

Ramadan is a month of fasting, and only after dusk and the evening prayer are the faithful allowed to take nourishment in food and drink. Id al Fitr, the final day of Ramadan, would come on the last day of June.

I was sitting in the back of a jeep in full battle dress, racing though the lawless streets of Beirut. I was shotgun for the second jeep of a three-jeep convoy headed for French headquarters. Our passengers were three U.S. Navy commanders, the French liaison officer, and Major Converse, who spoke some French.

I had been warned that evening excursions were usually boring. "You get to sit in the jeep for three or four hours, while the officer goes inside and has a good time." But I hadn't had any choice; Major Converse had selected me for the trip.

I wasn't disappointed not to be behind the wheel. Only one traffic law prevailed in Beirut; every man for himself. The concept "lane" didn't exist, and drivers wove through traffic like adversaries in the Daytona 500. I kept a close watch for snipers on nearby buildings, attempting not to cringe as we careened around corners.

The convoy turned right off a boulevard lit by street lamps and halted. In front of us, two sandbagged sentry towers armed with machine guns stood above a large gate. Concertina wire ran along the top of a stone fence on either side. The gate swung open.

Two French soldiers emerged carrying FA MAS automatic rifles slung so that the weapons were at hip level. One soldier pointed at the magazines in our rifles, indicating we should remove them. I took mine out and shoved it in my flak jacket pocket, then yanked my rifle's charging handle to the rear with a snap. Peering into the chamber, I confirmed there wasn't a round in it and slammed the bolt home.

The convoy drove into the French compound. A palatial mansion stood among gardens of palm and orange trees. The jeeps stopped by a sweep of stairs that led to the entry hall and discharged the passengers. I glimpsed a glittering chandelier of crystal through a picture window. The scene looked like something out of Scheherazade and *Tales of the 1001 Arabian Nights,* but the illusion shattered when I realized the building's façade had been strafed with machine gun fire. The chandelier was cracked and dirty, the grounds ill-kept.

Major Converse and the Navy commanders were greeted warmly by French officers waiting on the steps. They went inside. The driver of the jeep I was in ground gears as he reversed and parked under a huge tree next to some tents in front of the headquarters building. He killed the motor, and I sat in silence listening to the ting-ting of the cooling engine.

"Bonsoir!" a small-framed but exuberant Frenchman exclaimed, taking my hand and shaking it vigorously. He handed me a patch then went on to the next Marine and made the same gesture of good will.

I took a look at the patch in the dying light. It was a stylized man in profile, possibly Neptune, holding a trident. Two white stars were in the upper right corner.

"Merci," I said. The Frenchman smiled broadly. He was wearing the tightly cut, dark green fatigues all the French soldiers wore. His trousers were bloused above odd-looking boots laced shut with straps and buckles.

Three more soldiers joined us. They didn't speak English, and I quickly exhausted my limited French vocabulary asking them how they were. But that was enough to make me the unofficial translator for the Marines, and I was soon dredging French words from the back of my mind that I didn't even know I knew.

"Ask them where they're from."

"Ask them how long they've been in Lebanon."

"Ask them if they think we'll see any action."

"Ask them..."

"I don't know how to say that," I frequently had to respond.

The language of weapons is common to all soldiers, and we began examining each others' automatic rifles. The French FA MAS was extraordinarily light and compact. It fired the same size round as our M-16. The exuberant Frenchman told me it was made entirely of plastic and fiberglass. The Marines were impressed with the French weapon and pointed out some of the deficiencies of the M-16.

"Pepsi? *Bière?*" one of the soldiers asked. We all answered "beer," and the soldier left, returning a few minutes later with a dozen cans of warm Almaza on a tray. He passed them out, and we popped the tops.

"Bonne vie!" the French soldiers toasted.

"Cheers!"

Dividing into smaller groups, two or three Marines to a Frenchman, we continued communicating at a rudimentary level. The more beer I drank, the better my French got, and I was soon giving the other Marines a lesson in French 101.

"How do you say 'How are you?'"

"Comment allez-vous."

"How do I tell him my name?"

"Je m'appelle."

"How do I ask him if he likes being in Lebanon?"

"Try pointing."

I spoke with a young, blond soldier. I learned his name was Henri Bergot and that his father farmed in the Normandy region of France. He was in the military for two years of mandatory service and anxious to return to France and civilian life. He wanted more from life than being a radio operator and driver for his *capitaine.* He sounded just like a typical Marine.

I asked him why some of the soldiers wore maroon berets, like his, while others wore dark green. He explained that the maroon berets were for regular French Army troops while the green were for the *Légion Etrangère.* I had met and was talking with French Foreign Legionnaires!

One of the Marines had an extra American flag and traded it for one of the patches the French soldiers wore on their sleeves. The Frenchman who had given us the patches wore a green beret. I pointed at it, then at my cover, asking him if he would like to trade. He agreed and removed his beret. I placed my Marine cover on his head, showing him that it should be worn squarely. He put the beret on my head at a jaunty angle with the brass emblem facing forward. The emblem was a circle. Inside at the bottom was a round grenade from which seven flames rose, the outer two curled back.

A stocky, muscular legionnaire strode over to the jeep. He had close-cropped, firey-red hair.

"How's it going?" he asked in a thick, German accent. He was drunk.

"Good!" I answered. I drained the last of the beer from my can.

"Come," he insisted. I followed the legionnaire to a nearby tent. He went inside, then emerged carrying two canteen cups and a bottle. He handed me one of the cups and sloshed in four fingers of dark rum.

"Drink! Gut!" he said.

I took a swig. The rum burned a firey trail down my throat. We sat on a bench and I asked him how he liked the Legion.

"It's a good life. Tough, but good," he proclaimed. "The Legion is my family."

I discovered the legionnaire was a sergeant for the third time and had been in almost fourteen years. In another year he would be eligible to receive a small pension and was going to collect it in Tahiti. He had been stationed in the African desert in Djibouti and had seen action in Kolwezi in '78 when the Legion landed to protect Europeans from the Katangan Tiger rebels.

He told me about Camerone, a Mexican battle enshrined in Legion legend, where fewer than sixty legionnaires—reduced to three—stood against an entire army, keeping their vow to fight to the death rather than surrender. He spoke of the wooden hand of the commanding officer, Capitaine Danjou, later found on the battlefield, as though it were his own. The hand, he said, was on display in Aubagne, France and was paraded each year on Camerone Day, 30 April. He spoke in a voice heavy with pride, making the battle sound like it had occurred yesterday, rather than in 1863.

"Honneur et fidélité," he said. "It is our way of life." He had a rough face, ravaged by sun and time, but there was a softness in his eyes.

I didn't tell him I had wanted to be a legionnaire. It didn't seem right.

"My most proud moment," he said, "was receiving my white kepi." The *kepi blanc*, the white, flattopped hat, was an object he held in near veneration. His had been awarded in a torch-lit ceremony at sunset. He had sung *"Le Boudin"* and placed the hat on his head for the first time, bound by his pledge of honor and fidelity. "I was truly a legionnaire," he said.

He stood and loudly began to sing the Legion marching song in off-key, German-accented French:

> *Nous sommes des degourdis,*
> *Nous sommes des lascars,*
> *Nous sommes des Légionnaires.*
> *Nos anciens ont su mourir*
> *Pour la Glorie de la Légion,*
> *Nous saurons bien tous périr*
> *Suivant la tradition.*

> *Au cours de nos campagnes lointaines,*
> *Affrontant la fièvre et le feu,*
> *Nous oublions avec nos peines*
> *La mort qui nous oublie si peu*
> *Nous, la Légion.*

> (We are sharp,
> We are warriors,
> We are Legionnaires.
> Our forefathers knew how to die
> For the Glory of the Legion,
> We shall know how to perish,
> Following tradition.

> In the course of our far-off campaigns,
> In the face of fever and fire,
> We forget, along with our sorrows,
> The death that so seldom forgets
> Us, the Legion.)

He had tears in his eyes, and it struck me he was the loneliest man I had ever met.

I drained the last of the rum from my canteen cup and staggered to my feet. I shook the legionnaire's hand, thanked him, and rejoined the others.

Major Converse and the Navy commanders flowed liquidly out of the headquarters building and into the jeeps at ten o'clock. They had enjoyed the French wine and were laughing. I had never seen Major Converse in such a good mood. He slapped me on the back and gave me a thumbs up sign.

The French soldiers and legionnaires we had met waved goodbye. Two French jeeps escorted us out of the compound and led the way home.

I couldn't help thinking it could have been me living in the French compound. It could have been me talking with the visiting Americans, speaking fluent French, and singing *"Le Boudin"* with *"honneur."* I touched the beret on my head fondly, knowing this was the closest I would ever come to being in the French Foreign Legion.

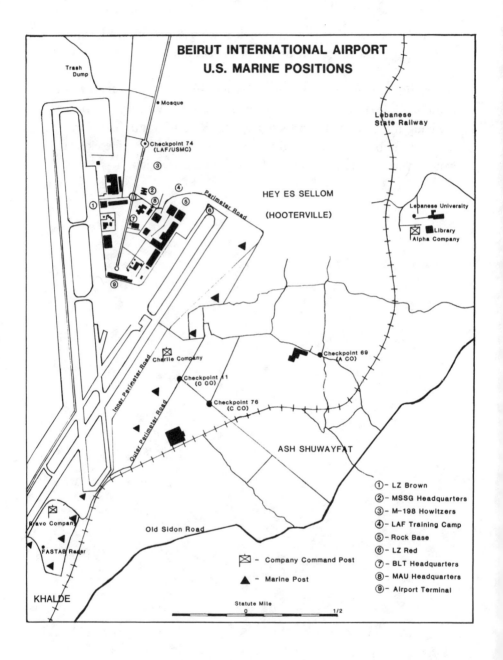

BEIRUT INTERNATIONAL AIRPORT
U.S. MARINE POSITIONS

Trash Dump

Mosque

Checkpoint 74 (LAF/USMC)

Lebanese State Railway

③

② ④

① ⑧ ⑤

⑦ ⑥

⑨

Perimeter Road

HEY ES SELLOM

(HOOTERVILLE)

Lebanese University

Library
Alpha Company

Inner Perimeter Road

Charlie Company

Outer Perimeter Road

Checkpoint 69 (A CO)

Checkpoint 11 (O CO)

Checkpoint 76 (C CO)

ASH SHUWAYFAT

Bravo Company

FASTAB Radar

Old Sidon Road

KHALDE

① – LZ Brown
② – MSSG Headquarters
③ – M-198 Howitzers
④ – LAF Training Camp
⑤ – Rock Base
⑥ – LZ Red
⑦ – BLT Headquarters
⑧ – MAU Headquarters
⑨ – Airport Terminal

☒ – Company Command Post

▲ – Marine Post

Statute Mile
0   1/2

8

"Formation!" Staff Sergeant Summers shouted. "Let's go.
Formation!" It was almost 0800 and time for morning formation
in front of the command post. Summers strode through the CP,
badgering the enlisted troops to get outside. "Let's go," he droned.
"Formation!"

"Why do we have to have these stupid formations?" I asked
Mudfart. "They're a complete waste of time."

"The sergeant major wants to talk to us this morning."

"Oh, no. Not again!" June was ending on a sour note. I was
wrestling with a hangover, and the thought of listening to one of the
sergeant major's speeches made my head throb. Mudfart and I
grabbed our covers and went outside. Twenty of the enlisted troops
were already in the parking lot lined up in three ranks, and I claimed a
spot at the end of the last row next to Ben.

" 'Bout time you got out here," he said. Everyone was talking and
joking. Formations in boot camp had meant standing at the position of
attention without moving or speaking, for hours if necessary. That sort
of nonsense had worn off us long ago.

Summers, a frown pasted on his face, emerged from the CP and
stood in front of the formation. He glanced at his watch repeatedly.
"How about it, Cavendish?" he finally said, noticing Colonel Geraghty's
personal driver in a jeep outside the CP entrance. "Formation. Now."

"I'm on standby to drive the colonel to the LZ," Cavendish
protested. Cav polished the windshield of the colonel's jeep everyday as
he waited, until it gleamed in the bright sunlight. He had been using
the I'm-on-standby excuse to get out of morning formations since our
arrival.

"You can standby in formation," Summers insisted.

A shrill whistle blast cut off Cav's reply. "Colors!" a voice shouted.

Summers called the platoon to attention then saluted as he faced
toward the two flagpoles partially hidden behind the senior staff NCO
tent. The American and Lebanese flags were jerkily raised into view.

The American flag fell from sight as it neared the top of the pole. After a moment, it was briskly raised to the top.

"Silone," Summers murmured exasperatedly. Summers was responsible for insuring that the flags were raised each morning at eight o'clock and lowered each evening at sunset. It was a struggle to find someone for flag detail, and Summers was always on the prowl. Summers shanghaied Silone for a month's worth of flag detail when he overheard Silone boasting that he hadn't raised a flag once during his two floats and didn't intend to start now. Silone had already served most of his month's sentence, but despite lots of practice raising the flag, he always got it wrong. Two days before he had flown the Lebanese flag upside down.

Three whistle blasts sounded. Summers cut his salute and faced the formation. The three Marines on flag detail marched from behind the tent and halted a dozen yards in front of the formation. Everyone began to cheer and clap.

"Way to go, Silone!" someone shouted.

"I didn't do it! Honest!" Silone claimed. "I blew the whistle today." He dangled the olive-drab whistle at arm's length. "See!"

"Knock it off!" Summers said. The flag detail got in line at the end of the formation.

"Here comes the Smaj," whispered Ben. "Smaj" was an exceedingly disrespectful term for sergeants major and one most hated with a passion.

"Pleh me!" Ross groaned in a voice a little too loud. A titter went through the formation. The sergeant major was a pompous, little man with the tightest high-and-tight in the unit. He had two folds of skin on either side of the back of his neck that looked like a cobra's hood. "The sergeant major's neck is so tight," Ross had once claimed in Branigan's after a few beers, "that it puts pressure on that pea-sized brain of his. He tries to call 'Help me!' but instead it comes out backwards, 'Pleh me!' That's why no one ever listens to him." Since then, Ross was guaranteed an easy laugh with his Smaj imitation.

The sergeant major marched to the front of the formation. "Men," he said in a gruff voice. "You've been screwing up! This place looks like a shit pen." My eyes glazed over as I stopped listening to the Smaj's discourse on how screwed up we were. All I could do was stare at his tobacco-stained mouth and missing front tooth as he ranted.

A few minutes into the familiar speech he had us gather around him in a semicircle. "Now, you all know there's a whorehouse just outside the compound, men." That was news to me. My ears perked up. "Two boys from Alpha Company got caught going over the wire last night."

I looked at Ben and smiled. Scuttlebutt like this made our day.

"Don't do it!" the sergeant major admonished. "I know you want to get your wick dipped and play a little hide the sausage. Your gal Suzy Rottencrotch is probably back home screwing your best friend Jody, while you're over here defending your country. But don't think those are good enough reasons to go over the wire. You're not going to get away with it, and if I catch you, I'll make damn sure Colonel Geraghty comes down hard.

"A while back some Italian soldiers paid a visit to that whorehouse. They got their throats slit and their wangers cut off. Believe me, men, no piece is worth that." The sergeant major held up his right hand and pointed to it. "Just keep saying hello to Mr. Happy." Everyone laughed.

"That's it, men. Get back to work. Summers, get this place cleaned up, goddamnit!" The sergeant major swaggered back to the senior staff NCO tent.

"Do you believe that about the Italian soldiers?" I asked Ben.

"No. Do you?"

I shook my head. "Not a word."

Summers had us line up at one end of the parking lot for police call. We walked toward the senior enlisted tent, picking up paper and cigarette butts as we went. The day's working party, Silone and Scaly, began sweeping the lot with two straw brooms.

After police call I went to the operations office to get my helmet, flak jacket, and rifle. I was scheduled to drive the photographers around the compound.

"Ready to go, Big Guy?" I asked Ross as I stepped into the supply tent. Ross was sitting on Staff Sergeant Tolbert's cot in the back of the tent loading his movie camera. The supply tent was our sanctuary. For some reason Gunny Thorn steered clear, and it was a good place to hang out. There was a table with chairs for card playing, a cache of pornographic magazines, and always a couple of bottles of booze stashed in one of the big wooden supply boxes.

Tolbert had excellent liaison with the cooks at the BLT—the "hook up" as Mudfart called it. He could get anything. We frequently dined on cheese, salami, and crackers washed down with the white wine Tolbert got from his British friends. He made chili occasionally, and once he even appropriated a huge pan of lasagna. But the best of his hook ups was the watermelon he got from some Lebanese soldiers. Tolbert cut a plug at one end then sloshed in a half bottle of vodka. He talked Archie into chilling the melon in Branigan's refrigerator, and we slurped it down one evening behind the supply tent as we watched the "fireworks display" in the mountains.

Tolbert had named the tent "Chester's Place" after a *Hustler* magazine cartoon character who was a sex pervert. I wondered if it wasn't Tolbert who was the pervert. He talked of nothing but sex and narrated in graphic detail what he was going to do to his wife when he got home. He claimed his marriage worked well because he had a seven-inch tongue with a wart on the end. His greatest boasts, however, came when he talked about the size of his organ. "It's so big," he declared, "when I get a hard-on all the blood rushes out of my head, and I faint."

The least entertaining thing about the supply tent was Tolbert's bunkie, a staff sergeant named Cummings. Cummings was twenty-eight but acted like an old man. He had a game knee when he wanted a little sympathy or needed a convenient excuse to get out of work. His arms and legs trembled like a palsy victim's, and he walked as though he were constantly on the verge of falling down. Corporal Bradley, one of the supply clerks, had dubbed Cummings "Wheebles" because, Bradley had explained, "Wheebles wobble but they don't fall down."

Wheebles lost bowel control at least twice a month. "Damn chow hall," he would whine as he hobbled toward the head to wipe himself. Tolbert loudly announced he was going to make Wheebles wear a diaper if he didn't learn self-control. I felt sorry for Wheebles when he wasn't getting on my nerves. He had never been away from his wife more than a few weeks at a time and missed her terribly. Tolbert told us Wheebles cried himself to sleep most nights. I'd heard he'd already had one nervous breakdown, and I suspected he was in the middle of his second. I kept waiting to hear the news that he was being given a medical discharge.

Ross finished loading his camera. "Be with you in a sec, Albert," he said. He put on his flak jacket and slapped a helmet on his head. We walked outside, and I climbed into the driver's seat of the jeep we had been assigned. Ross got in back.

I spotted Tolbert sashaying across the parking lot, grinning sheepishly. His eyes were bugged out a bit, and as he climbed into the jeep he slapped me on the back. "Hit it!" he shouted.

"You're certainly smug today," I said.

"The Thorn and I got into it again, and he lost for a change. He didn't want us to make this little trip but I told him otherwise. Major Converse had to settle it."

I turned on the jeep, pumped the gas pedal a half dozen times, and pressed the starter button. The jeep wheezed twice then roared to life. Grinding the gear shift into first, I took my foot off the clutch. The jeep lurched forward, and we were on our way. First stop, the BLT.

❦   ❦   ❦

The Battalion Landing Team was headquartered in a huge mausoleum of a building. At four stories it was the largest in the vicinity of Beirut International. Concrete abutments supported each side, and the long rows of windows that encircled the building had long since lost their glass and been covered with plastic. The building, a former PLO headquarters, was scorched black in places and pockmarked inside and out with gunfire. The front entrance sported a tan sign with a large Marine Corps emblem in its center. BEIRUT HILTON, MILITARY DISCOUNTS AVAILABLE, it read.

The ground-floor lobby was a vast atrium the height of the building. Balconies on each level offered a view of the supply and administrative offices below. One section of the lobby was the weight room, and the clang of Nautilus machines was accompanied by the grunts of Marines working out at all hours. An old Lebanese man nicknamed Shuffles sold sodas for fifty cents and candy bars for forty in a small walled-off area in one of the stairwells.

The Combat Operations Center and the Peacekeeping Chapel were on the second floor. Father George Pucciarelli, the MAU chaplain, held services in the chapel on Sundays. The intelligence section and a small Staff NCOs and Officers Club was on the fourth floor.

Marines lived in a honeycomb of rooms throughout the building. Mudfart had shown me the cubbyhole he'd cleared out during the previous float. "I took out wheelbarrows full of rock," he'd said. "It was a lot of work, but I had my own room when I was done." Living in the BLT, Mudfart insisted, was much better than living in the musty basement of the Safety Center building.

The enlisted Marines' club was in the basement of the BLT. Much larger than Branigan's, it sported several wooden picnic tables and a real bar with stools. There were even a couple of archaic video games in one corner. The walls were decorated with drawings of gung-ho Marines in combat, and underneath were written quotes from the Code of Conduct:

> I am an American fighting man. I serve in the forces which guard my country and our way of life. I am prepared to give my life in their defense.

Another section of the basement housed the Battalion Aid Station as well as the medical and dental records for most of the Marines on shore. Seventeen Navy corpsmen ran the station, taking care of Marines from the line companies when they got sick. Doctor John Hudson, the only medical officer ashore, was the officer in charge.

❦   ❦   ❦

Lebanese Armed Forces (LAF) soldiers were rappelling down the face of the BLT when the photographers and I pulled up in front of the building. Ross and Tolbert hopped out and started taking pictures.

The Marines had been training the LAF through the Office of Military Cooperation for over six months. The soldiers were taught courses in diesel mechanics, cannoneer techniques, and artillery procedures. The rappelling exercise was part of a program to train the soldiers in basic infantry skills. They looked like they were enjoying themselves as they jumped off the roof, some in a barely controlled headlong fall to the ground. I remembered the rush of adrenaline the first time I clamored down the four-hundred-foot rappelling tower in boot camp.

The Lebanese Army had a long way to go to overcome its troubled past and establish itself as a credible, cohesive national force. It had split along religious lines during the 1975 Civil War, and discipline had broken down within the Muslim ranks. The army was known as a corrupt, pro-Maronite Christian organization, and even the Army Law of 1979, intended to begin reconstruction, did little to change its reputation.

In November 1982 the Lebanese Parliament gave President Amin Gemeyal emergency powers to reform several Lebanese security organizations including the LAF. Gemeyal selected General Ibrahim Tannous to command Lebanon's Army. Tannous, a Phalangist during the civil war, had been removed from his assignment as commander of the Lebanese Army garrison at Rumiyah Barracks because of his ties with the Christian militia. Despite this, he was considered a political moderate with a strong desire to work for the good of Lebanon and was officially "reassigned" and "at the disposal of the Defense Ministry." Respected by radical Christian elements and some of the Muslim sects, his appointment helped stop further polarization of the LAF.

Gemayel and Tannous immediately began to seek out corruption within the army. The director of general administration was fired and charged with malfeasance. Some Army officers were forced to retire, including the former commander of the LAF, General Khoury. Conscription of troops began, with the initial goal of 2,700 needed to bring four brigades up to 70 percent strength.

The "new" LAF passed its first test on 15 February 1983 when it peacefully deployed into East Beirut. Nevertheless, the force was still incapable of spreading its influence outside the city and into the Chouf and southern Lebanon. It still needed expansion, training, planning, and political agreements with the various factions before it was capable of that.

The LAF troops looked up to the Marines as demigods. Most of the Lebanese soldiers wore solid green uniforms, but the soldiers wearing camouflage uniforms like those of the Marines strode about with a special pride in their walk. Some wore high-and-tights instead of the longer haircuts Lebanese regulations allowed. The soldiers were always friendly and waved, frequently bellowing out a "Hurrah!" in imitation of the Marine Corps' famous Devil-Dog grunt.

Most Marines, on the other hand, scoffed at the Lebanese soldiers behind their backs. "We are da Webanese," they would parrot as the soldiers ran by the command post in formation. "Da mighty, mighty Webanese." We called them the LAUGH, not the LAF. The consensus was we couldn't count on them. If things got tough, we'd be on our own.

👑   👑   👑

Ross and Tolbert finished taking pictures of the rappelling soldiers, and we headed out of the compound to perimeter road. It was a hot day, and we kicked up a cloud of red dust as the jeep bounced over the road. Lebanese soldiers practiced their low crawl through tall grass nearby, firing blanks with their M-16s. To our left I could see "Hooterville," the sprawling Shiite Muslim slum that surrounded the airport to the north and east.

We drove past Charlie Company. Sentries on guard near sand-bagged outposts saluted the jeep. Other Marines, filling sandbags and burning shitters, glanced up as we passed. A string of Marines ran along the right side of the road singing as they did their daily physical training. A shot-up building on the left, sprayed with a big 1.5 MILE in red paint, denoted the halfway point of the PT course. These were the "real" Marines, I decided, toughing it out on the front line, living in tents without showers and running water—Marines whose idea of a big night on the town was drinking a beer at Branigan's.

I turned left at the end of perimeter road, and we were flagged through the last Marine checkpoint. Staff Sergeant Tolbert slammed a magazine into my M-16. We were entering no man's land, the hotly contested area under Israeli control. The security of the compound was far behind us.

The Israelis, at best, had a poor reputation in Beirut. Subject to frequent attacks, the Israeli Defense Force (IDF) responded with indiscriminate, high-volume fire in all directions. Many innocent Lebanese civilians had become casualties, and although no Multi-national Force members had been hit, it was only a matter of time. Machine gun rounds had already impacted Marine positions near the Lebanese University. Two weeks earlier, on the night of 15 June, the IDF had fired tank rounds into buildings west of the railway line near the compound, forcing the Marines on the perimeter to scramble for their bunkers. Despite promises made to Colonel Geraghty that it wouldn't happen again, the firing was repeated on the night of 22 June—reportedly with the direct authorization of the IDF division commander.

Only three channels existed for communications between the IDF and the Marines: the government of Lebanon, the Multinational Force

Military Coordinating Committee, and an emergency radio hot line. None of the methods had worked, and Colonel Geraghty concluded the only recourse to stop the indiscriminate fire was for U.S. diplomats to approach the Israelis at a high political level in Washington and Tel Aviv. The MAU fired off an angry sounding message to the secretary of state in Washington, informing him of our predicament.

I didn't feel much comfort about the diplomatic efforts as I turned onto Old Sidon Road, the highway that had marked the route between Beirut and Damascus since antiquity and the site of recent attacks on the IDF. Several Israeli tanks were in the distance, and I knew their Rules of Engagement didn't stop them from patrolling with a round chambered. I didn't want to think about being caught in the cross fire between an Israeli tank and a Muslim grenade launcher. The Israeli soldiers would not hesitate to fire; their unique method of dealing with car bombs had proven that. When they spotted a suspect vehicle, it would immediately be riddled with machine gun fire. If it blew up the suspicion was confirmed; if not, too bad for the car.

Old Sidon Road was peppered with craters half-full of muddy water. I skirted them carefully until we picked up an Israeli tank on our tail. Then it was every man for himself as I raced through the craters, splashing water over the windshield and into the jeep. Ross whooped like a cowboy breaking a wild bronco. I handed him my camera and shouted, "Get some pictures!" The Israelis weren't happy with the idea. Wearing solemn frowns, they stared at us with disdain, a hateful glare in their eyes.

We finally arrived at Marine Checkpoint 35.

"If we make it back to the CP in one piece," Ross promised, "I'm going to get out and kiss the ground!"

Checkpoint 35 was a forward observation post in the middle of Hooterville. A dozen Marines assigned to Bravo Company lived in the two-story, cinder-block building. They waved to us from the second-floor balcony as they ate an MRE lunch. The Marines had painted a red sign on the wall, renaming the checkpoint COMBAT OUTPOST. They frequently received pot shots from the surrounding buildings, and the post, fortified with sandbags, was well-named. A smelly creek, little more than a drainage ditch, ran alongside the checkpoint. The Marines called the creek "Shit River," and the Lebanese used it as a sewer. Ross and Tolbert took pictures of the outpost for historical documentation, then we headed for the next Marine position on our list, Checkpoint 69.

Checkpoint 69 had been dubbed THE FIRING LINE by the Marines who lived there. Two tents pitched amid scrub and withered trees, the checkpoint seemed isolated and alone. It was a joint LAF-Marine forward observation post, but I didn't see any sign of Lebanese soldiers. We spotted a few Marines playing cards inside one of the tents. It was a hot, lazy day, peaceful and serene. Lebanon's troubles seemed far away as we took pictures of one another standing in front of a gnarled cedar tree; but Checkpoint 69 was to be the site of some of the heaviest fighting in the months to come.

Our last stop was Alpha Company, positioned at the Lebanese University. The University had been a beautiful campus at one time, but now the buildings were covered with bullet holes. Great chunks of plaster had fallen from the side of the library where Alpha was head-quartered. The Marines were happy to see fresh faces; one invited us to the NCO club in the basement and treated us to cold sodas.

The University was near Israeli headquarters. I could see the blue-and-white Star of David flag flying on a nearby hill. The flag, waving peacefully in the breeze, seemed symbolic of the fighting and the power struggles that had marred the Chouf for the past decade.

During the 1975 Lebanese Civil War, two parties had struggled for power in the area: the Christian National Liberal Party (NLP), led by former Lebanese President Camille Chamoun; and the Druze Progressive Socialist Party (PSP), led by Kemal Jumblatt. The Druze forced Chamoun and the NLP out of the area in early 1976. Kemal Jumblatt was assassinated in March 1977, and his son, Walid Jumblatt, became the leader of the PSP and the dominant political figure in the area.

Bashir Gemayel had gained leadership of the Christian Phalange Party during the civil war. His philosophy was that for the Christian community to maintain control of Lebanon, they would have to be united under a single party. Building a loyal militia he called the Lebanese Forces (LF), Bashir Gemayel overpowered the Phalange Party's major rival, the NLP, in 1980.

The Israeli invasion, two years later on 6 June 1982, helped Bashir Gemayel and the Phalange Party gain political superiority. Although the Phalange did not have a political base in the Chouf, they saw the Israeli invasion as an opportunity to alter the status quo and impose their military-political supremacy on the region. The LF moved into the Chouf soon after the invasion. The local inhabitants, viewing this as a threatening development, mounted organized resistance.

Bashir was elected President of Lebanon in August, giving him the power of the state to consolidate his control of the Phalange Party. Bashir thought that under his guidance the Phalange would dominate the Lebanese Christian community, and the Christians would then have the upper hand on the entire Lebanese political system.

That was not to be the case, however. Bashir was assassinated on 14 September and replaced by his brother Amin. The Phalange Party viewed Amin Gemayel as a weak moderate and feared he would negotiate away hard-won Phalangist power to other factional leaders. From the Phalangist perspective, Amin as president meant that although the party would maintain control of the Lebanese government, without the leadership of Bashir and his close supporters it would be weakened and changed beyond recognition. It was necessary for the LF to fight, first to preserve its authority within the Phalange party and second to ensure that Bashir's policy of Christian dominance was maintained.

The LF viewed themselves as the custodians of state authority. Any resistance against them was a rebellion against Lebanon, and President Gemayel could do little to enforce government authority except on the terms demanded by the militia. By winning control of the Chouf, the LF would broaden its political base and establish itself as the supreme force in Lebanese politics.

Since early October, outbreaks of violence between the LF and the PSP occurred with increasing regularity. Israeli forces occasionally intervened to stop some of the heaviest bloodshed but generally pursued a policy of restraint. Some factions accused Israel of actually perpetuating the fighting to justify their continued occupation of southern Lebanon.

For Israel, the fighting in the Chouf between the Phalangists and the Muslim sects created both opportunities and problems. Israel supported the objectives of the Phalangists who wanted to eliminate the PLO and other forces in Lebanon hostile to Israel. Yet, by supporting the activities of the LF, Israel did little to win the support of the moderate Muslim elements.

The Phalangists, even with Israel's tacit approval, were not successful in their bid to establish political supremacy over the PSP. Walid

Jumblatt's militia, fighting on Muslim territory, offered stiff resistance to Phalange attacks. Israel, in an attempt to keep the violence from escalating, refused to give the LF free reign, and rather than break the PSP they succeeded in only strengthening Druze resolve. The outlook for halting the fighting between the Phalange and the PSP was not good.

"Violence in the Chouf district is likely to continue and perhaps even spread," I had read in a Defense Intelligence Agency appraisal.

> Setbacks experienced by the [Phalange] are likely to make it more determined. The political philosophy of the militia is to achieve political domination, not to strike compromises that could involve sharing political power with other groups. Israeli forces in Lebanon will probably act to keep the fighting from escalating to serious levels, but they will not react to every incident. The violence probably would end if the [Phalange] were to withdraw from the district. But Israel is not likely to force the militia out, nor is the militia likely to depart on its own initiative. . . . Only a wider regional agreement resulting in the withdrawal of all foreign forces from Lebanon is likely to make possible an end to the continuing pattern of violence in the Chouf region. . . . The total withdrawal of Syrian, Israeli, and PLO forces from Lebanon would. . . transform what is now an international problem into a domestic one, and the Lebanese would have to look to their own resources to solve it.

The Israelis didn't look like they would leave Beirut or southern Lebanon any time soon. Continued occupation was necessary to keep the PLO out of southern Lebanon and thereby increase the security of Israel's northern border. Like the experts, I too thought that with the IDF's departure, Beirut would be on the road to peace. We were to find out how disastrously wrong that idea was when the Israelis did eventually stage a pullback two months later.

In the meantime, the Christians and the Muslims fought in the mountains, the Israelis continued to fire at anything that moved, and the Marines were sitting ducks in the middle of it all.

⚜   ⚜   ⚜

Ross greeted the command post upon our return to the compound with the same enthusiasm he would have greeted a Big Mac and a Coke. True to his promise, he got out of the jeep and made a great show of kissing the parking lot. "You're a nondriving SOB, Albert," he declared. "I thought that tank was going to run us down."

"Next time I'll leave you standing in the middle of Old Sidon Road," I threatened. "You can walk back."

"There's no need for that. I'll never get into a jeep with you again. Not if I value my life!"

Ross and Tolbert headed for the supply tent, and I went into the CP to give the jeep's trip ticket and mileage to Ben.

"You missed a good one while you were gone," Ben said. "Gunny Sparks and my major sent Lieutenant Block on a secret mission."

"What?"

"They got tired of hearing that 'Da Nang, '69, rainy season' crap. Gunny did two tours in Vietnam and has a Purple Heart to show for it, but Block made it sound like that was nothing compared to his heroics. Hell, Block wasn't even ten years old in '69! Gunny Sparks and Major Melton gave Block a sealed envelope and told him they were sending him on a top-secret mission. You should have seen Block's face. Gunny had him so worked up I thought he was going to shit."

"What was the mission supposed to be?"

"They told him he was going to Hey es Sellom as a forward observer. They claimed the latest intelligence report said the Druze were planning a big initiative against the Marines, and Block's mission was to infiltrate them to find out what they were up to."

"I can't believe anyone's that stupid," I said. "Where's our fearless hero now?"

"They had him throw some stuff in his ALICE pack. Told him he wouldn't make it back for at least a couple months, if ever. Then they had him camouflage his face with war paint. He was so nervous his hands were shaking. He kept pulling his .45 out of its holster while he was packing to make sure it was loaded and dropped it twice. Then they had him get into a jeep with orders not to open the envelope until he was ready to head for the Chouf. He started the jeep then tore open the envelope. You should have seen his face when he read what they'd written. You could see crimson under three layers of green paint."

"What did the note say?"

"HA-HA-HA, STUPID! in big, red letters. I don't know if Block was more embarrassed or relieved. He headed for the company grade quarters and hasn't come out since. He'll probably spend the rest of the float hiding in his rack. If anyone deserves to be played with it's Block. He's ten times worse than a private right out of boot camp."

Ben and I had a good laugh. It was close to chow time, so we headed to the BLT for dinner.

Another workday in the 'Root was over. It had been a good day. The Thoreau Theory was working better than I had ever hoped. The mass of men might be living lives of quiet desperation, but I was in Beirut, Lebanon making history and living a life of adventure in the United States Marine Corps.

Ben began to whistle a tune. I started humming along, then we both launched into the words of a World War I fighting song that somehow seemed appropriate. It was as if we, as Americans and Marines, by maintaining the same esprit de corps of those who fought on Iwo Jima and in Belleau Woods, could make everything in Lebanon all right.

> Over there, over there,
> Send the word over there!
> That the Yanks are coming,
> the Yanks are coming,
> And we won't come back
> till it's over, over there!

9

I WAS A CELEBRITY once again. This time I was going to be a "star" for three seconds on the news program "Good Morning America." Rehearsing the words that would bring me fame and fortune, I stood in front of MSSG's motor pool with forty other Marines. We wished America a happy Fourth of July a dozen times before the captain from public affairs was satisfied our performance was up to David Hartman's standards. He finally told the Navy cameraman to begin taping.

"One, two, three, action!" the captain shouted. He was enjoying his role as director, no doubt envisioning himself as the next Steven Spielberg.

"From the Marines serving in Beirut, Lebanon, Happy Birthday, and Good Morning, America!" we thundered in unison.

"Cut! More energy!" Captain Spielberg ordered.

We shouted the words again on cue. It sounded pretty good to me, but the captain decided we might look better if we were rearranged. I ended up squatting in the second row on the left next to Mudfart; my legs fell asleep as we repeated our spiel several more times for the camera.

Two sailors from the *Iwo Jima* were in charge of the video and sound equipment. They were assigned to the Armed Forces Radio and Television Service, affectionately called "AFARTS" by U.S. troops stationed worldwide. AFRTS had a small transmitter van parked behind the CP, and during the evenings and on Saturday mornings we could watch television reruns from the States in Branigan's.

The radio station broadcasted all day long. Some of the shows starred local disc jockeys, but most were recordings of programs produced in the U.S. The best part of AFRTS was the hourly newscasts that were transmitted over an open telephone line from the States to the BLT, then over a ground line to the transmitter van. Mudfart and I always stopped whatever we were doing to hunch attentively over our transistor in the office and listen to the five-minute news spots. Other than weeks-old newspapers and magazines, the broadcasts were our only window to the outside world.

We finally finished taping the "Good Morning America" segment. Being a TV star was hard work, and Mudfart and I headed to the "Hey Joe" for a cold soda. The Hey Joe was a small store run by some enterprising Lebanese. They had hung a large, red-and-yellow sign above the entrance of the squat, windowless building that identified it as the Marine Corps Exchange. No one called it that, though. It was the Hey Joe because that's what the Lebanese called us when they wanted to sell something. "Hey, Joe. I got very nice souvenir for you. You like, no?" or "Hey, Joe. You buy cold soda from me. I give you good price, special for you."

The Hey Joe sold a vast assortment of junk. Tables were piled high with cheap brass ashtrays, Arab headdresses, Multinational Force T-shirts that shrunk six sizes after a single washing, and postcards of Beirut in the early '70s when it was still a beautiful city. Mudfart and I went to the Hey Joe every few days to sort through the piles, looking for some missed tidbit worth buying. We rarely bought anything other than a soda or a box of cookies to break the monotony of MREs, but it was worthwhile going just to escape the Thorn. Besides, Mudfart was in love with one of the Lebanese girls who worked in the store. That every other Marine in the compound was in love with her too didn't seem to bother him.

Her name was Liliane, and she had long, dark hair that hung to the middle of her back. Her olive complexion and almond-shaped eyes gave her an exotic look, but it was her dazzling smile and shy demeanor that endeared her to everyone. She was working the ancient cash register as Mudfart and I bought a Pepsi.

"*Keefuk,*" Mudfart said as he handed her fifty cents. It was the only Arabic he knew, a greeting for "How's it going?" that sounded suspiciously like a dirty word. Liliane smiled shyly and batted her lashes, but then she did that with everyone. Mudfart, feeling encouraged, brushed his mustache with a forefinger in a dapper gesture. "How about you and me later?" he asked suavely. The girl kept smiling. I don't think she understood English very well.

I grabbed Mudfart's arm. "You're holding up the line," I said and dragged him outside. We sat under a large shade tree and drank our sodas. Mudfart and I had become close friends even though we squabbled like brothers. I was supposed to be the NCO in charge and got mad when he had other ideas or didn't want to do what I said. He thought I was too bossy. It was our common nemesis, the Thorn, that pushed us together, and we always covered for one another whenever Gunny was on the prowl.

"When Gunny first started dogging me," Mudfart said, "I thought it might have been because I'm black." Mudfart and I talked a lot about prejudice. The Marine Corps had had serious race problems ten years before on its large base in Okinawa, but relations between the enlisted troops of the MAU were good despite the occasional mumblings from some of the whites that Staff Sergeant Summers favored blacks on working parties. Mudfart's comment about Gunny made me wonder about Gunny's integrity.

"What makes you say that?" I asked.

"No matter what I did, the Thorn was always standing over my shoulder. I couldn't do anything good enough to make him happy, and he definitely didn't trust me to get a job done."

"Maybe he thinks blacks are shiftless and not to be trusted," I joked.

Mudfart was serious. "Looking back, I don't think that's true. Sometimes I did try to avoid work—who doesn't?—and I would have done just about anything to get out of this float. I wish Gunny would forget about that and look at my job performance now. I've been working hard, but once the Thorn gets an idea cemented into his head, it's there to stay." Mudfart was getting desperate to make corporal, but Gunny had recommended low proficiency and conduct marks for him, ruining any chance of promotion for quite some time. Mudfart had been a lance corporal for two years, and with only a year to go in the Corps, it looked like that might be his terminal rank.

"Things will get better," I said. "George knows you're doing a good job. Gunny will get off your back, and you'll get promoted."

"I sure as hell hope so."

I clasped Mudfart's shoulder. "We better get back to work before you-know-who starts looking for us." Gunny never wanted us when we were in the office, but as soon as we tried to take a break, that was when he'd show up with another stupid job. Mudfart and I tossed our empty soda cans into the pile of trash next to the Hey Joe and headed back to the CP.

❧   ❧   ❧

The Fourth of July is a special holiday for Marines. Patriotism, at least in the Marine Corps, was back in style. With Reagan as president, there was a new feeling America was at last back in the saddle and on a rebound from the disasters of Vietnam. The defense budget was up, our foreign policy seemed stronger than ever, and the U.S. was again a symbol to the world and a beacon of freedom.

For me, the Fourth of July meant holiday routine, and I was already taking advantage of it. At a quarter past seven, an hour after I'd normally gone to the office, I was still lounging in the rack thinking about the scheduled picnic and a whole day free from work. Mudfart had talked of nothing but the big Fourth of July basketball game against MSSG for days. The MAU headquarters' team was terrible and lost every game, but Mudfart loved to play. He shot hoop on the BLT's court every chance he got.

I heard the pleasant voice of the sergeant major coming from the next room. "Goddamnit, Summers, this place is a shitpen. I want it cleaned up now!"

Summers stuck his head in the door. "Holiday routine's been cancelled," he said. "Petit, you've got field day at the CP. Ross, you're in charge of burning shitters."

Ross sighed and swung his legs out of his rack. "Damn," he moaned. "Can't we even get one day's break?"

"You know the sergeant major," I said. "I figured he'd freak when he found out another congressional delegation was coming. I hate to see how he'd react if something important actually happened."

"I love the Corps," Ross said. "It's not just a job, it's burning shitters on the Fourth of July."

I spent the next hour wiping dust from the tops of doorways in the CP just in case some congressman felt like putting on a white glove and checking for dirt. According to the sergeant major, things couldn't be too clean. Of course it was easy for him to have that attitude; he wasn't the one who had to do the work. "I bet the Smaj's mother doesn't keep house this clean," I mumbled to myself.

VIP visits were always a pain. The Smaj seemed to go into a wilder frenzy each time someone of importance came. This was the second or third congressional visit since our arrival, and so far no congressman had bemoaned the reality that the CP wasn't spotless. They were too interested in having a good time and chalking up another country on their junket list at taxpayer expense. They never inspected the Marine positions for long. After interjecting a few "uh-huhs" or a "that's interesting" as Colonel Geraghty gave them a tour of the compound, they'd leave for the American Embassy. That was where the real action was, the big parties.

By the time I'd finished cleaning in the CP, Ross was outside helping with the food preparation. He was wearing his glasses upside down and generally acting silly as he sliced bread rolls in half to make hamburger buns. It was impossible not to get filthy when you were burning shitters, and Ross looked like he had been rolling around in diesel fuel and sand.

"I hope you washed your hands before you started cutting the bread," I said. He looked at me and grinned. Putting his knife down, he wiped his hands on his sweaty T-shirt.

"See that bun?" he asked, pointing to one on top. "That one's for the sergeant major."

"Remind me not to eat a hamburger today."

A working party had erected camouflage netting over part of the parking lot for shade. Picnics were normally held under the trees behind the command post, but nothing was too good for our congressmen. The fifty-gallon barrels we used for grills had been hauled to the front of the building, and Nels and Silone were dumping in the bags of charcoal we bought on the Lebanese economy. Hadley taped American flags to the poles that supported the netting, giving the CP a festive look.

Staff Sergeant Tolbert sashayed across the parking lot from the supply tent carrying an armload of serving utensils. He dropped them onto the food table, then picked up two silver ladles and held them to his chest so they looked like breasts.

"Yoo-hoo, big fellow," he said to Ross, winking. "How'd you like to show me a good time?"

"Sure, if you think you can handle this huge love muscle," Ross answered, pointing, as usual, to his groin.

"That tiny thing? Let me get my microscope first."

"You won't need a microscope, baby. Just ask Albert."

"Leave me out of this one," I said. "I don't want to have anything to do with you two."

The picnic started in early afternoon. We ate hamburgers and hot dogs, pork and beans, and corn on the cob. Chocolate cake was for dessert. The food had been distributed through the BLT mess hall, and each unit was responsible for preparing its own picnic. Everyone got one free soda or beer. Profits from the clubs financed the drinks, but most of the money was being saved for a big bash in Rota, Spain on our way out of the Mediterranean just before the float was over.

After the picnic, everyone but the congressmen and the top brass went to the BLT to watch MAU headquarters get trounced by MSSG in basketball. Mudfart claimed our team was gypped by the referees. I decided we were just plain bad but didn't say anything to Mudfart. He urgently wanted the team to win and vowed he'd practice more.

The congressional delegation left the next day but was soon replaced with another. Beirut in July, it seemed, was the place to be for American politicians. Secretary of State George Schultz toured the compound on the fifth while his wife lunched with Mrs. Gemayel, the Lebanese president's wife. Another congressional delegation, a Republican from Mississippi and a Democrat from Louisiana, arrived on the seventh for a briefing from Colonel Geraghty. They claimed to have come to Lebanon to meet with their constituents and insure our boys in green were being treated well, but the real reason they made the trip was because the Marines allowed them to purchase and wear camouflage utilities while touring the lines. The congressmen loved to parade around the compound in their new uniforms. It was their chance to play Marine for a day, then go back to the States and swap tall tales about their adventures in the 'Root.

I had been granted the distinction of ironing the secretary of state's new uniform and cover before it was presented to him. A Marine's cover is a badge of honor, a sign to the world of his true feelings about the Corps. A highly starched cover is a symbol of being a gung-ho super Marine; a trampled cover stained with sweat and grease is a sign of being a "shitbird." An important dignitary couldn't be allowed to parade around the compound looking dogeared, so the executive officer assigned the adjutant the important job of dewrinkling the secretary. The adjutant passed the "honor" to me. I didn't mind taking care of Schultz, but soon some of the officers discovered I had mastered the fine art of blocking a cover with a roll of toilet paper and then starching the creases until they were sharp enough to cut. They wanted me to iron their covers too. Even Colonel Geraghty asked me to iron his. I turned down the money he offered, but he was the only officer who didn't demand my services for free.

Ben teased me unmercifully when he discovered I was ironing the colonel's cover, accusing me of being a "bootlicking brown-noser."

"Look who's talking," I said. "The King of the Brown-nosers who's taken the art of ass-kissing to new heights!" Ben had been carrying a biography of Marine Corps hero Chesty Puller in his flak jacket pocket for weeks. I claimed he only pulled it out when some bigwig could see him read it, but of course Ben denied that.

As each new group of dignitaries arrived, the sergeant major became even more zealous about cleanliness. By the time the Chief of General Staff of the British Army, Sir John Stanier, visited on 9 July and Brigadier Generals Cook and Heinz from the European Command arrived to inspect on the twelfth, we were used to his screaming "field day!" as he ran about the compound, his cobra hood fully extended. Over beers in Branigan's the enlisted troops decided the Smaj was bored and didn't have enough to do. "I hope he finds a job soon," Ben said. "I'm tired of dusting the cracks in the walls."

Unfortunately for Ben, the sergeant major did find something to do; he made himself a nuisance in the logistics section. The Smaj decided Ben wasn't doing a good enough job dispatching jeeps and took over.

"I wanted three jeeps and six men to ride shotgun for the colonel at 1300," the Smaj would scream at Ben. "It's fifteen minutes till and nobody's out there."

"The shotguns and drivers are standing by in Branigan's, sergeant major."

The Smaj would stand a bit straighter. "Well, just see that they're ready," he'd bluster.

"I think the sergeant major's doing a hell of a job," Nels announced one day in Branigan's after the Smaj had chewed Ben's butt. Ben glared at Nels. Nels had just been meritoriously promoted to sergeant partly on the sergeant major's recommendation, and Ben thought Nels might actually be serious. "The sergeant major has inspired me to stay in the Corps for thirty years," Nels insisted. "I can only hope that someday when I'm forty-five my biggest aspiration in life will be to make sure some colonel gets his jeep on time."

❦   ❦   ❦

The days of July merged into one another, the routine of each day a carbon copy of the preceding. Antalya in Turkey and Catania in Sicily had been chosen as liberty ports, and ships from the Mediterranean Amphibious Ready Group departed the coast of Beirut one at a time to ferry Marines from the line companies to some well-deserved rest and relaxation far from the 'Root.

The biggest change in the MAU headquarters' routine was the arrival of a new executive officer. The old one departed with the new one's arrival on 18 July, and everyone was anxious to discover what our "newby," Lieutenant Colonel Harold Slacum, was like. He was a stern man who wore a hearing aid, but Hadley, assigned as his personal driver, immediately dubbed him "Slugo" and pronounced him "a good guy" after a few days of chauffeuring him around.

Doing laundry was part of the weekly routine I hated. The working party hauled the heavy bags full of dirty uniforms to the ship, washed all night, then returned the following day, and was cursed rather than thanked. The so-called clean clothes usually looked dirtier after they had been washed. Whites came back a dingy gray, and uniforms, when one of the washing machines on ship didn't devour them, came back grease-stained or with sand in the pockets.

The officers and staff NCOs complained the most even though their uniforms were pressed and hung on hangers. The enlisted troops' uniforms were shoved back into the laundry bag after being washed and were unceremoniously dumped on the basement floor so we could search through the pile. Archie and Scaly got stuck with laundry detail most often because they worked directly under Staff Sergeant Summers, but everyone had to take a turn.

Laundry was collected on Friday mornings. I had forgotten to get mine together the second to last week in July and told Mudfart I was going to the basement. It was close to ten o'clock, and Mudfart knew I wouldn't be back until after lunch. We took turns skating out of work, and as long as the Thorn didn't need me, I'd be safe taking a nap.

I was pulling a pair of dirty trousers from under my rack when an explosion shook the building. Alarmed, I ran into the larger room. Several of the off-duty communicators scurried about trying to find their flak jackets and rifles. I'd left mine in the office. Sergeant Layland ran down the stairs and into the room wearing full war gear.

"We're being shelled!" he shouted. "Get in the holes."

"I left my war gear at the CP," I said.

"Better get it and get in a hole," Layland advised.

Of course the basement was probably the safest place to be at the moment, but I charged up the stairs and sprinted toward the CP to recover my gear. I heard the whine of another missile as it flew overhead. They say you never hear the one that gets you, so I kept running as I heard a loud explosion behind me.

I'd almost made it to the CP when the gunnery sergeant in charge of the communicators screamed, "Get in a hole, Petit!" MSSG had dug several foxholes along the right side of the CP with a backhoe. We hadn't needed them, and they were never reinforced with sandbags, but I dove into the nearest one headfirst anyway.

Then Gunny pushed my head down as two more missiles exploded nearby. "Where's your flak jacket and helmet?" he demanded.

"I left them in the office."

"That's a good place for them."

I poked my head up enough to see the car that screeched to a stop on the road just outside the CP. A CBS camera crew jumped out and began taping. The shelling hadn't stopped, and already the news media were arriving.

My heart was pounding. This is fun, I decided, but when the camera lens turned in my direction I, like everyone else, assumed a studied expression of seriousness. It seemed like the expression a person being shelled should wear; having watched TV all my life, I knew what made good copy and wanted to make sure I was on the evening news.

The all-clear signal was sounded ten minutes after the shelling stopped. Eleven 122mm rockets had impacted near Marine positions, and the day's excitement gave everyone something to talk about for the next week. Ben and I examined the crater in the pavement between the BLT and MAU headquarters where a rocket had landed a dozen yards from a Marine sentry post. No one had been hurt, and the attack seemed to be nothing more than an aberration.

Nevertheless, formal guidelines that detailed alert conditions for the Marines on shore were implemented. The conditions were divided into four states of readiness. The lowest state, normal operations, was termed Condition IV, under which the two mobile and five foot patrols could be conducted daily by the BLT without special precautions. There would be one man assigned to sentry posts during daylight hours and two on each post at night. The Combat Operations Center was to be manned with a normal watch, and civilian cars chosen at random would be spot searched.

Condition III meant an attack against the Multinational Force was possible. Once the watch officer in the command post declared Condition III, travel outside the compound would be restricted to essential missions with a minimum of two security jeeps and four armed guards. Marine snipers would be placed in designated positions, physical training along perimeter road would immediately cease, and one out of every five civilian cars would be searched.

Once the intelligence section determined an attack against the Marines was probable, Condition II would be sounded. The AH-1T Cobra helicopters on the *Iwo Jima* would be armed with missiles and placed on a fifteen-minute standby. Other air operations would be limited, and the secondary reaction force would be activated. Off-base travel would be restricted to emergencies only, and all civilian cars attempting to enter the compound were to be searched.

Condition I was the highest state of readiness, meaning an attack against U.S. positions was imminent or in process. The Marines on shore were to be on full alert with the Cobras on a five-minute standby. After the medevac helicopter moved ashore, all other air operations would be limited to emergency use only. There would be no travel outside the compound under any circumstance, and all artillery and mortar nets were to be activated.

The ships had their own alert conditions and Rules of Engagement as well:

1. Any small boat/craft within the Beirut anchorage area must be assumed to be a potential terrorist threat until positively identified and shall not approach closer than one hundred yards to any ship of the task force without the permission of the commanding officer of the unit.
2. Every attempt will be made to stop small craft from approaching U.S. Navy ships by friendly, nonforceful means.
3. If the approaching craft reaches four hundred yards: notify

ship's officer in charge, intercept with picket boat, challenge via light/voice, warn away by loud hailer, and illuminate by light.

4. If craft continues to approach to a distance of three hundred yards despite warnings: call away security force, illuminate with searchlights, attempt to fend off approaching craft with picket boat.

5. Craft approaching reaches one hundred yards: activate fire-hoses, load weapons, and fire warning shots in the air.

6. Craft approaching reaches fifty yards: engage with minimum force to prevent craft from closing further. Deadly force will be used only as a last resort to protect the ship.

The Navy commanders also had to worry about underwater swimmers and speedboats approaching the ships. They were authorized to deal with unidentified swimmers by using concussion grenades if the swimmers failed to halt and surface after appropriate warnings. Stopping a speedboat, however, would be tough. "High-speed small craft," the rules acknowledged, "can compress the time of reaction to such a degree that obtaining permission for forceful acts will be virtually impossible. Nothing herein should be construed to limit the authority of the commanding officer to defend his ship. His decisions in the face of hostile or neohostile craft will be defended."

Marines have always had a tough time accepting the idea that wars should have rules, particularly when the enemy doesn't seem to operate by humane codes. Every Marine is introduced to the laws of war during boot camp and learns that it is morally wrong to kill or torture prisoners of war, to treat civilians inhumanely, and to destroy life and property to a greater extent than a mission requires. But the issues were clouded, and each of us in Beirut had our own idea of what was morally right and wrong and how far we'd go to save our own life. War was a big topic of conversation in Branigan's the evening after the shelling.

"I think we should go up in the mountains and kick some butt," Chase said.

"Who are you going to fight, Space?" Beckford asked. "We don't know who did it. Are we supposed to kill everyone in the Chouf?"

"Why not?" Chase asked. "Get them before they get us!"

"We're going at everything all wrong anyway," Nels said. Nels was a bit of a military historian and had read widely on the subject. "This isn't how you fight a war, sitting in one position. It's like Ulysses S.

Grant said: 'The art of war is simple enough. Find out where your enemy is. Get at him as soon as you can. Strike at him as hard as you can and as often as you can, and keep moving on.' We have no choice but to strike back against whoever is responsible, otherwise we're going to get hit again and again and again."

"But we aren't in that situation," I objected. "This is a peacekeeping mission, not wartime."

"True," Nels agreed. "We aren't at war, but the problem is they sure as hell are at war with us. And if we don't wise up, we're going to be in deep trouble."

"I hope you're wrong." Unfortunately, Nels was very much right, and in the weeks to come his point would be driven home again and again.

The Marines continued to train LAF soldiers through the Office of Military Cooperation as July faded into August. The LAF's 3d Company, 1st Air Assault Battalion finished their training course, and Colonel Geraghty presented diplomas to the top thirty graduates. Mudfart and I had designed the certificates, lettering them in Old English, and the class of 280 soldiers must have been intensely proud of their official-looking diplomas, even though most couldn't read English.

The operations office kept busy planning training maneuvers with other members of the Multinational Force. We scheduled parachute jumps and a heavy-caliber live-fire exercise with the Italians. The BLT demonstrated their TOW (Tube-launched, Optically guided, Wire-controlled) missiles, capable of being fired from the back of a jeep, to the French, and HMM 162 set up an equipment display for General Angioni, the commanding general of the Italian contingent.

Ben heard a rumor that the new executive officer was planning a PFT for the end of August. A Physical Fitness Test is a training requirement Marines face every six months and consists of pullups, situps, and a three-mile run. I dreaded the run more than death, but because neither Ben nor I had done much exercise since our arrival in the 'Root, we decided it was a good time to start running just in case the scuttlebutt was true. We ran only a mile down perimeter road before turning around our first time out, but within a few evenings we were

up to the required three miles. I decided Ben's rumor had to be true
because George began a running program with one of the other officers.
That was a sure sign a PFT couldn't be far away, and Ben and I resolved
to get gung-ho and run our three miles wearing flak jackets and boots.

Our lofty plans for a training program, which Chesty Puller would
have envied, crashed to an abrupt halt less than a week later. Ben and I
got back to the CP after our evening run, hot and sweaty. I spotted
Silone leaning against the colonel's jeep in the parking lot. "Why don't
you run with us next time, Silly?" I gasped, feeling like I might throw
up. "You could use it."

"Didn't you hear the news?" he asked.

"Hear what?"

"Someone shot at two Marines running on the outer perimeter road
less than ten minutes ago."

"You're kidding."

"Nope," Silone said, shaking his head. "There's no way I'm going
to run out there. I'd rather stay fat."

I frowned at Ben. "I think it would be better if we planned on
failing the PFT," I said. Ben immediately agreed, and although the
inner perimeter road wasn't closed to runners after the sniping
incident, I decided being in shape wasn't worth dying for.

Confrontations between the Marines and the Israeli Defense Force
continued despite Israel finally deciding to withdraw its occupation
force from the Beirut area. A Marine convoy was stopped by an IDF
patrol near Israeli headquarters and later released at the direction of
Israeli command. Bravo Company caught an eleven-man IDF patrol
as it crossed the railroad tracks that marked the eastern boundary of the
U.S. lines. The patrol was escorted back to Old Sidon Road via Checkpoints 11 and 76 without incident, but it was clear the Israelis were
seeing how far the Marines could be pushed.

On 1 August, the BLT began to rotate its line companies to new
positions in order to maintain the alertness of the troops on the front
line. Bravo Company moved into Alpha's old position at the Lebanese
University library, while Alpha moved into tents stretched along the
perimeter. Charlie Company's Third Platoon was assigned to embassy
security, and the troops manning the seven joint-Marine/LAF checkpoints were shuffled. The rotation was complete by the afternoon of the
third.

The U.S. Army's Field Artillery School's Target Acquisition Battery (FASTAB) arrived three days later. Deployed with them were two AN/TPQ-36 counter-mortar/counter-artillery radars designed to provide data on incoming mortar, artillery, and rocket rounds. Using a triangulation method, the radars could pinpoint the location of enemy launchers and give our guns a grid coordinate on which to return fire. The Army unit had been assigned to the MAU after the shelling incident in July, and as it turned out their arrival on 6 August occurred when needed.

On the night of 8 August, two more rockets impacted near the airport. "The rocket attack on 22 July," the report I typed for Major Converse read, "was no longer an aberration, and these impacts signaled that more attacks were likely and, in fact, were becoming standard operating procedure." It was at this time Colonel Geraghty decided to move the remainder of the BLT support personnel and a reaction platoon of 150 men into the BLT headquarters. The BLT was one of the safest buildings in the compound. It had endured earlier fighting and survived Israeli artillery barrages without being harmed. Even a minor earthquake in June had caused no structural damage.

At 0525 on the morning of the tenth, a single 122mm rocket landed between the MAU and BLT headquarters, and First Lieutenant Neal Morris had the dubious distinction of becoming the first Marine to be wounded by flying shrapnel. An hour later, the airport came under a Druze rocket barrage aimed at the Lebanese Air Force flight line east of Marine positions and Lebanese Army camps located immediately to the north. Whoever was firing could not aim very well, and within an hour, twenty-seven 122mm rockets fired from the Chouf had landed around Beirut International. The U.S. Army radars, along with sightings made from the roof of BLT headquarters, enabled us to determine the grid coordinate from which the rockets were being fired. At 0725, our 81mm mortar platoon fired four illumination rounds over the suspected firing grid. The rounds were a calling card to make the Druze aware we knew exactly where they were firing from and that live rounds would follow. Within ten minutes the shelling stopped.

During the attack, two AH-1T Cobra helicopters were launched to answer calls for fire. The ships went to General Quarters, and the naval gunfire vessels moved into position to fire should it become necessary. The use of the mortar illumination rounds was the first time since the

Marines had landed almost a year earlier that indirect fire weapons had been used in self-defense. It would not be the last.

Major firefights between the LAF and the various militias in the Chouf continued through the following two days. I spent most of the time in the basement listening to the explosion of rockets. Condition I had been sounded, and this time I realized the safest place to be was in the basement, not charging around outside looking for my flak jacket and helmet. The airport was in the middle of the gun target line between the LAF and the militias, and dozens of spillover rounds landed near Marine positions.

The government of Lebanon was forced to close Beirut International, and, with no air traffic coming in, the mail flights from Rome stopped. The Druze threatened to shell the airport if it was reopened, and a contingency plan to bring mail through Cyprus via MAC (Military Airlift Command) aircraft was begun. We knew it might be weeks before mail from home arrived, and I felt cutoff, knowing my parents were frantic.

The fighting in the hills tapered off the afternoon of the twelfth, only to increase gradually in intensity for the next two weeks. Isolated rounds occasionally landed near Marine positions and the American ambassador's residence. The IDF commenced redeployment of nonessential equipment in preparation for their withdrawal, and our patrols in the city were occasionally harassed by Muslims. The other members of the Multinational Force received occasional small arms and mortar fire.

The enlisted troops of the MAU settled back into a routine that was intermittently interrupted by the Condition I siren. The sergeant major had attached an air raid siren to a pole outside the supply tent, and whenever a round exploded nearby, Wheebles would limp out of the supply tent, crank the siren's handle a few times, and dive into a nearby foxhole. Because Mudfart and I worked just outside the Combat Operations Center, we usually knew Condition I was going to be sounded before we heard the siren's wail. We would quickly shove the confidential material on our desks into the safe, grab our gear, and head for the basement. We preferred the basement because at least there we could lie on our racks as we counted explosions rather than sit in the sand of a foxhole. The excitement of being shelled had long since worn off, and it was a drudgery to lock up and head for the basement, sometimes two or three times a day.

Mudfart and I were assigned to working parties daily. I spent many hours filling sandbags to reinforce the CP and the foxholes, which were strategically placed around the building. We had been caught unprepared by the 22 July rocket barrage, but now each foxhole had a sandbag roof reinforced with plywood. A case of emergency MREs and a ten-gallon water jug were placed in each hole. In addition to the foxholes, Colonel Geraghty decided a secondary command post would be needed if anything happened to the main Combat Operations Center. A working party cleared part of the basement of the building across the street, and the communicators placed radio gear inside.

The new commandant of the Marine Corps, General P.X. Kelly, arrived to inspect the troops on 16 August. The sergeant major had gone on the warpath, and I did nothing but field day the CP during the three days before the commandant arrived.

The night before the big day I was in the supply tent getting sloshed with Ross, Tolbert, and Wheebles, talking about how much I wanted to be free of the Marine Corps. I had to be careful what I said. Although Ross was desperate to get out, Tolbert and Wheebles were career men and had joined the Corps immediately after graduating from high school. They complained about the Marine Corps as much as the rest of us though, and I couldn't understand how they had stuck it out for so long.

"When you've got a wife and two kids to support," Tolbert was saying, "you don't have much choice."

"I'm never getting married," Ross claimed.

"I know that," Tolbert said. "Assholes usually don't."

"You must be the exception then," Ross shot back.

I took another swig of beer. Branigan's was running a special. The club had bought a keg of beer, and Archie would fill your canteen cup to the brim for fifty cents.

Listening to Tolbert and Wheebles, I realized how lucky I was. My experience in the Marine Corps was part of a broader plan, the Thoreau Theory, and I knew I'd go on to other things; for them the Corps was their life. They didn't like it any more than I, but they had nothing to look forward to except ten more years until retirement. I suddenly felt sorry for them.

I stood up and announced I was going to the head. An uneven pathway of brick led from the supply tent to the piss tubes, and I had only walked a few feet when I twisted my ankle in a crack and fell into a bush. Laughing, I hobbled back to the supply tent. "Just call me Wheebles," I said. Everyone but Staff Sergeant Cummings roared.

The next morning I couldn't walk. Ross lent me his shoulder and I limped to the Battalion Aid Station. A corpsman wrapped my swollen ankle in a bandage and told me to stay off it for a few days. I managed to secure a ride back to the CP, but before I could tell Gunny Thorn I wouldn't be in the office, Mudfart and Ben grabbed me.

"What happened?" they demanded.

The truth didn't sound particularly interesting. "There I was," I said after a moment's thought. "Druze on the right, Phalange on the left, armed with nothing more than a pocket knife. I killed six of them before they finally got me."

"Yeah, sure," Ben said and walked away. I told Mudfart to let Gunny know about my predicament then limped toward the basement. Space Chase was on the path behind the CP.

"What happened?" he asked.

"There I was. Druze on the right, Phalange on the left, armed with nothing more than a pair of fingernail clippers. Ten confirmed kills before they finally got me."

Chase stared at me with his mouth open. I think he believed me.

I spent the next day and a half in the rack. Sick of MREs, I finally limped to the chow hall for the evening meal. Steak and lobster was on the menu in honor of the commandant's visit. We NCOs had to give our mess hall to the VIP party, but despite the long line to get into the main mess hall, the wait was worthwhile. Anything for a decent meal. We knew we would be served cold cuts and beans as soon as the dignitaries left.

The Secretary of the Navy, John F. Lehman, arrived for a briefing a few days after the commandant's departure, and the enlisted troops were subjected to another frenzy of "Field day!" by the Smaj. Our only consolation was that the float was half over. "It's downhill from here!" I enthusiastically told Mudfart on the halfway day.

The BLT began another air-assault course, on 22 August, training the LAF's 2d and 3d Companies, part of the 3d Air Assault Battalion. But within a week the class would end. The LAF soldiers would no longer need training; they'd be in the Chouf fighting. In the meantime, the MAU operations section scheduled parachute jumps with the

Italian and French, and Hadley got permission from Slugo to jump with them. Hadley had completed the U.S. Army's jump school in Georgia. He told everyone in Branigan's how much fun sky diving was.

"I wish I could give it a try," I said. Bravery was easy in Branigan's, especially after a few beers.

The day after Hadley's jump, my wish to fly through the air with the greatest of ease came true. Major Converse strode into the office. "You two have been working too hard," he told Mudfart and me. "Everyone in the office is going SPIE (Special Patrol Insertion and Extraction) rigging this afternoon."

"We've got a lot of work to do, sir," I protested.

"That can wait. You need a break."

I didn't want a break, but Major Converse didn't give options. I had seen other Marines SPIE rigging, and while it looked exciting to hang suspended in midair from a flying helicopter, I was suddenly nervous.

"Have you ever gone SPIE rigging?" I asked Mudfart after Major Converse had left.

He shook his head. "I'm afraid of heights, and I hated rappelling in boot camp so much that my drill instructor kicked me off the tower. I swore I'd always keep two feet on the ground after that."

After lunch, the operations office took three jeeps to LZ Golfball, a large field alongside perimeter road. I noticed Gunny Thorn had somehow gotten out of coming, but everyone else in the office was ready.

Ross was excited. He'd brought his movie camera and was planning to shoot film while he flew underneath the helicopter. "Don't worry about a thing, Albert," he assured me. "I'll get a great shot of you when you fall."

"Try to bounce when you hit the ground," Tolbert added. "It'll make a more interesting picture."

"Thanks a lot, guys," I said.

Close to one hundred Marines and fifty French soldiers were at the landing zone when we arrived. The operations office split into two groups of eight. Ben, Silone, and two clerks from the supply section had ridden out with us; Mudfart, Ross, Tolbert, and I joined their group. Major Converse and the other officers and staff NCOs from the operations section made up the second group.

We watched as a CH-46 Sea Knight helicopter hovered overhead.

Eight Marines, each wearing a harness, stood underneath the helicopter. A thick rope hung from an opening in the helicopter's belly,
and two instuctors attached the Marines to it. The helicopter lifted,
jerking the Marines off the ground, and I could hear the shouts of the
dangling men as the Sea Knight flew away.

The purpose of SPIE rigging is to place a reconnaissance patrol
behind enemy lines and later retrieve them. The troops are normally
combat-ready, carrying weapons, ammunition, and ALICE packs, but
because this was only a training exercise with the French, we didn't
have any gear.

The helicopter circled the airport and started coming back. It was
almost my turn to defy gravity. Two Marines from the BLT strapped
Ross into a rope and D-ring harness and then moved on to me. One
shouted a few hasty instructions: "Keep one arm around your partner
and the other arm fully extended," he said. "Otherwise the rope will
start spinning and you'll get dizzy."

"What happens if the rope snaps?" I asked.

"Don't worry, Albert," Ross chimed in. "The fall won't kill you.
It's the sudden stop at the end."

The instructor moved on to Ben and started hooking him into a
harness.

The helicopter passed overhead, and the wash from the propellers
kicked up a storm of dirt and flying grass. The helicopter stopped its
forward motion and slowly lowered its cargo of Marines to the middle
of the landing zone. It was obvious that the pilot had to have a light
touch on the controls. If he came down too fast the Marines would end
up as mush on the landing zone. The pilot was right on the mark, but
the Marines fell in a heap anyway. Disentangling arms and legs, the
men quickly got to their feet. The instructors detached them from the
rope, and the Marines hurried to the sidelines so that their harnesses
could be used for the next group.

One of the instructors waved his arms, and I found myself running
toward the hovering helicopter. Ben and I stood together as the
instructor passed the heavy rope between us and hooked our harnesses
to the metal rings embedded in it. I put my left arm around Ben's
shoulder as instructed, keeping my right arm free for balance. Ross and
Mudfart were in front of me, Silone and Tolbert behind. The
instructor signaled the helicopter's pilot, and the Sea Knight slowly

rose. There was a slight jerk, then suddenly I was flying! Ben let loose a primordial shout of joy. Glancing up, I could see Ross' and Mudfart's feet dangling a foot above my head. Mudfart wore an ear-to-ear grin as he waved. "This is great!" he shouted.

The view was spectacular. The airport was laid out like a map beneath my feet. I saw a plume of smoke from a mortar explosion in nearby Hey es Sellom, but it seemed unimportant. I felt like Superman, invincible, as the cool wind rushed by.

"I can fly!" Ben shouted. I knew what Ben meant. There was no feeling of strain from the harness, and it felt like I was flying on my on power. The noise of the helicopter was distant, and I could hear the thick rope that supported us creak as it slowly turned under the strain of our weight. Silone was below me. He looked up and smiled. "Don't get airsick up there," he cautioned.

The ride was much too short. The helicopter completed its circle of Beirut International, and after a few minutes of glorious freedom from gravity, we were hovering above the landing zone. The ground was a long way down, and the Marines below looked very small. The Sea Knight started to descend. I hoped the pilot wasn't coming in too fast; there weren't any points of reference by which to judge our speed.

The ground rushed up. I thought I was going to land on Silone's head, but the pilot of the helicopter was in complete control. The Sea Knight's descent slowed, and I gently stepped to earth directly in front of Silone. The instructors detached us from the rope. I felt exhilarated as I ran back to the starting point and removed my harness.

"Let's do it again," Mudfart said. Everyone shouted agreement, but there was only one ride per customer. We had to content ourselves with watching others experience the excitement.

That moment was the last bit of tranquility and fun the men of the 24th Marine Amphibious Unit would share.

IV

Peacekeepers at War

10

ANOTHER EXPLOSION ROCKED the basement. I was leaning against my rack, eyes riveted on the light bulb overhead as it flickered briefly then stabilized. Beirut had erupted into chaos the previous afternoon, Sunday, 28 August, and the fighting had gone on for almost twenty-four hours.

"Get out here!" someone shouted.

I grabbed my rifle and scurried into the other room. A crowd of Marines stood around Lieutenant Jacobs, the assistant logistics officer. Jacobs' face was grimy with sweat and dirt.

"What's going on, sir?" someone demanded.

"Are we moving out?"

Jacobs shook his head. "Men, I don't have to tell you things are pretty bad out there." Another artillery round exploded nearby. I hung on Jacob's words, afraid the rumors we had been passing back and forth for the last few hours were true.

"The whole city's fighting," he said. "We've been hit with over a hundred mortars and rockets. Checkpoints 35 and 69 are getting hit hard, and at 0940 this morning the M-198s fired six illumination rounds over a Druze position. Four minutes later Alpha Company got hit with mortar rounds. Two Marines are dead, three wounded."

There was an audible gasp. "Goddamnit," Ben said.

"The first Marine was killed instantly, the second died during evacuation to the ship."

"Aren't we firing back?" someone asked.

"The checkpoints have been firing small arms in self-defense since last night. We got the grid for a Druze position a couple hours ago, and Charlie Battery fired six illumination rounds over the target. The USS *Belknap* fired two more."

"What the fuck is a goddamn illumination round gonna do?" Chase demanded.

"Why aren't we killing some of the bastards?" I said. Everyone roared approval.

"At ease!" Jacobs yelled. "Colonel Geraghty's doing everything that can be done. The Cobras have been launched, and it looks like the colonel is going to authorize the battery to fire live rounds."

"About goddamn time," Chase sneered.

"That's enough," Jacobs said. "The colonel's in a tough political position."

"Fuck politics," Chase practically screamed. "I'm sick of this political trash. We're the ones who are sitting ducks, not the goddamn politicians in Washington."

Jacobs glared at Chase. Chase was on the verge of insubordination, and Jacobs, a former staff sergeant who had worked his way up to first lieutenant, wasn't the type to take any guff. Rather than being sympathetic to the enlisted troops' problems, he was an officer now and let everyone know it.

"Drop it, Chase," Sergeant Layland warned.

Chase stormed off.

Jacobs kept staring in Chase's direction. "I've got to get back to the CP," he finally said, putting on his helmet. He trotted up the basement stairs.

"Listen!" Mudfart whispered.

Quiet. The rockets had stopped. I listened, ears straining, but the only sound I could hear was the occasional patter of distant machine gun fire.

"Do you think it's over?" I asked Ben.

"You tell me."

The beginning of the trouble had started five days earlier on the afternoon I had gone SPIE rigging. Colonel Geraghty and the United States' special envoy to the Middle East, Robert McFarland, had overflown Israeli occupied territory as part of the coordination for the withdrawal of Israeli troops from Beirut. Israel had finally agreed that a pullback to the Awwali River in southern Lebanon would still allow her to maintain the security of her northern border. The thirty-minute flight over the area south of the village Ad Damur to the Awwali was conducted in an Israeli UH-1N helicopter and had been coordinated through diplomatic and military channels with both Lebanon and

Israel. Although the actual withdrawal wasn't scheduled to begin until early September, the Druze and the Phalange immediately started jockeying for tactical positions in the Chouf.

An aura of tenseness settled on the city the day after the flight. It had been exactly one year since the Marines waded ashore to execute the negotiated PLO withdrawal, but no special celebrations were planned to mark the event. The day was spent in normal routine.

Sunday, 28 August, dawned hot and sultry. Major Van Huss, the operations officer from the 22d MAU and Major Converse's counterpart, had arrived Saturday evening as part of 22 MAU's advance party. The advance party's arrival was another sign that our float was winding down, and I started a countdown to the relief-in-place scheduled for early November.

At 0800 Sunday morning, I drove the two operations officers to the Marine positions around the airport. Mudfart was our shotgun, but perimeter road was eerily quiet. Major Converse briefed the incoming operations officer as we drove past the line companies. Stopping at the U.S. Army's FASTAB radar outpost, we could hear the sound of ominous thunder in the mountains. It sounded like threatening rain, but the sky was clear. The thunder warned of another, far more deadly, kind of storm.

After the tour of the perimeter, we took a tour of the key positions in the city. Traffic was heavy as we slowly made our way through the streets of downtown Beirut. I kept a sharp eye on the cars that surrounded us, fully expecting a hand grenade to be lobbed in our direction at any moment. I cringed each time a Shiite woman passed. Dressed in black from head to foot with only their eyes showing, their way of life seemed alien and fanatical. I imagined that everything from an automatic rifle to a bazooka was hidden beneath their long robes.

Our route took us on Abdallah al Yafi Avenue, just north of the airport, and we passed the Italian contingent's position near the Sabra and Shatila refugee camps. The camps still housed almost thirty thousand Palestinian refugees, and somewhere in the jungle of shanties was the mass grave where the victims of the Lebanese Christian massacre lay. Nearby were the ruins of Kamil Stadium, an important PLO training ground that was bombed out of existence by the Israelis during their invasion of Beirut. The area had been riddled with tunnels, and the Israelis had seized a huge cache of weapons.

French headquarters was on our right next to Midan Sibaq al Khayl, a large hippodrome originally designed for horse racing. Now it was a training area for LAF armored personnel carriers. French and Marine engineers, after clearing hundreds of mines, had built a helipad in the center of the track in case it became necessary for the French forces to evacuate by air. We were near the "Green Line," the boundary that divided the city into east and west. West Beirut, the section of the city where the American Embassy and the airport were located, was predominately Muslim; the eastern side of the city belonged to the Christians. Many of the Lebanese government buildings, such as the Ministry of Defense and the Presidential Palace, were in East Beirut, and violent flare-ups between Christians and Muslims were common along the line.

Major Converse gave me directions to Martyrs Square, the center of the city and the site of intense fighting ten years earlier during Lebanon's civil war. The square, still a hotly contested area, was on the Green Line, but the narrow streets leading to it were filled with throngs of shoppers calmly going about their daily business. The square itself, however, was ghostly: no cars, people, or a single sign of life. The buildings were blasted-out husks and piles of crumbling ruins. A rusted bus, half-buried in rubble, partially blocked one street. An eerie shiver went down my spine; it was as if the ghosts of a thousand dead men haunted the square.

"Not much left, is there?" Major Van Huss said.

"It looks like the set for an end-of-the-world movie," Mudfart commented.

A winding street named Shari al Mina took us away from Martyrs Square. Major Converse knew the city well; I would have been instantly lost in the maze of streets without his directions. A few minutes later, we passed the old American Embassy. The seven-story building had been pronounced structurally unsound after the 19 April van bomb attack, and the Lebanese government planned to demolish it. Most of the debris from the explosion had been cleared from the ground level, but slabs of concrete still hung precariously from twisted steel rods on the upper floors. Major Converse pointed out the route the driver of the explosive-laden van had taken. It seemed unbelievable that the suicidal maniac was able to detonate his cargo directly in front of the building without being stopped.

The new U.S. Embassy was only a few miles from the old. The American ambassador's staff now worked in a complex of buildings that included the British Embassy and the Duraford Building. A mob of Lebanese nationals stood across the street, waiting to be admitted to the consulate so that they could apply for visas to the States. The Marine guards on duty allowed a few at a time to cross the street and enter the building under the watchful eye of an amphibious tractor. A glum sentry sat behind an M-60 machine gun mounted on top of the vehicle. A difficult lesson from the embassy bombing in April had been learned. Most of the street was blocked off, and we were forced to slow down to avoid rolls of concertina wire and huge cement blocks called "dragon's teeth." It would be almost impossible for a car bomb to make its way through embassy security now.

Immediately after the embassy bombing, steps had been taken to safeguard the Marines at the airport as well, particularly the BLT headquarters. Civilian foot traffic was prohibited near the building, all vehicles were searched, and over a quarter of a million sandbags were emplaced. For a variety of political reasons, extraordinarily stringent security measures were ruled out. For example, the parking lot adjacent to the headquarters was ideally suited for a mine field, but because the lot served the airport and was used by civilians, the idea was rejected. Instead, a concertina wire entanglement was built to barricade the parking lot, and a metal sewer pipe was placed in front of the building's entrance to act as a blockade for unauthorized cars. Tank ditches around the compound were contemplated but ultimately rejected because the threat of car bombs was not deemed serious enough for such strong action, and ditching would have destroyed the parking lot the Marines had built for the airport less than a year before. Given the Marines' mission to maintain visibility in Beirut, turning the compound into an impregnable fortress would have made that directive impossible. The Marines had already used every available fifty-five-gallon barrel in southern Beirut, filling them with dirt to act as barriers at the main avenues of approach to the compound.

It was close to noon as our expedition headed back to the compound, taking a more direct route along a corniche that provided a spectacular view of the blue-green Mediterranean. I could see some of our ships in the distance. This section of the city, a resort area dotted with luxury hotels and sidewalk cafes, seemed less hostile. Bikini-clad women sunned themselves on the beach, and an amusement park, complete with Ferris wheel, was jammed with people.

"See that Holiday Inn?" Major Converse asked, pointing to a twenty-story building. "It's pretty famous. It had just been finished and was ready to open when the civil war broke out. It was damaged extensively during the fighting, and the PLO had a command post there when the Israelis invaded. The Muslims liked to throw their Christian prisoners off the roof—alive."

"Pleasant thought," Major Van Huss mumbled.

Mudfart and I grabbed an MRE lunch from the supply tent when we got back to the CP. Ben joined us under the trees in front of the building, and we could hear sporadic gunfire coming from the direction of Hooterville as we ate. "Sounds like the natives are getting restless," Ben said.

I was mixing dehydrated strawberries with water when a round whizzed through the trees. "Maybe we should go inside," Ben suggested. Wood splintered as several more rounds hit the tree above my head. "Make that definitely."

I was gathering my gear as Wheebles floundered out of the supply tent and cranked the Condition I siren. Mudfart and I said "basement" at the same time and hurried to the berthing area. We wouldn't emerge again for almost twenty-four hours, and by then two Marines would be dead.

🏵   🏵   🏵

A local cease-fire was declared shortly after Lieutenant Jacobs had given us the news. Our M-198 howitzer battery had fired six live rounds at a Druze position with pinpoint accuracy, killing three militiamen and wounding fifteen others. The Druze battery immediately became silent, but it was too late to bring back the lives of Second Lieutenant Donald Losey and Staff Sergeant Alexander Ortega.

Mudfart and I went to the office. I was angry that we had waited so long to return fire, but the Rules of Engagement stated that response to direct fire would be initiated at the lowest possible level, with riflemen firing only in self-defense. It seemed ironic that overtures for a cease-fire commenced only after the Marines had fired their howitzers in anger. Violence was the only message the Druze were capable of understanding.

Captain Kettering came into the office from the COC. He had been up all night and looked exhausted.

"Any good MREs left?" he asked, digging in our box of food.

"A veritable gourmet's delight, sir," Mudfart said.

Kettering chose beef stew, his favorite meal, and held it up for us to see. "How's this one?"

"Excellent choice, sir, excellent," Mudfart and I said in unison. We went through the same ritual with Kettering every day. No matter which MRE he picked, Mudfart and I always raved over his choice.

"How did we get the coordinates for the Druze gun, sir?" Mudfart asked.

"It's a combination of several sources," Kettering answered, "such as observation from helicopters, known and suspected enemy positions based on intel reports, and interception of Druze radio nets. The FASTAB is good for targets at longer ranges, but the radars were swamped most of the time last night because of the sheer volume of rounds. We don't rely on a single source of information because we have to be positive we're hitting the right target.

"Don't want to hurt any civilians," he added sarcastically.

"What civilians?"

"Do you think we'll fire again, sir?" I asked.

"These things have a habit of escalating. Now that we've gotten our feet wet by firing back, the Druze will push to see how far we'll go to defend ourselves. It'll get easier for us to retaliate each time."

Condition III was set late in the afternoon. It looked like the cease-fire was holding, and the BLT dispatched an armed supply convoy to make contact with Checkpoints 35 and 69. The resupply went without incident, but 150 heavily armed, masked civilians "escorted" the patrol through the streets of Hooterville. The convoy arrived back within the perimeter at 1930 hours, describing the situation in the city as very tense. The remainder of the night was quiet with only sporadic fire fights and shelling in the city.

I took advantage of the relative calm to write my parents, telling them I was keeping my head down and not to worry. "I'm beginning to wonder why the Marines are in Lebanon," I wrote. "These people have no interest in compromise or in working out their problems. It is obvious that we are unable to do it for them, and if they have no interest in preserving their country, why should we?" I dropped the letter in the mailbox, not knowing when, if ever, they would receive it.

Fighting resumed at a high level at 0600 the following morning, Tuesday, 30 August. Checkpoint 69 came under heavy small arms fire, but when the Marines returned fire with an M-60 machine gun, the attack quickly stopped. Bravo Company was the next position to get involved in the renewed skirmishes. At 0655 the company came under heavy rifle fire, and a fifteen-minute fire fight ensued. Fighting also escalated in the northern sections of the city with rockets exploding near the British Embassy in West Beirut and the American ambassador's residence on the east side of the city.

The Combat Operations Center was an exciting place to be during the fighting. Communicators sat behind a long table at one end of the large room, receiving radio messages from half a dozen places. Each place had a code name. MAU headquarters was known as "Valuable," the *Iwo Jima* was "Ulcer," and the embassy was "Sugar Cane." Colonel Geraghty was referred to as "Red Man 6." Messages were transmitted on top-secret cryptographic gear, which scrambled the communications so that it was impossible for the enemy to intercept them. Several radio nets were up at all times, and the frequencies were changed on a daily basis.

A watch officer received the messages from the communicators first, passing a written copy to the appropriate section as well as maintaining a log of everything received. The intelligence section was in the far corner of the COC and had the difficult job of determining the grid coordinate of enemy positions. Trying to guess where the warring factions might strike next was an all but impossible task. Maps of Beirut covered the walls, and enemy positions were constantly updated as new information was received.

The operations section was in the center of the COC. Along with fire support coordination, operations decided when it was appropriate to return fire. Major Converse, in effect, ran the entire show. "Take this grid under fire," he would say after the decision to engage the enemy had been made. He would then hand the grid coordinate to a communicator for relay. The howitzer battery took it from there.

Converse normally sat in a large green chair at the table he used for a desk, but during the first live fire mission he had offered the chair to Colonel Geraghty. "You've got the hot seat," George said. From then on the chair was known as "hot seat six." One of the communicators immortalized the name on a sign and taped it on the wall above the chair. No one except Colonel Geraghty ever sat in it.

I was in the Combat Operations Center on the afternoon of the thirtieth, updating the daily message boards, when one of the communicators received an important message from the embassy. The PSP was making threats against a contingent of U.S. Army soldiers assigned to the Office of Military Cooperation. The men, protected by a company of LAF soldiers, lived in the Cadmos Hotel in West Beirut, and the PSP indicated that although they didn't want to harm the Americans, they were determined to attack the hotel and wipe out the LAF.

Colonel Geraghty and Major Converse discussed three options: evacuate the Army personnel by sea, evacuate them by ground to the Duraford Building and British Embassy area, or reinforce them with a twenty-seven man Marine detachment and provide the Army personnel with automatic rifles and ammunition. The USS *Austin* and *Belknap* assumed positions off the northern tip of the city, while heated negotiations between the PSP and embassy officials to permit the soldiers' safe passage began. In the meantime, the enlisted troops of MAU headquarters prepared to move out.

"Watson!" Staff Sergeant Summers yelled. "Blood type?"

"O positive."

Summers marked it down on a roster.

"Bradley?"

"B positive."

"Petit?"

"A negative."

I stood in the parking lot with the other enlisted troops of MAU headquarters. A security squad from BLT's dragon platoon had been inserted by helicopter to take up positions around the ambassador's residence, and we were the only ones available to go to the Cadmos. In a bandolier across my chest, I wore the extra hundred rounds of ammunition that supply had issued me, and my hands shook as I filled extra magazines with rounds. Getting ready was only a contingency plan in case the negotiations with the PSP broke down, but I had a hunch I'd be facing combat in downtown Beirut by dusk.

"I hope we come out of this alive," I said to Ben.

Ben slapped me on the back. "Of course we will," he assured me. He didn't sound very confident.

"I want to get at least a Purple Heart out of this mission," Cavendish, Colonel Geraghty's driver, said.

"Why?" Silone demanded. "I only want to get my ass out in one piece."

"I don't want to get hurt, just wounded a little," Cav explained. "Wouldn't it be great to have a whole row of medals on our chests when we get home? Especially a Purple Heart and a Combat Action Ribbon."

"Don't you mean if we get home?" Silone asked.

"Of course we'll get home."

"Tell that to Losey and Ortega."

"Who wants a medal anyway?" Nels said. "They're the ultimate irony of combat. You can beat a man and kick him, but he won't follow you unless he wants to. But offer him a bit of pretty cloth or a shiny piece of metal, and he'll follow you into combat and hand you his life on a silver platter."

"Hell, I don't want a medal," Ben said. "That little strip of purple cloth's not going to keep Ortega's wife warm at night or make her any less lonely. My wife would rather have me at home, and I want to be there in one piece."

We had been following the Marine Corps' hurry-up-and-wait policy for over an hour when Captain Kettering emerged from the COC to tell us the operation was off, at least for the moment. The USS *Portland* had relieved the *Austin*, and negotiations with the PSP were continuing; Colonel Geraghty decided to hold off on sending us. Cav may have been disappointed over the cancellation, but I felt nothing but relief. Longing for the thrill of combat and the excitement of living on the edge had been easy when it wasn't staring me in the face.

"Men, we're going to Condition I in a few minutes," Kettering announced. "Better move to the fighting holes now."

Alpha and Charlie Company had begun receiving small arms fire, and stray rounds started impacting near the CP. Ben and I jumped into the hole outside the supply tent. Ten minutes later, the airport was being shelled. I passed the time counting rounds until I heard a helicopter fly overhead. A CH-46 had been caught at Rock Base when the shelling began, and while it managed to make it back to the ship, we later learned it took a small arms round through the windshield in the process.

Artillery and mortar rounds continued to land around the airport until 7:00 P.M. Bravo Company at the Lebanese University was getting hit hard. Shells were landing all around the library building, and the battery was forced to fire two illumination rounds at a Druze gun position. The shelling stopped.

Condition II was set at 1926 hours, and Ben and I crawled out of our foxhole, grimy from sand. Being in a foxhole was boring. Conversation was quickly exhausted, and we had no way of knowing what was going on outside the hole. We could only wait and hope the fighting ended quickly.

Archie opened Branigan's, and Ben and I rushed in to buy a soda to wash down an MRE dinner. We had barely started eating when Condition I was sounded again. This time we headed for the basement. Checkpoints 76, 35, and 69 began receiving small arms fire and, fighting alongside LAF soldiers, engaged the enemy. Fighting at the line companies was to continue for the next eight hours.

I spent a frustrating night in the basement listening to what sounded like World War III outside. Conversations were limited to saying "that was a close one" each time a shell exploded nearby. All the contingents of the Multinational Force were being shelled sporadically, but Beirut's port area was hit with a massive rocket barrage. Sunken ships from the civil war still posed a navigational hazard in the small harbor, and from the reports received, it looked like a few more might be added.

The MAU identified two artillery positions firing at French head-quarters near midnight. The French were adamant that they weren't requesting the Marines to return fire on the positions, but in diplomatic double talk they stated they "would not oppose it." Because the volume of fire was so intense, Colonel Geraghty decided there was no choice but to try and reduce it. The howitzer battery fired two illumination rounds on both grids, and firing from the positions stopped for an hour before restarting at a subdued level.

Less than an hour later, the shelling of Beirut International picked up. The battery fired two illumination rounds at grid 405440, a PSP position near Hey es Sellom, in an effort to ward off the attacks. The strategy of firing illumination rather than live rounds was beginning to lose its punch, however. Moments later, the PSP target fired six rounds at the howitzer battery. One shell impacted within two hundred meters of the Marine position; a second exploded fifty meters to the north.

Although the PSP were becoming braver, they stopped firing and no further rounds impacted in the vicinity of the airport through the remainder of the night.

A dense smoke hung over the city the following morning. The LAF was running short of ammunition, and the MAU received orders from Sixth Fleet to transfer twelve pallets, five hundred thousand rounds of 5.56mm cartridges, to the LAF at Juniyah, a Lebanese naval base south of Beirut. The huge expenditure of ammunition around the city—over a million artillery rounds—was at levels rivaling major battles of World War II.

Negotiations with the PSP to evacuate the U.S. Army soldiers had continued through the night, and at 0840, the first twenty-six soldiers were allowed to move by van from the Cadmos Hotel to the Duraford Building. The evacuation ended moments later when a rocket-propelled grenade landed directly behind the van on its second trip. Fifty-three soldiers were still stuck in the Cadmos as fighting in the area renewed.

Much of the fighting in the northern part of Beirut was the result of a two-pronged sweep through the area by the 4th and 8th LAF Brigades. The sweeps were intended to divide the northern half of the city from the southern half, in which the 3d LAF Brigade was trying to maintain order. The LAF changed its tactic of leaving the militias in the Chouf alone and commenced rocket attacks on artillery and mortar positions. In response to the shelling, the PSP began firing on the Ministry of Defense. After several direct hits on the building, endangering the lives of both U.S. Army and Marine officers, the howitzers fired six live rounds on the PSP position. Just as Kettering had warned, it was becoming easier to return fire each time American lives were in danger.

The city settled into an uneasy silence at six o'clock that evening. The USS *Austin* completed an emergency resupply of water to the Marines on shore, and the embassy reported that an agreement with the PSP had been reached, allowing the U.S. Army personnel to return to the Cadmos. The MAU moved to a cautious alert Condition III, and the intense fighting, at least for the moment, was over.

11

MUDFART AND I were dancing with one another in the operations office as Ben walked by. "Have you been taking Lieutenant Block lessons again?" he asked.

"Gunny's going home! Gunny's going home!" Mudfart and I sang.

"Are you serious?"

"Hallelujah, yes!" I shouted as Mudfart and I stopped twirling around the room. "He's being medevaced to Wiesbaden, Germany today."

"Why?"

"His mouth is broken," Mudfart screamed. "Isn't it wonderful?" Gunny Thorn had a blocked salivary gland, and the left side of his face had swollen up like a grapefruit. He could barely talk, and because the doctors on the ship couldn't do anything for him he was being evacuated to an Air Force hospital in Europe.

"Is he coming back?" Ben asked.

"Doubtful," I answered. "This close to the end of the float they'll probably fly him back to the States after surgery."

"You mean he's gone forever?"

"Yep."

Ben hooked his arm around mine, and the three of us did a do-si-do around the office singing, "Gunny's going home!"

"Now if we can only get rid of the sergeant major," Ben added.

It was the morning of 4 September, and the Israelis had begun their withdrawal from the Beirut area at midnight. The withdrawal, although without incident for the Israelis, was accompanied by an immediate outbreak of Druze and Phalange clashes in the mountains and the shelling of East Beirut. The Chouf villages Suq al Gharb and Aytat were being pounded by artillery, but Beirut International had remained relatively calm since the cease-fire of 31 August.

Father Pucciarelli scheduled a memorial service for the two Marines killed in action. Correspondents from all over the world had arrived to cover the Beirut story, and press coverage of the ceremony was intense.

135

CBS, ABC, and NBC had cameras trained on us as we stood in formation outside the CP. I grimaced when I saw Wheebles was acting platoon sergeant. Staff Sergeant Summers had gone to MSSG on a supply run.

Colonel Geraghty and the executive officer marched to the front of the formation.

"Platoon," Wheebles anemically whispered, "Atten-hut!"

The formation snapped to attention and Wheebles, quivering like a mound of jello, reported. "Sir, headquarters platoon all present or accounted for."

"Post!" Slugo commanded.

Wheebles executed an about-face and lost his balance, stumbling backward half a dozen steps before he managed to regain control.

"Daffy Duck joins the Marines," Ben whispered.

I started to laugh. "Shush!" someone behind me cautioned. Wheebles lurched to his position behind the formation, somehow managing not to fall.

"Let us pray," Father Pucciarelli said. I bowed my head and listened attentively to the chaplain's prayer. Between invocations to God, Pucciarelli proclaimed that Losey and Ortega had died in the valiant effort to "protect this troubled nation's sovereignty."

"This isn't a memorial for the dead," I whispered to Ben. "It's a justification to the press on why we're here." Colonel Geraghty continued the "we must help Lebanon maintain her sovereignty" theme during his comments, barely mentioning Losey and Ortega. I slowly began to fume. Finally, a Marine on the roof of the building across the street played taps, signaling the end of the service. Wheebles dismissed the platoon without again making a fool of himself on the six o'clock news.

"At least the dog-and-pony act for the press is over," Nels said in Branigan's after the ceremony.

"That service should have been called 'The Howdy Doody Show,'" I said. "Watch the Marines dance like puppets while Washington pulls the strings."

"And of course we haven't been in combat," Space Chase added. "Losey and Ortega dropped dead from boredom, not massive shrapnel wounds to the head."

Despite our isolation, we were acutely aware that a storm of controversy was taking place in the American press. The Reagan administration insisted the Marines were not involved in combat, while much of Congress insisted that we were. Under the War Powers Act, Reagan would need congressional approval to keep us in Lebanon if we were engaged in combat, and determining our role in Lebanon was a presidential power he refused to relinquish. It was frustrating to sit in a foxhole day after day as missiles exploded around us only to hear on the radio that the Marines were not involved in Lebanon's civil war. I knew how often the line companies returned fire. The Marines were obviously in combat, but the politics of the situation forced our commanders to insist that we were not involved in the fighting, even as we became more embroiled each day.

"Did you see the message from the commander of naval forces in Europe?" Ben asked everyone. "It was a warning to Geraghty and Commodore France—something like 'The loss of life can be expected, but the loss of equipment, naval vessels, and aircraft is unacceptable.'"

"At least we know were we stand," I said. "Cannon fodder."

"I don't care what some idiot safe behind a big desk in Europe says," Space Chase exclaimed. "My life is worth more than a broken down old jeep!"

"Too bad your brain's a quart low," Ben commented.

           ✿   ✿   ✿

As a result of the heavy fighting at the end of August, the commander in chief of U.S. Naval Forces in Europe (CINCUSNAVEUR) had suspended the requirement for presence patrols within the city. Colonel Geraghty cancelled all mobile and foot patrols outside the perimeter until further notice and made plans to reinforce the Marines on shore should it become necessary. The USS *Eisenhower* Carrier Battle Group, along with the French aircraft carrier *Foch* and several Italian naval gunfire ships, moved closer to shore. The embassy planned for a possible evacuation of U.S. citizens, and a noncombatant evacuation communication net was established, linking the American Embassies in Beirut and Tel Aviv to the commanders of the U.S. task force.

Twelve hours after the Israeli withdrawal had begun, the Marines on the lines were fighting again. In an attempt to fill the void left by the withdrawing Israelis, the Lebanese Armed Forces began staging mechanized infantry troops at Beirut International for further movement south. The PSP wanted to prevent the LAF from establishing a position at all cost, and because the LAF soldiers were intermingled with Marines, Charlie Company began receiving small arms and mortar fire. The fighting escalated when the PSP broke out a 106mm recoilless rifle and started taking pot shots at the LAF's armored vehicles and Marine bunkers. Mortar rounds were landing on top of Charlie Company's position, and the BLT dispatched an M-60A1 tank to crush the recoilless rifle.

The LAF immediately launched an artillery attack on the PSP positions in the foothills, intending to move south behind the barrage. The fighting around Charlie Company gradually tapered off as the LAF's 4th Brigade moved its column of sixty mechanized vehicles into the Beirut suburb Khalde and away from Marine positions. An uneasy Condition II remained in effect until early evening when four rockets landed at the southern end of perimeter road. Sporadic shelling of the airport continued throughout the night, and the mortar platoon and M-198 howitzers fired illumination rounds over the PSP guns several times in a vain attempt to initiate a cease-fire.

The PSP rocket gunners continually moved their launchers, thwarting the intelligence section's ability to accurately locate the firing positions. At five o'clock on the morning of 5 September, Charlie Company again came under fire, and the mortar platoon responded with eleven live rounds on a previously identified PSP position. One Marine was injured in the exchange and was evacuated to the *Iwo*. MAU headquarters alternated between Condition I and Condition II throughout the remainder of the day as fighting in the nearby hills continued. An ammunition resupply of the LAF was conducted at Juniyah. The LAF was firing over two thousand rounds of artillery ammunition every twenty-four hours, and without the operation, the Lebanese government would have been completely unable to support its army.

The sixth and seventh proved to be a very trying time for the Marines. Shortly after midnight on the sixth, the first of several rocket barrages fell on the airport. The position from which the rockets were being fired was close; the time of flight was only two or three seconds, and at 0345 a second barrage consisting of twenty-one rockets began.

In the basement, I woke to the news that two more Marines were dead. Corporal Pedro Valle and Lance Corporal Randy Clark had been killed by shrapnel, bringing the total dead since the first attack on 22 July to four. The number of wounded stood at twenty-seven. The howitzers retaliated by firing illumination rounds at a suspected target, but determining the precise location of the firing battery in the dark was impossible.

At dawn, the Cobras were launched in an attempt to locate visually the artillery positions, but the massive amount of rocket launcher emplacements and impacts in the hills made it impossible to say which position was firing on the airport. Another barrage of rockets hit the airport at 1000 hours, and isolated rounds continued to impact around Marine bunkers throughout the day. By late afternoon, despite the inaccuracy of the gunners in the hills, over 120 rounds of artillery, mortar, and rocket fire had scored direct hits on Beirut International.

Political negotiations were ongoing throughout the day. Special envoy Robert McFarland flew to Damascus for cease-fire discussions with Syrian officials, and Lebanese president Amin Gemayel, in a political ploy, threatened to resign if the talks were not successful.

The night of 6 September was oddly quiet. The artillery and mortar fire died down in the hills, but the alert was once again sounded as shelling began anew at 0730 the morning of the seventh. Rockets impacted near Bravo Company at the Lebanese University and in the center of the city. One French soldier was killed and three were wounded when the French headquarters came under attack. At 1115, the French launched two reconnaissance aircraft from the *Foch* to take aerial photographs of the deadly artillery positions.

The French aircraft reconnaissance was quickly followed by U.S. F-14 photo missions flown from the *Eisenhower*. The TARPs (Tactical Air Reconnaissance Photo) missions were to become frequent during the following weeks, and the intelligence section of the MAU used the photos extensively to ascertain the location of enemy gun emplacements. SA-7 surface-to-air missiles, capable of knocking an F-14 out of the sky, were located in the hills surrounding the city, but the intelligence experts felt that their use was tightly controlled by the Syrians and did not pose a significant threat.

The F-14s were on a thirty-minute alert, and their photos could be processed within five hours of the aircraft's recovery. Because of the sensitive nature of the reconnaissance flights, multiple legs were flown over each target position to maximize effectiveness. After processing, the photographs were flown from the *Eisenhower* to the *Iwo Jima* and then ashore to the intelligence section. Four additional photo interpreters were assigned to the *Eisenhower* to help interpret the mission results.

The data culled from the aerial imagery was exchanged with the French. Brigadier General Stiner, the Department of Defense's military representative to the McFarland mission, requested that some TARPs missions be flown in direct support of the Lebanese government. His request was relayed to the commander of the Sixth Fleet. I was surprised when the *Eisenhower* was authorized to undertake the missions; the TARPs flights were supposed to be used for American defense, not Lebanese offense.

Shelling of the airport began again in the early evening of 7 September with three rounds landing just outside Charlie Company's lines. Six more rockets landed near Rock Base and the MAU headquarter's CP, wounding a Marine from MSSG. The howitzers fired six rounds of live ammunition on the suspected target; the USS *Bowen* prepared to fire more, but the artillery position fell silent. The Marines stood down to alert Condition II at 2038 hours.

Lieutenant General Miller, the commander of Fleet Marine Force Atlantic, and Major General Gray, the commander of Second Marine Division, arrived during the afternoon of the seventh to inspect the troops. Their first night in Beirut was calm although the city was filled with tension. The two generals toured the compound the following morning. Cav drove Colonel Geraghty's jeep and told me everyone on the line asked General Gray the same question: "Sir, are we going to get a Combat Action Ribbon?" The best answer the general could come up with was "Maybe."

"I hope we get it," Cav said just before he drove the generals to Rock Base to catch their helicopter.

"You should be happy we're going to get hostile-fire pay," I said.

"Big deal. Sixty-five bucks a month. I'd rather have the ribbon." General Kelley had issued a memorandum authorizing the Marines on shore a pay bonus because of the danger we faced. Sixty-five dollars a month hardly seemed just compensation for getting shot at.

Ten minutes after Cav left, three rockets landed at the edge of the runway. The jeeps raced back to the CP a few minutes later.

"The generals made their bird," Cav announced. "But you should have seen Gray and Miller hit the deck when that artillery hit. The rockets exploded a couple hundred meters away, and look at this!" Cav held up a small piece of shrapnel. "It landed in my jeep."

"You almost got that Purple Heart, Cav," I said.

"Next time I'll get it for sure. At least Gray and Miller know what it's like to be a sitting duck now. Maybe we will get that Combat Action Ribbon after all."

In response to the attack, USS *Bowen* fired a four-round salvo of five-inch 54-HE on the target, becoming the first U.S. Naval vessel to shell an enemy position in the Mediterranean since World War II. Sporadic shelling of the airport continued the rest of the night, but somehow being shaken awake by the constant explosions seemed almost normal.

On the morning of 9 September, twenty mortar rounds launched from the southeast landed in the airport's terminal building. The mortar position began to plague the Marines at Beirut International on a daily basis. Nicknamed "Achmed the Mad Mortarman," the Druze gunner responsible for the attacks would fire ten to twenty rounds and disappear. Varying the time of his attack, he effectively escaped retribution. After referring the culprit to the LAF, everyone watched in vain for several days as the LAF's artillery landed everywhere but in the vicinity of Achmed.

Achmed's primary target was the Lebanese Air Force, which consisted of five Hawker-Hunter aircraft. The planes had been trapped on the westmost runway of the airport since the shelling had begun, and now that the runways were full of craters it looked like the planes would stay stuck. The LAF, however, had been secretly turning a road north of Juniyah into an emergency airstrip, and for several nights Lebanese crews had been covertly repairing the runway so that the planes could take off. At five o'clock on the morning of the fifteenth, the aircraft managed to become airborne before Achmed knew what was happening.

The Lebanese Air Force's triumph was short-lived. The following morning, two of the planes were shot down by ground fire. One of the planes managed to land in a field on the island of Cyprus, but the other crashed in the sea four thousand yards from the *Iwo Jima*. Search-and-rescue aircraft from the *Eisenhower* fished the pilot from the Mediterranean, and Achmed the Mad Mortarman turned his weapon to new targets.

The news media had a field day covering the Marines at war. They smelled a good story and were everywhere. We shared our foxholes and MREs with them; they poked and prodded and asked all sorts of questions. The television networks, wire services, newspaper syndicates, and photo agencies sent dozens of correspondents, photographers, and TV crews to Beirut. News representatives from England, Norway, Switzerland, France, Germany, and Turkey arrived to record the action, and independent television stations sent crews to interview hometown Marines. Every reporter was on the lookout for a new angle, and Colonel Geraghty was bombarded with requests for interviews. He spoke with Tom Brokow and Ted Koppel by telephone and granted interviews to newspapers from Baltimore, New York, and Miami. The colonel maintained a nonchalant attitude through it all, as though he had lived in a fishbowl all his life, but deep down I think he was as excited about the news coverage as the rest of us.

The Public Affairs Office was responsible for keeping tabs on all the reporters. The staff of two officers and six enlisted men escorted thirty to forty reporters around the compound each day, frequently exposing themselves to hostile fire. The European print journalists constantly sought out the individual Marine's political viewpoint, and Major Robert Jordan, the officer in charge of public affairs, gave the reporters daily news bulletins to keep them from delving too deeply. The enlisted troops were carefully instructed not to divulge any confidential information but were never barred from voicing their opinions.

It was easy to be quoted in a newspaper article. Simply walk up to any one of a dozen reporters and say something controversial. But most of the Marines took their role in Lebanon seriously and shied away from the newsmen and cameras. Except for a brazen few, fame wasn't on anyone's mind, and despite Andy Warhol's claim that someday everyone will be famous for fifteen minutes, most were content to sit back and watch.

Still, there were plenty of chances for fame and fortune, but when my opportunity knocked I was napping in the basement.

Mudfart shook me awake. "A reporter was looking for you," he said. Mudfart sounded like he was speaking another language.

"What?" I asked groggily.

"Ross is behind the supply tent. He's going to be on TV!"

I sat up. "Why do they want me then?"

"A reporter came in the office and asked if you were the MAU's MRE connoisseur. I told him yes but that I didn't know where you were. Come on, let's go watch Ross."

I staggered out of the rack and followed Mudfart to the supply tent. Ross was sitting on a stool behind the tent expounding the virtues of meatballs in barbecue sauce. A video camera with CNN written on its side was recording everything.

"What I like about MREs," Ross was saying, "is that unlike regular C rations, you can carry a lot more in your ALICE pack, and MREs cook up to a nice meal to warm your tummy." Ross placed a canteen cup of water on a portable stove and put a foil packet of meatballs into the water to heat. Then he started spreading jelly on one of his crackers. "Before I eat my main dish, I like to have an hors d'oeuvre to whet my appetite. Cracker with apple jelly. Mmm-mmm! After you spread the jelly, you take a nice big bite of the cracker." Ross took a bite, slowly savoring the taste. "Good cracker," he finally announced.

The CNN reporter standing behind the cameraman was trying hard not to laugh. He covered his mouth to suppress his giggles, but he'd already lost any chance of controlling himself. Ross had taken charge of the piece and was even suggesting possible camera angles to the cameraman.

Ross shook a little salt into the packet of meatballs. "Now I'm ready to chow down on my main entree," he said. "How about you?" He started to pull the packet from the boiling water. "You've got to be careful during this time because this is a hot meal and you don't want to burn yourself," he warned. "I'm used to it because, well, I'm a tough Marine, and I can handle things like that. This hot meal doesn't hurt my hand at all." He yanked the packet from the water and mugged for the camera, pretending he'd burned himself. The reporter looked like he had swallowed his tongue to keep from laughing out loud.

"Mmm-mmm, that's good!" Ross exclaimed as he chewed his meatballs. "The only thing I can compare these meatballs to is the taste of a sirloin with fries. It's very similar to it."

Ross put down the packet of meatballs and opened his chocolate nut cake. "Sometimes I like to just wolf my dessert down," he said, "and other times when I feel in a mellower mood, I'll just break off a little chunk and taste it like this." Ross broke off a piece and popped it into his mouth. "The only thing that's missing—and I've saved up a lot of these chocolate nut cakes—is milk. I wish I had a cold glass of milk right now because then it would remind me of when I was a little boy back home on the farm, eating my chocolate chip cookies with ice cold milk. And let me tell you, if these chocolate nut cakes ever get on the open market, Famous Amos is in a world of trouble. This chocolate nut cake is darn good.

"After I finish my cake," Ross continued, "I put my wrappers back in the big plastic MRE package because it also doubles as a trash bag. Kids, you always want to remember to never leave trash hanging around. Keep America beautiful. Plus Beirut, Lebanon!"

The reporter was pleased with Ross' performance and shook his hand. Ross had turned what would have been a mundane report on MREs into a very funny piece.

"How does it feel to be a star, Big Guy?" I asked.

"I'll never forget all the little people who made me what I am today. What was your name again?"

                    ❦   ❦   ❦

The nature of the Marines' role in Lebanon changed dramatically during the second half of September. The U.S. Contingent of the Multinational Force could no longer claim it was neutral in the conflict between Muslims and Christians. During the night of the sixteenth, the Ministry of Defense and the American ambassador's residence came under heavy artillery bombardment. The USS *Bowen* and the *John Rodgers* fired six naval gunfire missions, expending a total of seventy-two rounds on six different targets.

The nearby village Suq al Gharb was quickly becoming a key battle-ground in the fight. The ridge near the village overlooked the entire city, and any militia whose artillery controlled the high ground of the ridge would control Beirut. PSP elements concentrated their efforts on taking the town, and Palestinian units fighting in the mountains joined the attack on the LAF with two battalions of infantry supported by tanks and intense preparatory artillery fire. The heavy fighting was clearly audible throughout Beirut. The LAF was so low on artillery ammunition it could no longer provide an adequate defense, and General Stiner requested that the ships fire in their support. Between 10:00 A.M. and 3:00 P.M. on the nineteenth, the U.S. naval gunfire ships *Virginia*, *John Rodgers*, *Bowen*, and *Radford* fired 360 five-inch rounds on Muslim targets. The PLO units broke and ran under the massive barrage, and the tide of the battle for Suq al Gharb turned in favor of the LAF.

The barrage turned out to be only a temporary measure, however. Artillery and rocket fire continued to threaten the Ministry of Defense and the ambassador's residence. On the evening of the twentieth, the ambassador's residence was hit with artillery rounds, which started several fires. After the fires were extinguished, all personnel except the Marine guards and a radio watch were evacuated to the relative safety of the Presidential Palace, and the *John Rodgers* and the *Virginia* engaged the enemy's artillery by firing thirty rounds each. The naval gunfire ships bombarded three different gun positions with ninety additional rounds the next evening.

Listening to the fighting from the basement was an exercise in futility and helplessness. I was becoming adept at differentiating between incoming and outgoing artillery rounds. Rounds heading our direction had a special whine to them, and I counted the seconds with my head down until I heard the explosion, feeling safe until the next rocket.

Ben and I passed the time by talking on the basement stairs as the fighting raged around us, but everyone reacted to the artillery barrages differently. Some of the troops seemed unconcerned; others, their nerves worn raw, jumped at every sound.

Beckford seemed especially poised for some sort of breakdown. Sometimes he would join Ben and me on the stairs. "They're coming," he would whisper. "I know they're going to sneak through the lines. It would only take a single grenade tossed down the stairs and we'd all be dead." Beckford loaded his rifle once and was ready to charge outside blasting away like John Wayne until Ben calmed him down. A minute later, he was cowering in his rack with the covers pulled over his head screaming, "Shut up! Shut up!"

Several songs written by anonymous Marines circulated through the basement. "The Chouf Shuffle" and "Don't Drop the Bomb on Me, Baby" were popular, but "I Love Beirut in the Mornings" was

Beckford's favorite. After his strange outbursts he'd join the others as they sang it:

Mothers, tell your sons to beware,
Bombs are bursting everywhere;
See Beirut go up in flames,
See Marines get blown away.
I don't know what to do,
But if you shoot at me, I'll shoot at you.
I love Beirut in the mornings,
I just wonder if it's still there.

I was confused by the subtle changes in U.S. policy. I feared we had lost sight of our original mission and questioned our motives. But there were no simple answers; everything was shrouded in shades of gray. "Whatever happened to popular, clearly defined conflicts such as, Hitler advances on Europe?" I wrote in an angry letter I wanted to send to the *New York Times*. "The Marines in Lebanon are on a nebulous, ill-advised mission which, for lack of a better term, is defined as 'peacekeeping.' Unfortunately, there is no peace to keep. Lebanon is embroiled in civil war, and the Marines, forced to play the diplomatic game of waiting, sit at a highly visible airport, an easy target for every religious nut with a cause and an AK-47."

Retaliation was like a drug. It was becoming too easy for the naval gunfire ships to answer calls for fire in support of the LAF. If the U.S. is going to be in a war, I thought, then let's not hide under a banner that proclaims Peacekeepers! with our hands tied behind our backs. Send in more Marines and push the Muslims back to Damascus. The Syrians' attempt to shoot down two of our reconnaissance aircraft with their surface-to-air missiles only served to reinforce my opinion. "The United States has gone to war over less than this," I proclaimed after the incident. "If the Syrians want war, let's give it to them."

At the same time, despite my bold statements, I was afraid that we were indeed poised for war. As one of the Marines who would be on the front line, I wanted to damn foreign policy and just go home. But every sign pointed to a U.S. war in the Middle East. The 31st Marine Amphibious Unit, normally deployed in the Pacific, had transited the Indian Ocean and Suez Canal and was waiting off the coast of Lebanon. Officially known as "Ready Group Alpha," its presence meant another 1,800 combat-ready Marines could move ashore at a moment's notice. Over a dozen American warships sailed up and down the coast, and the United States' only battleship, the USS *New Jersey*, was scheduled to arrive before the end of the month to, as the Pentagon put it, "send a message to Syria." *New Jersey's* firepower alone was enough to destroy half of Beirut.

❧   ❧   ❧

The city had been quiet for two days, but by noon, 23 September, Beirut was again at war with itself. Rockets hit the Italian position, igniting their ammunition dump and destroying over twenty vehicles. Miraculously, no one was killed. The French headquarters was also hit hard, seriously injuring one soldier and wounding three others. The French responded by launching an airstrike on Muslim strongholds in the Bekaa Valley.

Fighting broke out between the LAF and the Muslim militias in Hooterville during the early afternoon. Small arms fire and mortars impacted near Checkpoints 69 and 76, and the mortar platoon returned fire with twelve rounds of live ammo. The assault on the checkpoints did not stop, however, and an hour later the mortar platoon fired an additional twenty-eight rounds on the attacking militias. The checkpoints were originally set up to act as a buffer between Israeli forces and the Hey es Sellom area, but with the withdrawal of the IDF they no longer had a clearly defined purpose. The isolated checkpoints were vulnerable, and Colonel Geraghty decided it would be impossible to reinforce them or evacuate any wounded without placing other Marines in extreme jeopardy. The risk was unacceptable, and plans were drawn to move the Marines to safer positions as soon as the fighting slowed enough for a tactical retreat.

At 7:00 P.M., the M-198 howitzers engaged an active mortar position with six rounds of HE/PD, and the *Virginia* fired thirty more rounds on artillery positions that were shelling the airport. The LAF commenced an intense barrage of massed artillery and mortar fire into the same area, but unfortunately, their aim was not very accurate. Two Marines at Rock Base were wounded by the LAF guns before MAU headquarters could get them to stop.

The Ministry of Defense came under artillery attack at 10:00 P.M.

the USS *Radford* responded with twenty rounds on the suspected rocket launcher and was joined by the *Bowen* to fire an additional 120 rounds at four separate targets. Fighting around the airport gradually tapered off, and by morning the Marines at Checkpoints 69 and 76 were able to redeploy to safer positions at the Lebanese University.

The *New Jersey* arrived off the shore of Beirut as scheduled on 25 September, and I thought it was a humorous coincidence that the factions in the Chouf had agreed to a cease-fire coinciding with the battleship's arrival. The "Big J" was formidable. Each of her nine, sixteen-inch guns could deliver a 2,700 pound armor-piercing round on target every thirty seconds, and her twelve, five-inch guns had a range of nine nautical miles and could fire twenty rounds per barrel per minute. Major Converse felt the actions of the Multinational Force had given the factions no choice but to call a cease-fire. In a report to Headquarters Marine Corps, he wrote, "The arrival of the 31st MAU and USS *New Jersey*, the willingness of the U.S. Multinational Force to use naval gunfire in support of the LAF, and the air strike by the French on the twenty-third indicated to the opposing factions the readiness of the Multinational Force to escalate the fighting beyond the capabilities of the militias and directly contributed to the willingness of all parties to call a cease-fire."

The fighting continued up to the last minute, however, as all sides jockeyed for the best possible position. The cease-fire was slow to take hold, but fighting throughout the city gradually tapered off until, on the morning of the twenty-sixth, the Marines crawled out of their fighting holes and bomb shelters to face a quiet but still deeply divided city.

Mudfart and I celebrated the cease-fire by filling sandbags. A CBS camera crew caught us in action.

"Yes, we're still digging in," Mudfart said in response to a reporter's question. "The cease-fire will never hold. There's too many crazies up in the hills wanting to kill each other, and as far as I'm concerned, let 'em. I just want to make sure I've got a good bunker to dive into."

I agreed with Mudfart, but as the fighting slowed then stopped, I became optimistic that September would end on a positive note. I was wrong. On the second to last day of the month, two U.S. Army soldiers assigned to the FASTAB were kidnapped by the Amal after making a wrong turn off the main north/south avenue in the center of Beirut.

The Amal was a powerful Muslim militia led by Nabih Berri, and although they viciously fought against the LAF, their attitude toward the Marines thus far had been moderate. Nevertheless, I figured the Army soldiers would be dead by the end of the day.

Colonel Geraghty was sitting in hot seat six when I went into the COC to see what was happening. His face was a mixture of anxiety and concern. The kidnapping was the culmination of weeks of life-and-death decisions, and for the first time I saw the colonel without a look of self-assurance. He was approaching his limit, and the sleepless, agonizing nights had taken their toll. Major Converse was talking on one of the radio nets in an effort to discover the fate of the soldiers. I quickly left the COC, but seeing Colonel Geraghty with that strained look on his face was a demoralizing blow.

I picked up bits and pieces of the kidnapping story as they filtered out of the COC. A green Mercedes had blocked the Army soldiers' jeep when they tried to return to the main road. The driver of the Mercedes pointed a pistol at the soldiers and ordered them to get out. A second vehicle carrying four men armed with AK-47 rifles roared up, and the two soldiers were disarmed and taken to a schoolhouse. Half an hour later, they were taken to Nabih Berri, who apologized for the incident. Berri indicated that the Amal had no antagonism against the Marines and released the two soldiers to a French liaison officer.

The soldiers were unharmed, but the incident marked an ominous change in the strategy of the factions opposed to the presence of the Marines. The heavy fighting was over, but the sniping and terrorist attacks had just begun.

12

ROSS' NIGHTMARES STARTED in October. He would wake in the middle of the night gasping for air, his hand muffling a ragged scream. The 26 September cease-fire had brought a fragile and uneasy peace to Beirut, but unknown to us we had merely entered a new, even more dangerous phase in our mission. During August's heavy fighting, the intelligence section continually warned that terrorist attacks were an active threat, but the threats were nonspecific, overshadowed by the very specific and active reality of artillery rounds killing Marines. The terrorist warnings began anew with the cease-fire. Perhaps Ross, at some subconscious level, sensed the ominous fate that hung over us. His nightmare was always the same: shadowy figures bulldozing tons of dark red earth into the basement as we slept. The earth would rush down the stairs in a torrent, crash through the door to our room and engulf our racks.

Ross' nightmare was prophetic; the warnings became reality on 3 October with a minor incident. An unidentified man fired three rifle shots at Bravo Company in the early morning hours before disappearing into the slums of Hooterville. No one was wounded as the Marines dove into their bunkers, but the torrent that would eventually sweep away so many lives had begun.

The line companies rotated to their final positions during the first week of October, and Alpha moved back to the Lebanese University library building. On the fifth, a UH-1N helicopter transporting the U.S. Defense Attache and an aide to the McFarlane mission was hit by sniper fire. A single round passed through the cockpit. Upon landing at the Ministry of Defense, the pilot was unable to restart the aft rotor, and the disabled aircraft was forced to return to Rock Base on its remaining PT6 turboshaft engine. The vulnerability of helicopters using standard transit patterns over the city was reevaluated, and actions were taken to protect U.S. aircraft. Staggered flight times and routes, terrain flying, and limiting nonessential helicopter trips did little to stop the snipers, however. The following day, a second Marine helicopter was taken under fire. The pilot of the CH-46 Sea Knight, noticing a shudder followed by airspeed loss, aborted his mission. Post-flight analysis revealed that a small arms round had hit an aft rotor blade.

Sniper fire directed at the Marines slowly started to escalate. Bravo Company sentries observed three men entering a building under construction in Hooterville on the morning of the seventh, and moments later sniper fire from the building began to hit Marine bunkers. The firing stopped after several rounds, but armed militiamen were observed throughout the area constructing barricades and manning checkpoints. The cease-fire meant nothing to the militias; it was merely an opportunity to dig in deeper before beginning the war anew.

Scandal rocked the MAU headquarters in early October. The "love that dare not speak its name" had started talking and wouldn't shut up. I got up one morning to discover that one of the officers was simply gone. He had vanished without a trace, and no one, not even Silone who knew all the good gossip, could explain why. The mystery was the major source of conversation for a week. Everyone agreed that the officer had been a bit strange. He'd crane his neck in the shower tent like a tourist on a sight-seeing bus and was always taking pictures of anyone who had his shirt off. I figured the story would break any day, but Colonel Geraghty managed to keep the lid on the report that one of his officers had been dismissed because of suspected homosexuality. After a few days of rumors, we turned our attention to more pressing problems; the continuing war around us.

A full-scale battle between the Phalange and PSP militias erupted on the morning of the eighth, ending thirty-six hours of relative calm. The factional fighting along the Green Line was pushing the cease-fire to its limit. Alpha Company reported that stray rounds were impacting the library building, and one Marine from Bravo was wounded in the foot. The fighting diminished to sporadic small arms exchanges during the night, and quiet prevailed until the following morning when Alpha again came under sniper fire. One Marine was hit in the right shoulder, but his wound was not serious enough to warrant evacuation. An hour later, a CH-46 flying to the Ministry of Defense drew sniper fire, and the helicopter's fuselage was pierced by several rounds.

Mudfart and I went to the BLT headquarters late in the afternoon for a memorial service honoring Corporals Valle and Clark, the two

Marines killed in action a month earlier. Without the press hovering about, the ceremony in the Peacekeeping Chapel was almost propaganda-free. Captain Paul Roy, the commander of Alpha Company, delivered the eulogy. "By their ultimate sacrifice," Roy said, tears in his eyes, "they have given this land a chance to find its own destiny. It was evident from my conversations with both of them in times past that they cared deeply for their families and loved ones back home. It showed in their performance and attitude. I'm confident they are beside us now, giving us courage to march on."

The propaganda came after the ceremony. A boyish lieutenant stood in front of a TV camera in the BLT lobby. The glare of the bright lights highlighted his blond hair, and the American flag behind his left shoulder made him look like part of a Norman Rockwell painting. A dozen Marines stood behind the cameraman and reporter, and Mudfart and I squeezed in to watch the interview. The lieutenant was saying that the Marines shouldn't feel sorry for themselves. "To see people who merit pity," he said, looking directly into the camera, "go into Hooterville and look at what the people live in, the food they eat, and the clothes they wear. Look at the faces of the children and realize the death, destruction, and poverty many have experienced. For some, it is all they know and possibly all they'll ever know. Yet they appear happy, rather than pitiful and dejected."

"Happy, hell," I whispered to Mudfart. "Who's he trying to kid?"

"Why do you think the Marines are here?" the reporter asked.

"The Lebanese people are depending on us to help restore peace so they can rebuild their economy, their city, their homes, and their lives. As a result of our efforts, Beirut someday will be a comfortable home for its people just as America is for us!"

"Let's get out of here," Mudfart said. "I think I'm going to throw up."

Mudfart and I sauntered outside the building to the basketball court. A hot and furious game was in progress, and several of Mudfart's buddies called to him to join them.

"I'll be back later," he shouted. "We're headed for chow."

A huge line confronted Mudfart and me outside the chow hall. It took us nearly half an hour to get inside. The artillery and sniping had closed the wooden shacks in front of the BLT, and now everyone had to eat in the main mess hall. There was very little room, and the wooden picnic tables were jammed so closely together that it was difficult to squeeze between them. The food had gone from bad to inedible. We could no longer buy fresh fruits and vegetables from the Lebanese economy, and the unchanging menu of mystery meat stew or slices of baloney on a stale roll was miserable. I often thought fasting would be better than the slop the BLT cooks served.

Chili mac, the Marine Corps staple of ground beef mixed with macaroni in tomato sauce, was on the menu. One of the servers plopped a big scoop on my paper plate. "Here's a nice thick steak for you," he said. "Smothered in mushroom gravy."

"What else you got, Red?" I asked. I didn't know the server's real name, but he had flaming red hair and a face covered with freckles. He had been on mess duty for months. Marines are normally stuck working in the chow hall for four weeks before returning to their unit, but Red must have been a bad boy. He was always being punished with mess duty.

"How about a steaming baked potato swimming in butter and sour cream?" he asked.

"Sure, I'll take one of those."

Red dropped a dallop of half-cooked home fries on my plate. "We're running out," he said apologetically, "but we've got plenty of vegetables." He scraped up a ladle of a green viscous material from another pan. "I think it used to be broccoli. Want some?"

"No, I better pass. I want to save some room for my crêpes suzette."

Mudfart and I found a seat next to the Kool-Aid stand. "I'll get the bug juice," Mudfart volunteered. The line wasn't too long, and he waited only a few minutes for the privilege of filling two paper cups with orange Kool-Aid. Mudfart handed me one of the cups, and I took a sip. "How is it?" he asked, squeezing into his seat.

"Tastes just like orange water."

Mudfart and I finished eating within a few minutes. He headed for the basement to change into his basketball shorts, and I strolled over to Branigan's. Nels was sitting at the bar eating an MRE. I told him about the silly lieutenant I'd seen at the BLT.

"Some people will sell their souls to be on TV," Nels commented.

If the Lebanese people were as anxious for peace as the blond lieutenant had claimed, they sure didn't show it. The Phalange and PSP were at it again early the next morning. The LAF finally intervened during the evening, using tank rounds on the militias' hardened positions, and the fighting diminished and finally stopped near midnight.

At eleven that morning, Alpha Company had been fired on with rocket-propelled grenades by three armed men from the nearby suburb Ash Shuwayfat. The men retreated into a bunker partially sheltered by houses, and no fire could be returned without endangering civilian lives. The hostile bunker was a continuing source of harassment. The following day it again fired on Alpha, hitting the company's CP with four rifle rounds before falling silent. The snipers began again in late afternoon, and at 1934 hours, Alpha fired one illumination round over the bunker. The bunker stopped firing until 2200 when Charlie Company's sentry post was hit by two rounds. The sentries fired pop-up illumination and saw three men armed with rifles and rocket-propelled grenades thirty-five meters outside the perimeter fence. The sentries fired twelve rounds of M-16 ammunition at the fleeing men who escaped down an alley into Hooterville. The snipers then turned their rifles back to Alpha Company. An illumination round warning was completely ineffective, and the sniping continued for the rest of the night.

♧   ♧   ♧

After all the VIPs that had traipsed through the MAU headquarters, I thought the Smaj had finally learned to relax. I was wrong. He went into his typical field-day frenzy when he heard the commandant was scheduled to arrive. The MAU was in a continuous Condition II alert because of the sniping, but the Smaj insisted that Silone stay outside to sweep the parking lot.

The commandant arrived just in time to witness a major cease-fire violation. At 1700 hours on 12 October, PSP forces launched a surprise mortar attack against the LAF positions in Suq el Gharb, and the LAF returned automatic weapons and artillery fire. The fighting was the heaviest since the cease-fire agreement began, but the sniper threat continued to be foremost on Colonel Geraghty's mind. Major Converse, in a report to the commandant, stated, "The trend of terrorist 'hit and run' activity directed against the U.S. Multinational Force contingent continues to be one of cautious but definite escalation. The areas of Ash Shuwayfat and particularly Hey es Sellom are being used as a base of operations against the U.S. presence in Beirut."

The American Embassy was attacked the next day. A hand grenade thrown from a speeding car heading west exploded near a BLT sentry post at the Durrafourd Building. One Marine was wounded and evacuated to the *Iwo Jima* after treatment at the American University of Beirut. The car, a dark maroon foreign model, escaped around the corner at a high rate of speed. Less than two hours later, Rock Base was the site of another attack. Three rocket-propelled grenades aimed at a helicopter parked for repairs impacted in the landing zone. Minutes later, a man threw a grenade into the Lebanese Army training camp near Rock Base and escaped on foot to the north along perimeter road. The Marines were helpless. Charlie Company fired an illumination round over a sniper position in Hooterville, but the Muslim militiamen ignored it and continued to shoot into Marine lines.

The commandant held an awards ceremony in the BLT headquarters that afternoon, handing out more than a dozen Purple Hearts to Marines who had been wounded during the August fighting. I watched the ceremony from an upper balcony as the general shook each Marine's hand. The press was there in droves, and with all the talk of heroism and of writing a new chapter in American history, I was swept up by feelings of patriotism. I overheard someone comment, "It's so clear to me now, freedom isn't free," and I asked myself again why we were in Lebanon. "Lebanese stability" and "sovereignty" didn't sound like very good reasons for which to fight and die, yet in that moment, watching the Marines being decorated and described with words like gallantry and valor, I wanted to be down there.

Visions of being a war hero continued to dance in everyone's heads after the ceremony. Even Major Converse was affected. "I should get a Purple Heart," George told Mudfart, Ben, and me as we sat around the operations office swapping war stories.

"Why, sir?" I asked.

"I was on the CH-46 that got hit by sniper fire. A little piece of metal zinged by and cut my arm." I must have looked skeptical. "Look, I'll show you," George joked. He pushed up his sleeve and pointed to a small red spot on his bicep. It looked like a pimple.

"Sure, sir," Ben said. "That looks like Purple Heart material to me."

"I can kiss it to make it feel better if you'd like," Mudfart said.

"When they start giving Purple Hearts for boo-boos we'll let you know," I added. George turned an off-shade of red, but managed to keep his sense of humor and laugh with us; he quickly found an excuse to escape into the COC.

A Marine earned a Purple Heart the next morning the hard way by getting splattered by deadly accurate sniper fire. Traveling along perimeter road near Bravo Company, the jeep driver was shot in the chest and flipped his jeep. At the same time, a second driver just beyond Rock Base was wounded through both legs. Rock Base and Charlie Company returned fire at the snipers in Hooterville, but it was too late. The Marine shot in the chest died during evacuation to the *Iwo Jima*.

Active measures had to be taken to protect Marine lives. Perimeter road was immediately closed to all traffic—no exceptions. Even Rock Base was too exposed to the crazies in Hooterville, and Colonel Geraghty ordered it moved. The helicopters changed their base of operations to the western side of the airport and a new landing zone, LZ Brown. The support personnel moved out of their tents and into a huge hangar that couldn't have been very comfortable. It was peppered with bullet holes, and part of its corrugated iron roof flapped in the wind. But at least it was far from the snipers.

The militia activity in Hey es Sellom continued to escalate. The night of 14 October was punctuated by bursts of sniper fire aimed at sentry posts on Alpha and Charlie Companies' perimeters. The hostile fire continued the next morning, and a Marine sniper team was dispatched to deal with the threat. The team surveyed the area with sniper scopes for several hours, pinpointing those actively firing at Marine positions. Then the team opened fire with eighteen rounds of ammo at fourteen separate targets. Their success was immediately evident by the sudden silence from each enemy position, but despite Marine countermeasures, the firing into friendly positions continued to be hostile and unpredictable.

A Shiite religious celebration on the fifteenth brought huge crowds and processions to the southern suburbs. More than a hundred armed civilians, some wearing red armbands, marched through the streets of Hooterville. The demonstrations, while increasing tension, were orderly, but they served to point out a dangerous situation; because of Rock Base's tactical retreat to a more defensible position, nothing except the Lebanese Army training camp remained between the Shiite community to the north and MAU headquarters.

Colonel Geraghty decided to form what was supposed to be a crackerjack squad of Marines to defend the CP should the Muslim militias overrun the training camp. Mudfart and I were assigned to the unit that was led by Staff Sergeant Summers. We called ourselves "Death Squad," and whenever Condition I was sounded we were to report to the secondary command post. Some of us would move to the roof of the building to act as snipers if necessary, others to the field behind the Hey Joe. I didn't want to take the Death Squad seriously, hoping as I filled sandbags to fortify bunkers on the roof of the secondary CP that the squad was nothing more than a fancy working party.

On the afternoon of the sixteenth, the hostile bunker near Alpha Company began firing heavy weapons at the library building. The Marine sniper team returned scattered rifle fire over the next few hours, but by early evening the exchanges had become intense. Five rocket-propelled grenades exploded around the library, and one scored a direct hit in the building's breezeway, wounding three Marines. Alpha returned fire with M-16s and M-60 machine guns but was unable to reduce the volume of fire enough to allow a medevac helicopter to land nearby. The British offered the assistance of their armored Ferret scout cars, which were used to escort a convoy carrying two seriously wounded Marines to the Ministry of Defense for evacuation.

The firing directed at Alpha continued to increase in intensity until the Marines were forced to retaliate by firing two anti-tank missiles at a machine gun emplacement. A few minutes later, Captain Michael Ohler was hit in the head and killed instantly by a rifle bullet. By 2230 hours, the fire fight had spread to the south and west, and Alpha Company was virtually besieged. The fighting finally began to taper off after midnight, but low-level sniping continued throughout the night.

Late the following morning Alpha was quiet, and a BLT resupply and medevac convoy made its way to the company to bring Captain Ohler home. Beckford knew Ohler and somehow finagled a seat on the convoy to be with a friend on his final journey. I saw Beckford sitting under the trees in front of the CP after the convoy returned. His head was cradled in his arms, and he was crying. I knew there was nothing I could say that would comfort him. The deaths of the six Marines had hit me hard, but I didn't know them; they were only names. To Beckford, their deaths were vastly more personal, and I could only hope that I would never feel his torment.

Later in the day, Mudfart and I got some bad news. I was filing messages when the adjutant, a lieutenant named Davis, called me into his office. "He's back," Davis said simply. He may as well have slugged me in the gut.

"No."

Davis nodded.

"When?"

"He's on the ship now. He'll probably fly in on the next bird."

I told Mudfart the bad news. An hour later, Gunny Thorn, his mouth repaired, strode into the office.

"Goddamnit, Petlick and Mudfart, how the hell are you? Been getting any?"

"Welcome back, Gunny," I said through clenched teeth. "I thought you were headed for the States."

"I couldn't stay the hell away when I knew you needed me."

"Everything's settled down now, Gunny," Mudfart said. I could tell he wanted to scream "so go home!" but didn't.

"Where's the sergeant major?" Gunny demanded. Before I could answer, the Thorn stalked out of the office. A second later, he stuck his head over the sandbag wall and grinned. "Get to work, goddamnit. Your goofin' off days are over." Gunny disappeared for the rest of the day, but knowing he was in the compound was enough to make me want to join the PLO.

"Let's hope the snipers get him," Mudfart said.

"Shooting's too good for him, but it would be nice to use him for target practice."

The day after Gunny's triumphant return, the LAF units in Suq el Gharb came under increased pressure from the PSP. Fighting in the Chouf was particularly heavy during the afternoon of the seventeenth when the LAF was bombarded with mortars. The fighting within the city intensified late on the eighteenth. Armed militiamen tried to barricade a traffic circle near the Shatilla refugee camp, but the Lebanese Army units broke up the barricade and reopened the road.

Colonel Geraghty's weekly military coordination meeting was scheduled for two o'clock the following afternoon, and the colonel decided to take a heavily armed jeep convoy to the embassy instead of flying. The intelligence section predicted that the threat level for a quick jaunt through the city was low. Ben had plenty of volunteers to act as shotguns. After weeks of hiding underground, everyone was going stir crazy and wanted to get out of the compound. I volunteered to go, but by the time I found out about the trip the shotguns had already been selected.

Ben was giving the drivers a last-minute brief on the convoy route in the parking lot when the sergeant major strolled out of the staff NCO tent and took over. "Gather around, men," he growled.

I broke off my conversation with Nels and stared in the sergeant major's direction. The Smaj had assumed his John Wayne pose: one foot propped up on a jeep with both hands resting firmly on his hips. When the shotguns had formed a semicircle around him, he began. "Men, there's two things you got to watch out for when you're in this city, ragheads and camel jockeys. There's a goddamn raghead sniper in every window and a camel jockey around every corner just dying to blow your shit away. I don't want no heros out there. You've got one and only one job to do. Protect that man in the passenger seat."

"The voice of Mr. Potato Head," Nels whispered.

"So keep your eyes open!" the Smaj ordered. "And I don't mean to be looking at the ladies either. I don't care if every woman out there's stripped stark naked, your eyes belong on the street, the buildings, and other cars. If word gets back to me that you're out there sightseeing, your ass is going to belong to me."

The Smaj, at least in his own mind, had put the fear of God into the shotguns. "There's one more thing," he added. "Be careful out there." His work done for the day, the Smaj strutted back to the staff tent.

"I've always suspected it but now I'm sure," Nels said. "That man's brain dead."

Colonel Geraghty emerged from the CP carrying an M-16. Instead of sitting in the passenger seat of his jeep, the colonel climbed into the back, looking like any other shotgun. Chase slid into the front seat next to Cav.

"Space Chase has finally found his calling," Ben commented as he walked by Nels and me. "The perfect decoy."

The convoy raced out of the parking lot, and I returned to my typing in the office. Major Converse was leaving for Norway in a few days to be briefed on an operation scheduled for the next float, and I had a lot of work to do. The MAU had also been tasked with a week-long operation in Morocco before we sailed home, and although I dreaded the thought of any delay, George's trip to Norway meant we were officially "short" and almost homeward bound.

I was sitting with Hadley in Slugo's jeep after work when I heard Cav's call on the radio net. It was almost 4:30, and the convoy was overdue.

"Valuable, valuable, this is red man six, over." Cav's signal sounded a little weak, but the CP's response was loud and clear.

"Red man six, this is valuable. Go ahead, over."

"Be informed we are en route to position 309496 to assist BLT supply convoy. ETA five minutes, over."

"Roger, red man six. Valuable out."

"What do you think happened?" I asked Hadley. We knew a few minutes later when Cav reported. "Valuable, valuable, this is red man six, over."

"This is valuable. Go ahead red man six."

"Be informed we are in the vicinity of car bomb pos and are pinned down by heavy sniper fire. Four casualties, one medevaced to Italian pos, over." Cav's voice sounded strained, and I could hear the pop of rifle fire in the background.

"It's a goddamn car bomb," I told Hadley.

"Roger, red man six. Be informed BLT reaction squad is en route your pos. ETA ten minutes, over."

"Roger. Red man six out."

Hadley and I spent a long ten minutes waiting for Cav's next radio message. He finally called in to say the convoy was headed back to the CP. It was close to dusk when the jeeps pulled into the parking lot. Space Chase was excited that he'd seen some action, but Cav was shaken up. "It was pretty damn scary," Cav finally admitted. "There were pieces of car bomb all over the street, and the lead truck in the convoy was totaled. It had to be towed away."

"Who got hurt?" I asked.

"The one truck driver was the worst off. He had blood streaming down his face, and I think the explosion made him deaf. They took him to the Italian field hospital. I hope he makes it. He looked pretty bad."

The intelligence section later learned the remotely detonated car bomb was the work of a fanatical, pro-Iranian Islamic fundamentalist group. The group was obviously quite professional, and it was only luck that the car bomb hadn't been successful in destroying the convoy. The wounded Marine at the Italian hospital was eventually medevaced to the *Iwo*.

Branigan's was rowdy that night. Ross downed half a dozen beers and started writing on one of the walls. The scribblings that didn't boast about the size of his male organ belittled the size of the sergeant major's. Everyone joined in, and soon the wall was covered with comments:

JOIN THE MARINE CORPS:
TRAVEL TO EXOTIC, FAR AWAY LANDS.
MEET INTERESTING PEOPLE
AND KILL THEM.

DEATH TO THE RAGHEADS!

THE 'ROOT SUCKS!

WHEN I DIE, DON'T SEND ME TO HELL.
I'VE ALREADY SERVED MY TIME IN LEBANON.

Cav's contribution was a large WE'RE DOOMED!, which he colored in with a black felt-tip pen. I bought two cans of Almaza and handed one to Cav. "Still want that Purple Heart?" I asked.

Cav looked up from his work. He seemed surprised by his answer. "No, I don't think I do."

The Smaj was furious when he saw the wall the next morning. He ordered Archie to scrub off the more savory comments, and most of Ross' handiwork was lost to posterity.

The mad car bombers struck again. A French jeep crossing an overpass near the Green Line was destroyed by a command detonated mine hidden in a garbage can. Fortunately, the driver was only slightly wounded.

The twenty-first and twenty-second of October were remarkably quiet. Saturday the twenty-second was practically a holiday routine, and an American band hired by the Department of Defense was even scheduled to play in the afternoon. Mudfart and I drove Major Converse to Beirut International early in the morning for his flight to

Norway. George wasn't too happy about taking Trans Mediterranean Airlines, but with the airport open one day and closed the next because of the shelling, Air France and TWA had stopped flying into Beirut. It was TMA or nothing.

"I hope the plane isn't hijacked," George said. He was wearing civilian clothes so he couldn't be readily identifed as a military commander.

"Just don't sit by anyone named Achmed, sir," Mudfart encouraged. "And if they've got a strange bulge under their coat, jump out the window."

"I hope you packed a parachute, sir. But I wouldn't worry about getting hijacked. You better worry about the food. They'll probably give you sheep eyes and curried goat gonads. Don't forget this is the Middle East."

"Thanks," George said. "That's what I like about you two. I can always count on a little disrespect."

I stopped in front of the airport terminal, and Mudfart and I said our goodbyes to Major Converse. Turning back into the traffic flow, I sped down the boulevard, anxious to get back to the safety of the command post. Being outside the compound made me nervous, and I felt relieved as I drove through the main gate.

Gunny Thorn was surprisingly nice that afternoon, for Gunny. Mudfart asked him if we could knock off work early to see the band. "Goddamnit, you're always wantin' something, Mudfart," Gunny complained.

"It is Saturday," Mudfart said, "and we have been working pretty hard."

"You can go, but only under one condition. I want you to field day this office tomorrow morning. It looks like a shitpen, goddamnit."

"I've had about as much of him as I can take," Mudfart told me later. "He doesn't do a damn thing around here but bitch, and you do his job most of the time. I don't think Major Converse even knew he was gone."

Mudfart was right about one thing. We had been working pretty hard. Before returning to the States, all naval units in the Mediterranean are required to do a "washdown." Tiny snails cling to vehicles and equipment and, if allowed back into the States, are capable of damaging U.S. agricultural products. Everything has to be scrubbed thoroughly. Mudfart and I had been cleaning mount-out boxes all week. We had a neat stack in one corner of the office with a plastic sheet draped over the top. The boxes were scheduled to be backloaded onto the ship the following Wednesday, and there was only one thought on my mind each time I looked at them—I was going home.

The city was quiet that evening with only an occasional flash of light and the distant thunder of artillery. I watched a movie in Branigan's with Hadley and downed a couple of beers. After the movie, we joined Mudfart and Silone in the operations office. The conversation turned to what we wanted to do with our lives. Silone had two big goals: getting laid and clearing up his face.

"Don't worry about that, Silly," Hadley said. "The first time you get laid your acne will clear right up."

Mudfart wanted to buy a nice car and "meet some serious freaks." All four of us definitely planned to get out of the Marine Corps. Hadley wanted to go to school in California, and Mudfart wanted to study architecture.

"What are you going to do?" Hadley asked me. "What's your next life going to be?" The gang knew about the Thoreau Theory and how I wanted to cram ten lives into one. I hadn't thought about my theory for awhile, and Hadley's question made me think.

"I don't know," I finally answered, "Adventure's not quite like I thought it'd be."

"Nothing ever is," Mudfart said.

It was getting late, and the four of us headed for the basement, unaware of the catastrophe the morning would bring. "Hold fast the time!" the writer Thomas Mann warned. "Guard it, watch over it, every hour, every minute!" But the Marines had run out of time. Even at that moment, a truck was being loaded with tons of explosives. I wonder now how its driver spent his last night. In a way he was lucky. He knew the fate that awaited him. The 350 Marines getting ready for bed in the Battalion Landing Team building had no idea that most of them would be dead by morning.

The basement was a zoo. The lights were on, and everyone was talking. Saturday night was party time, and with several cassette players blasting I knew I'd never get to sleep. It wouldn't do any good to demand quiet either. That always made the uproar worse, and the only way to get to sleep was to wait everyone out.

I went into the back room. The lights were already off, and I got undressed and climbed into my rack. Ross was in his rack reading a dirty magazine by flashlight.

"Taps, taps! Lights out!" I heard Hadley yell in the other room. "Maintain silence about the decks!" It didn't do any good, and the noise level actually increased. "How 'bout it, guys?" he pleaded. "I've got to get up early tomorrow to drive." Hadley's was a voice crying out in the wilderness. "Come on, please?" he begged.

"Say goodnight, Hadley," I heard someone shout.

"Goodnight, Hadley," a dozen voices roared.

"What is this, the Waltons?" Hadley demanded.

"Goodnight, Silone," someone called.

"Goodnight, Mudfart."

"Goodnight, Scaly."

"Goodnight, Archie." The liturgy of voices continued.

"How about, goodnight, peacekeepers?" Hadley yelled.

"Goodnight, John Boy."

I rolled over and went to sleep.

V
23 October 1983: Catasrophe

ROUTE OF BOMB-LADEN TRUCK

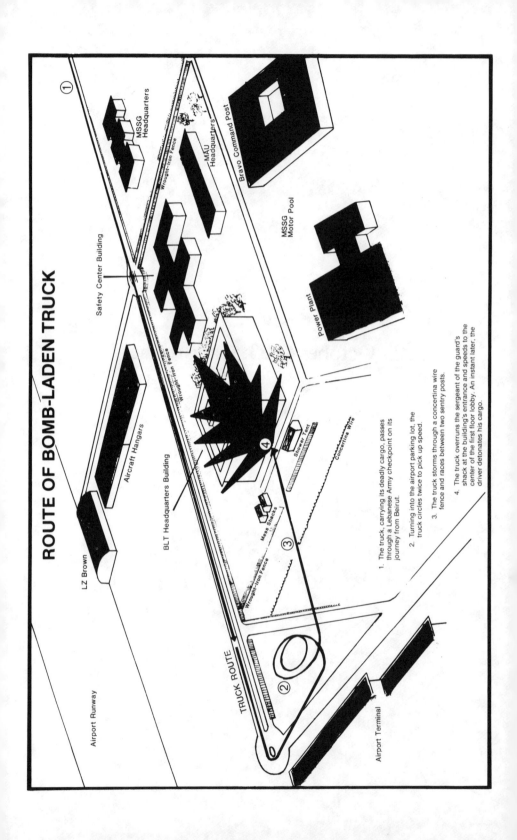

1. The truck, carrying its deadly cargo, passes through a Lebanese Army checkpoint on its journey from Beirut.

2. Turning into the airport parking lot, the truck circles twice to pick up speed.

3. The truck storms through a concertina wire fence and races between two sentry posts.

4. The truck overruns the sergeant of the guard's shack at the building's entrance and speeds to the center of the first floor lobby. An instant later, the driver detonates his cargo.

LZ Brown

Safety Center Building

MSSG Headquarters

Wrought-Iron Fence

MAU Headquarters

Bravo Command Post

Aircraft Hangars

BLT Headquarters Building

Wrought-Iron Fence

MSSG Motor Pool

Power Plant

Airport Runway

Wrought-Iron Fence

Mess Shacks

Shower Tent

Concertina Wire

TRUCK ROUTE

Airport Terminal

13

FACTS AND FIGURES never tell the story of human suffering. Two-hundred and forty-one is only a number, but it represents the lives of so many more. The 132,000 pounds of medical supplies, emergency excavation equipment, and rations flown in by the air squadron to support the rescue operation is phenomenal, but the single vial of morphine needed to ease the torment of one wounded Marine has more emotional impact. That debris hauled from the building stretched along one of the runways for 300 meters is impressive, but a friend dying in your arms is unforgettable. A crater forty-feet across and ten-feet deep created by five thousand pounds of explosives is monstrous, but the vacant space left by the husband or son who isn't coming home can never be filled.

Disasters taking place half a world away lose their immediacy. Unthinkingly, I have read banner headlines over breakfast that screamed "50 Killed in Coal Mine" or "Plane Crash Claims 100," turned the page, and reached for the jam. Suffering and death in monumental proportions, unless you are there, strike no nerve. A fleeting wave of sympathy may pass, but then it's on to the next story, the next crisis.

That fateful morning in October took my complacency and slapped my face with it.

"How could this happen?" I wailed with anguish as I surveyed the carnage moments after the blast. I felt devastated. Furious. Friends lived in the BLT. Co-workers. Marines who were in Lebanon on a *peacekeeping* mission.

I picked my way through rubble and stumbled down the hill to the building. Debris and bodies littered the path I had taken so many times before. The flight of stairs at the bottom of the hill was pitted from the blast and barely traversable. I skirted mangled jeeps that blocked the way.

The left side of the building was a darkened cavern billowing gray smoke. I made my way in that direction. Marines were hauling out bodies on makeshift litters. Others frantically moved rock to reach those buried.

I entered the gloom, choking on the smoke. As my eyes adjusted, I saw Hadley. He had tied a bandanna around his face to breathe more easily. Sweat was pouring down his forehead, and dirt encircled his eyes.

"This is awful!" I cried. There were no words to describe my feelings. Hadley looked past me with piercing eyes filled with shock, anguish, and disbelief.

I moved unsteadily about the area. At first I couldn't see any bodies. Then suddenly everywhere I looked a dust-covered arm or leg jutted from the rocks. I saw an arm and dug frenziedly. Then I spotted a foot and bounded madly in that direction. I was becoming confused and disoriented.

"I think this one's alive!" Hadley screamed.

I ran to the body over which Hadley stood. The Marine was face down in the rubble, and his lower torso and legs dangled in a huge pit that must have been the bomb crater. I hesitated a moment, almost afraid to touch him, then bent down and took one of the limp wrists. I squeezed it desperately. The body was warm.

"I think I feel a pulse!" I shouted. "Corpsman!"

A corpsman finished splinting the broken leg of a Marine sobbing in pain and rushed over.

"Pull him out of the pit," he ordered. "Call me when he's where I can get to him." The corpsman hurried to another wounded Marine.

Hadley gingerly tried to pull the Marine up by his midsection but couldn't budge him. He carefully climbed into the crater and began pushing up on the legs. Heavily insulated electrical cables and twisted steel rods stuck out at odd angles in the crater. The intact drive shaft of the suicide truck bomb lay at the bottom.

Two Marines carrying a bloody but empty cot bolted over and tried to help. Hadley and one of the Marines pushed on the legs; the other Marine and I pulled on the arms. We managed to drag the body out of the pit. Hadley and his helper scrambled up the steep incline of the crater, and the four of us flipped the Marine onto the cot.

A gaping hole with brains bulging out was all that was left of the side of his head.

"He's dead, Hadley," I sobbed. "He's dead."

I glanced around and found a torn bit of camouflage uniform. It was small but mercifully covered what remained of his head.

Hadley and I each took an end of the cot and began a long struggle through the rubble. Small stones shifted under my feet making it tough going with the heavy body. My M-16 was cumbersome and kept slipping off my shoulder. We had to stop twice to rest but finally made it up the hill to where they were placing the dead. The jumble of cots stacked with corpses was rapidly growing.

Hadley and I charged back down the hill, but I lost him in the confusion. Three Marines were standing around a huge slab of concrete. A pair of legs poked out from underneath. The four of us strained to lift the slab. It wouldn't move.

"We'll have to free the other end by moving those rocks on top before we can lift it," one of the Marines suggested. I looked up and saw it was Bradley.

I began scooping out handfuls of rock, but the end of the slab was wedged under layers of debris.

"Let's try it again." We used all our strength. The slab lifted a bit. Bradley grabbed one of the legs and pulled, a fierce look of determination on his face.

"Don't pull on his leg!" I shouted. For some perverse reason I thought Bradley was hurting him. Bradley pulled, straining until I thought the leg would come off in his hands. Finally he quit. Exhausted, we dropped the slab with a sickening thud.

"We can't get him out until we dig out the other end of the slab," Bradley said.

I staggered away, unable to deal with the death that surrounded me.

A bulldozer moved in and began to clear debris fifty feet from where I stood. Its blade caught one of the overturned jeeps partially buried in rubble, and the tearing sound of metal was followed by a roar as the punctured gas tank erupted into flame.

I darted to the retaining wall to my right at the bottom of the hill. A black Marine, his naked body a mass of torn flesh, lay on top of the wall in a crumpled heap. The middle toe of his left foot was gone.

A fire truck raced down the boulevard that led to the airport and slowed as it turned onto the access road next to the BLT. It edged as close as possible to the jeep and sprayed a thick, white foam on the blaze.

Lebanese rescue workers and Italian soldiers began arriving. Red

Cross ambulances careened up and discharged medics. A hasty cordon was set up to keep the press away from the building. Bulldozers and dump trucks to remove debris came. Shovel and picks were passed out, and the sound of jackhammers starting up could be heard. Like an ant hill that's been stepped on, the area was swarming with workers.

I stared with horror at the corner of the building above the chow hall. Sandwiched between thick reinforced concrete floors were rubble-filled spaces no taller than a foot. In those spaces Marines had lived and worked, shared hopes and dreams, and anxiously waited for their time in Lebanon to be over. In those same spaces defenseless men were crushed to death as they slept. The building had folded in upon itself like an accordion, and the men hadn't had a chance.

A knot of Marines swarmed part way up the side of the building. One dropped to his knees and poked a flashlight into a crevice.

"There's someone alive in there!" he shouted. "I can hear him calling for help."

An avalanche of rock cascaded down as the men widened the crevice entrance. Digging madly with their hands, they enlarged a crawl space barely big enough for someone to wriggle into. A Marine precariously wormed his way into a tunnel that might collapse at any second. Only his feet dangled out. He shouted something and was yanked from the hole.

"There's two in there still alive!" he announced.

I couldn't believe anyone could possibly be alive inside the building, but a Marine emerged, blinking rapidly in the bright sunlight. He was helped to his feet, then slid down a loose pile of rubble at the side of the building.

"Oh, God, I'm alive!" he exclaimed. He didn't have a scratch on him. Barefooted, he wore the lime-green surgeon's top and trousers in which he had slept. He rubbed the back of his head. Dust peppered his dark skin and hair.

"I'm alive! I'm alive!" he sobbed repeatedly. Tears streamed down his face.

A nearby Marine embraced him like a lost child. "It's okay," he comforted. Tears ran down his face too.

A group of Marines stood around the embracing pair, touching the one who was miraculously alive. Tears unashamedly rolled down their cheeks.

I clasped the rescued Marine's shoulder. "You're alive," was all I could say, my voice breaking with emotion. I was crying tears of jubilation and anguish, desolation and horror, all at the same time.

I wandered away from the group, unable to keep my eyes off the building. Space Chase was standing on a slab halfway up.

"There's a body here," he called. "Give me a hand." I ignored his plea for help as I stumbled past what had been the entrance to the chow hall. My mind was blank, and my feet surged forward on their own. Lebanese Red Cross workers wearing white T-shirts bumped into me as they bolted past.

Mudfart! I suddenly thought of Mudfart. He hadn't been in the secondary command post with the rest of the Death Squad. I spotted Staff Sergeant Summers a half-dozen feet away standing with his arms crossed. His face bore a hardened, heavy expression like it was chiseled from black granite. "Have you seen Mudfart?" I asked.

He shook his head.

"Mudfart!" I called, tears welling in my eyes. I ran back to where I had seen Chase. "Have you seen Mudfart?"

"No."

I ran to the cots piled with bodies. "Mudfart!" Hadley and a Marine I didn't know pushed past me carrying a litter. There was a headless corpse on it. The corpse of a black Marine. "Mudfart?" A nauseating jolt slammed into my gut.

The body's too big, I realized. It wasn't Mudfart. "Have you seen him?" I asked Hadley.

"Who?"

"Mudfart."

"No."

I ran back to the corner of the building that had been the chow hall. Between two cement slabs was a narrow space that led into the building. The smell of gas was overpowering. A Marine on his hands and knees peered into the opening. "We're going to need gas masks and flashlights to get inside," he said.

I turned and ran back to the cots. "Mudfart," I screamed, my voice growing hoarse. Six Marines were transferring the naked and mutilated bodies still on their litters to a flatbed truck. "Where are they taking them?" I heard someone ask. "To the hangar at LZ Brown."

"Mudfart? Have any of you seen Mudfart?" I called.

Someone grabbed my shoulder from behind. I spun around, elatedly thinking, Mudfart!

It was Ben.

"Take it easy," he said. "I'm sure Mudfart's okay. There's no reason on earth he would have been in the BLT."

Ben was right. I was panicking over nothing.

A Marine ran up to us from the building. "We need blankets, sleeping bags. . . anything," he shouted.

"I've got some extras stashed at the radio station," someone to my left said. It was a sailor off the *Iwo*, and Ben and I followed him to the transmitter van near the Safety Center building. The front of the building I lived in had been destroyed by the explosion. Twisted sheets of metal and shards of glass covered the ground. My foot kicked something soft and yielding. I glanced down. A severed hand, palm up, lay next to my boot. It wore a wedding ring. I swallowed hard, forcing down the bile that had risen to the back of my throat.

The sailor went into the van and pitched out several sleeping bags. Ben and I swept them up in our arms and rushed back to the building. Other Marines grabbed them from us to use as litters.

A nearby cordon of Marines was trying to keep the press back. One persistent cameraman tried to push past, and I heard the snap of the charging handle of an M-16 being pulled back followed by the click of the bolt going home. The Marine who had locked and loaded pointed his rifle at the cameraman. "Goddamn, motherfucker," he said. "Take one more step and I'll blow your fuckin' head off, you goddamn vulture." The cameraman backed away.

One of the slabs of cement blocking the way into the chow hall had been moved. Marines inside wearing gas masks sifted though the rubble.

"Where's your gas mask?" I asked Ben.

"In the basement."

"Mine too. Let's get them."

Ben and I ran past the transmitter van and headed for the basement. We had to take the long way around because the shortcut through the Safety Center building was blocked with debris.

The basement was pitch black. The power had gone off with the explosion, and I had to grope through my gear to find a flashlight. My rack was gone. Someone had already taken it to use as a litter, and all that was left was the mosquito netting. I found my flashlight. My gas mask was at the bottom of my sea bag, and I dumped everything out to get it, then rushed back into the main room.

"Did you find yours?" I asked Ben.

"Yep." We ran back to the BLT. A crane borrowed from the Lebanese construction company Oger Liban was making its way to one of the building's corners. The shattered cement walls and columns were no doubt trapping survivors, but there wasn't nearly enough heavy equipment to move the tons of rubble. A Marine on a stretcher, supported by a dozen workers, was slowly being lowered from the top of the building. He was covered with gray dust. His face and chest were caked with dried blood, but he was alive. Four of the workers rushed him to a waiting jeep that was standing by to take the wounded to LZ Brown for air evacuation to the ships.

Ben and I went into the hole that had been the chow hall. It was unrecognizable. The picnic tables were nothing more than splinters of wood, and the smell of gas was noxious and stung my eyes. Several small fires still burned, and the thick haze made it hard to see. Ben was in front of me when he tripped over a serving pan filled with what would have been breakfast. The cooks must have already started preparing it when the truck bomb hit, and an hour later I would have been in the chow hall eating a Sunday-morning meal of Canadian bacon and pancakes.

It became almost impossible to breathe as Ben and I moved deeper into the chow hall. "Let's get out of here," Ben suggested. "There's so much gas in here there may be another explosion." Several Marines were in another part of the chow hall. Ben and I tossed them our gas masks and stepped outside into the fresh air, but even outside the smell of fire and blood and death was oppressive.

A Red Cross medic team ran past us carrying a Marine on a stretcher. One of the medics was frantically pounding on the Marine's chest, trying to get his heart started. Another Marine, half-conscious and wearing a pair of blood-soaked gym shorts, was being taken to the ambulance jeep. His arms were wrapped around the shoulders of two Marines, and a third held his ankles. He had a tourniquet on his leg. A big chunk of his right thigh was missing, and a stream of blood trailed behind him.

I felt numb, my brain paralyzed. Nels and another Marine rushed by struggling with a leg partially wrapped in a blanket. Tears creased the gray dust on Nels' face. I looked for Ben, but I had lost him in the chaos. I began walking around the building. The mess shacks on the front side had been obliterated; nothing remained but a heap of mosquito netting and broken plywood. The steel flagpole that had been to the left of the main entrance was gone, and the shower tent was a twisted tangle of pipe.

One of the construction workers hooked a chain from a bulldozer to a huge chunk of concrete embedded with steel reinforcement rods. The bulldozer revved its engine and slowly pulled the chunk away from the face of the building. A storm of dust and smoke poured out from the interior. The parking lot the truck bomb had crossed was filling up with rescue vehicles. Red Cross workers were setting up a tent, and an ambulance, its siren a plaintive wail, raced out of the compound with a load of wounded.

The BLT motor pool was on the right side of the building, and the jeep mechanics had been housed in tents. They had written EIGHTH MOTOR T BATTALION on the retaining wall behind them next to a drawing of the Marine Corps' mascot, a bulldog. Each mechanic had painted his name underneath. The sign was all that was left. The tents were collapsed shreds of netting and canvas covered by shards of concrete. A jeep with a bloody cot on its hood slowly drove by me. A Marine whimpering in pain, pulled from the wreck of the motor pool by two Red Cross workers, was placed on the cot. He was covered with blood and his arms trembled. "I'm so cold," he cried. His entire body shuddered, and he fell still.

I found Ben staring at the ground near the rear of the building. "I just found out Lieutenant Jacobs wants me at LZ Brown," he said. "Will you ride along as shotgun?"

I glanced at the building. An arm jutted from between two of the floors. "Yes," I said quietly.

Ben and I walked up the hill to the CP. The shock wave from the explosion had blasted pieces of concrete all the way to the parking lot, and the corrugated iron doors that covered the bays were bent and off their runners. I scurried into the office to grab an extra magazine of ammunition. The inside of the CP was a mess. The glass windows on either side of the main door had shattered, and paper was scattered on the floor. The ceiling fan in the operations office was a crumpled pile in the middle of my desk, and a wooden partition that had separated two of the offices had been hurled twenty feet.

I ran back outside and climbed into the passenger seat of the jeep. LZ Brown was outside the compound and across the boulevard that led to the airport. I slammed a magazine into my rifle and locked and loaded it. Ben didn't say anything. Even though a loaded weapon in the compound was against the rules, I wasn't taking any chances.

It took only a couple of minutes to get to the hangar next to LZ Brown. We raced past a cordon of Marines who kept the press as far from the hangar as possible, and a medevac CH-53 lifted off the Tarmac as we screeched to a stop and jumped out. Two clerks who worked in the administration section were sitting outside the hangar.

"What are you doing here?" I asked.

"Body counts."

Ben and I went inside the hangar. The right side was being used as a morgue. It was already filled with cots, and the tangle of partially clad bodies was ghastly. I saw unattached arms, legs, and heads. Some of the faces wore looks of shock and pain, but those who had been sleeping when the bomb exploded were frozen in a bizarre repose of tranquility. All were caked with blood and dirt. Some were crushed, the bodies twisted beyond the recognition of human form. A few were little more than lumps of charred flesh.

The smell of blood, the reek of vomit and urine and excrement, the bittersweet odor of death clung to the air, cloying and heavy. I turned my back on the carnage, gasping for air to keep from retching. The horror was unspeakable. What a piece of work is man, I thought bitterly, to be capable of such a vicious, monstrous act.

I heard Lieutenant Jacobs giving Ben instructions. "I want you to act as a relay with the CP until we get some communication set up."

"Yes, sir," Ben said.

"Then once we get organized down here, I want you to take charge of putting the bodies into bags. The ships have only fifty body bags and eight transfer cases, so that's going to be a problem. In the meantime, I want you to get some blankets and poncho liners if you can find them and start covering the bodies."

"Right away, sir."

I stepped outside. "Have you seen Mudfart?" I asked one of the admin clerks.

"No. I just came in off the ship," the clerk said. "I'll tell him you're looking for him when I see him."

I glanced at my watch and thought about my parents. It was after eight o'clock, and that meant it was after 1:00 A.M. in the States. There was no way I could send my parents a message to say I was alive, and I knew they would be frantic when they woke to the news of the disaster. Then I remembered the press. I marched around the corner of the hangar and stood where I hoped one of the cameramen could get a shot of me.

"We have to go back to the CP," Ben called.

I rushed to the jeep, and Ben drove us to the command post. "Here," he said, handing me a slip of paper. "It's a count for the watch officer in the COC. I'm gonna run to the supply tent to see if I can get some blankets and poncho liners from Wheebles."

I glanced at the slip of paper. On it, neatly written in pencil, were two numbers: 67 KIA, 84 WIA.

The COC was a madhouse. With the destruction of the BLT's Combat Operations Center, the MAU headquarters had assumed control of the line companies and the separate platoons scattered around the compound. Every communication went through the operations section, and because Major Converse was in Norway the responsibility of being the officer in charge of not only the MAU operations, but the BLT as well, fell to Captain Kettering. Kettering already looked exhausted; his body was running on sheer willpower.

The radio communicators were swamped. The intelligence section had dozens of messages that needed to be relayed, and hundreds of calls were coming in from the perimeter. The three communicators on duty looked like each was handling two radio calls at the same time.

Lieutenant Davis, the adjutant, was the watch officer. His desk was at the COC's entrance, and I handed him the slip of paper.

"Sixty-seven dead?" he asked, a look of shock on his face. He had been on duty when the truck bomb detonated and had no idea of the magnitude of the catastrophe.

"Yes, sir," I said. "And eighty-four wounded, but I'm afraid this is just the beginning." I glanced around the COC, hoping Mudfart was helping Captain Kettering. Mudfart wasn't around.

"What are you doing now, Corporal Petit?" Kettering asked.

"I'm working at LZ Brown, sir."

"Think you can man a radio?"

"Yes, sir. I'll give it a try."

I stepped behind the communicators' table and sat in one of the empty chairs. Sergeant Layland was on duty and showed me how to work the radio's handset. I immediately received my first call.

"Valuable, valuable, this is tango victor papa, over."

I pressed the button on the handset and spoke into the microphone. "Tango victor papa, this is valuable, over." I took my thumb off the button. "Who's tango victor papa?" I asked Layland.

"That's Bravo Company, first platoon. Just write down whatever they tell you." He handed me a yellow radio message book.

"Valuable, prepare to copy," the voice from Bravo Company told me.

"Roger."

"The following personnel are reported missing at this time. Sefron, Roger A. Sierra, echo, foxtrot. . ." The communicator slowly spelled each name using the phonetic alphabet to make sure no copying error was made. I knew only a few of the alphabet's words, but I scribbled the letters as quickly as I could. Once I had transcribed the message, I passed a copy to the watch officer.

The sergeant who worked in the intelligence section handed me a message to relay. Sergeant Genet was a slender, slightly timid Marine who had managed to weather the severe razzing the rest of the enlisted troops gave him. He'd been crying. Staff Sergeant Garcia and two others who worked in the intelligence section had lived in the BLT. I relayed the message to one of the platoons at Alpha Company requesting their list of missing.

"Valuable, valuable, this is valuable mobile," I heard my handset say. I recognized Nel's voice.

"Roger, valuable mobile. Go ahead."

"Be advised we have two reports of sniping at BLT headquarters from the airport terminal building. Also be advised corpsman at site is requesting an oxygen regulator for first-aid treatment. Request you pass message to valuable afloat as soon as possible. Over."

"Roger, valuable mobile. I will pass your request, over."

"Roger. Valuable mobile out."

"Captain Kettering," I called. "I just got a report from the BLT that they're being shot at by snipers."

"Sir, Alpha Company CP has informed me that the library building is being hit with small arms fire," one of the other communicators reported.

"Damn," Kettering said. He walked back to the intelligence section.

"Those bastards are nothing more than animals," I said. I told Layland about Nel's request for the oxygen regulator. Layland got on another radio net and relayed the message to the *Iwo*.

I worked in the Combat Operations Center most of the day, too busy to even stop and think. At 1200, the first C-9 airplane arrived to medevac twenty-four of the most seriously injured to Frankfurt, Germany, and two hours later a C-130 left for Cyprus with twenty more. Most of the medical personnel had lived in the BLT. With 126 Marines wounded, some critically, the remaining corpsmen on shore had their hands full. By the end of the day, medical supplies, particularly narcotics, were completely used up and required emergency resupply.

I was relieved from duty late in the afternoon, and when I stepped outside the CP, I could hear the sound of jackhammers coming from the BLT.

"Did you hear about the French?" Cav asked me. He was sitting in Colonel Geraghty's jeep.

"What happened?"

"They got hit a few minutes after us. Blew up an eight-story building."

"Goddamn, when will this nightmare end? Have you seen Mudfart? I can't find him anywhere."

"I've been driving Colonel Geraghty all over the place. I haven't seen anyone."

I wandered back into the CP. The logistics office was filled with dozens of plastic bags stuffed with paper. Sergeant Genet was picking through one bag.

"We've got to go through all this and pull out the confidential material and personal stuff," he said. "It's going to be a big job."

Two Marines marched in carrying a crushed foot locker. "Where do you want this?" one asked.

"I guess over there," I answered, pointing to the operations office. More Marines followed carrying plastic bags, which they dumped next to the foot locker. I found a chair, sat down, and opened my first bag.

The smell of the bombing—the smell of dirt and blood—assaulted my nostrils, and it was as if I was back at the building. I battled with my stomach, trying not to gag.

I pulled a torn leather satchel from the plastic bag, gently rubbing the outside. This is a man's life, I thought. All of it that's left. The satchel was encrusted with blood, and inside were letters. I pulled one out. It was a hand-drawn birthday card from a little girl. The outside was covered with bright red hearts, and inside it read simply, "I love you Daddy." Blinking back tears, I put the card into the satchel and set it aside.

I reached inside the plastic bag and pulled out a sheaf of papers. Some I tossed aside to be burned, but anything personal that might help confirm a Marine lived in the building I put in a pile with the satchel. There were so many letters. I read a few, realizing I would never be able to forget their contents. Some of the letters were just fragments:

> I miss you and am very worried about what I read in the newspapers. I hope you are safe from danger, but I feel much better now that you told me how secure the building you live in is. I would just die if anything happened to you. I love you so much.

The blood-stained first page of one letter was still intact:

> Dear Son,
> All is well here. Your Uncle Willy has been sick with the flu for the past few days, but it looks like he's getting better now. The big excitement is that Todd finally got a job. I'll let him write and tell you all about it. Your mother was really happy. I was starting to think he was going to be a bum all his life.
> Son, I don't have to tell you how proud we all are of you. I know things must be pretty tough over there, but I know you're going to come through it okay. You're fighting for your country and what's right, and I know that. . . .

I fished a badly burned greeting card from the plastic bag. A cherubic baby's face announced: It's a boy!

Going through the bag was too emotional. Seeing the small glimpses of other men's lives before they were so brutally ended made me feel like an invader, a ghoul robbing a dead man's grave. I threw down the stack of papers on my lap and rushed outside. As I raised my hands to my face to wipe away the tears, the smell of death overwhelmed me. It was ground into my hands and clothes, and there was no way I could escape it. I doubled over, vomiting onto the dark red earth outside the CP.

"Are you okay?" I heard Staff Sergeant Summers asking.

I straightened up. "Yeah, I think so."

"This is the duty roster for tomorrow," he said. "I've got you scheduled from two in the morning until eight o'clock—six hours."

"What am I supposed to do?"

"You'll be security in BLT's parking lot. We're short of people, and we can't break anyone away from the line companies. You'll be standing guard with someone off the *New Jersey*. Better get some sleep. I'll wake you at 0130."

I went back into the command post. Sergeant Edwards, one of the administration clerks, was typing the names of the missing, wounded, and known killed on the green machine. The green machine was capable of cutting messages on ticker tape, which the communications center could read and transmit. The message was addressed to Headquarters Marine Corps.

"Mind taking over?" Edwards asked. "My eyes are getting blurry."

I sat in the seat in front of the green computer screen. A roster of names had been found in the wreckage of the BLT. Unfortunately, it was a month old, and with the transfer of personnel and movement of individuals back and forth from the line companies, it was completely out of date. Combined and cross referenced with the personnel rosters of the other units, it was all we had to make a missing-in-action list. Edwards had already typed in over two hundred names, and there were at least that many more to go.

"It might be easier if I read the names to you," Edwards suggested.

"Okay, I'm ready."

"Macroglou, John. Major. Social security number 346-56-4367. Status: missing.

"Maden, Charles C. Corporal. 023-45-3546. Missing.

"Mandenheart, Alan C."

"That's Mudfart. There must be some mistake."

Edwards shook his head. "Lance Corporal," he continued, his voice thick with emotion. "478-92-0454. Missing."

The names went on and on. Near midnight we finally ran out. "I better try to get some sleep," I told Edwards. "I've got guard duty at two."

Lying on the floor in the basement, I could hear the dull throb of jackhammers. The rescue workers were still tearing at the slabs of concrete that buried so many.

"Are you okay?" Ross asked. He was lying on the floor on his side of the room.

"I don't think I'm ever going to be okay."

I closed my eyes but sleep wouldn't come. It could have been me in the building, it could have been me, my mind droned over and over. The walls of the basement felt as if they were closing in.

Staff Sergeant Summers was shaking my shoulder. "Wake up. It's time for your guard duty," he said softly.

14

THE BUILDING WAS behind me, starkly lit by floodlights, as the
rescue workers continued to dig for survivors. It was almost four,
and first light was still two hours away. Guard duty passed slowly. As I
stood in the same sandbagged sentry post the truck bomb had roared
past the previous morning, I thought about the Marine who had been
on duty. I wondered how he felt as the truck slammed into the building
and exploded. I replayed the scene in my mind, viewing it in slow-
motion from different angles: me in the mess hall eating breakfast, me
standing in the central lobby watching as the truck raced toward the
building, me sleeping in one of the upstairs rooms.

I glanced over my shoulder at the monstrosity behind me. It was as
if I kept expecting to find the building whole once again, but each time
I looked, the horror and grief remained. Cranes to remove debris stood
at each corner, and the pervading rattle of jackhammers was a death cry
for those still buried. A dump truck full of bent steel and crushed
concrete roared past me on the way to dump its load, and a dozen
mangled jeeps pulled from the wreckage were lined up across the
basketball court.

"Look out for snipers," Staff Sergeant Summers had warned when
he placed me at my post. I spotted a man walking down the boulevard
in the darkness and flipped my rifle's safety off. I no longer cared that
our weapons were supposed to be unloaded; I was prepared to shoot
anyone who looked suspicious. The man, dressed in jeans and a black
shirt, strolled leisurely past the BLT, but before he disappeared in the
distance it struck me that he was admiring his handiwork.

The sun began to rise over the mountains, suffusing the air with a
pink glow. I kicked at a pair of camouflage trousers on the ground near
the sentry post before realizing they had been blown clear of the
building. The name Prevatt was stenciled inside the waistband. I
remembered the name from the list of missing and thought how ironic
that the trousers had survived but not the man.

I was relieved from duty at eight. Drawn irresistibly to the building, I watched silently as the workers uncovered another dead Marine. Scooping handfuls of rock from the area around the body, a sailor wearing a mask over his nose and mouth sifted through the debris for anything that might identify the person—a dog tag, military I.D. card, wallet, even a picture. Once the search was finished, four others gently, almost lovingly, picked up the dead man by his arms and legs and slid him into a body bag. Each of the four grabbed a corner of the bag and hauled it to the makeshift morgue near the rear of the building. A corpsman wearing a surgical mask and gloves tagged the bag, and two others placed it on the van that would take it to LZ Brown. The van was already half-full of dark green bags.

I walked up the hill, taking the path that led to the basement. Lebanese soldiers were sifting through the rubble scattered between the BLT and the Safety Center building. One, his eyes full of sympathy, handed me a cardboard box. Inside the box were correspondence course manuals from the Marine Corps Insitute in Washington and a half-dozen personal letters. A snapshot of smiling, happy people lay on top. A Marine in the center of the picture proudly wore a sweatshirt with USMC emblazoned on it.

Ross was sitting on the floor of our room when I got to the basement. The power was still off, and he'd lit a candle. "I've been sitting here thinking about death," he said. Ross and I had talked about a lot of things—about how screwed up Gunny Thorn was, about sex, about how much we hated Beirut—but never about anything deeply personal or emotional.

I sat on the floor across from him. "I'm so afraid of dying," he said. "I can't look at the ceiling without imagining it's going to collapse on me. I've never thought much about God. I don't even know if there is one, but if there is how could He let something like this happen?"

"I don't know."

"I've never really believed that I'm actually going to die. That was something that always happened to someone else, and somehow I knew when the grim reaper came I'd be able to talk my way out of it. I don't think that any more, and god am I scared."

"I think we're all scared."

"Everyone except Mudfart."

"Have you heard anything?" I asked anxiously.

"No, and I can't understand why he would have been in the building."

"I can only think of one reason. That he was on his way to play basketball when it went up."

"I keep hoping he's going to walk through that door any minute. He'll say, 'Yo, blood, what it be like?' and we'll all have a good laugh. Then maybe death won't seem so close anymore, and things will get back to normal."

"Life's never going to get back to normal, Ross."

"I know. All life is is a wild and crazy footrace to the grave. Mudfart beat me, but I'll be there soon enough. I'm beginning to think there's not much worth living for anyway, but I damn well intend to hang on for as long as I can. The alternative isn't very appealing."

I had wanted to take a nap, but I knew closing my eyes would be useless. I told Ross I was going to the CP and left him sitting alone in the darkness.

Staff Sergeant Summers stopped me outside the command post. "This is PFC Spenser," Summers said, introducing me to a skinny, pug-nosed kid. "He was in the BLT's basement storeroom when. . . He's going to be sleeping in the secondary CP now. Would you help him get settled in?"

"Sure." I carried one of Private Spenser's sea bags across the street to the entrance of the secondary CP. I felt apprehensive being with someone who had been brushed so closely by death. I was curious, but I treated him as though he were fragile, afraid I might interrupt a private thought or dredge up a horrid memory he was trying to forget. I wanted to scream a thousand questions: What does it feel like to be alive—to know that men who slept on the other side of a wall from you are dead? How long were you buried in the rubble? Did you think about dying?

"This is it," I said instead, stopping outside the command post's entrance. "You climb down the ladder, and I'll toss you your gear."

"I'm celebrating a bit," Spenser said. "My wife just had a baby." He opened one of his sea bags and took a cigar out of a box. "Have one," he said. I took the cigar. It was wrapped in cellophane with white lettering that read It's a boy!

"Thanks," I said. "And congratulations." I stuck the cigar in my flak jacket pocket, and Spenser climbed down the ladder into the basement command post. A few others who had survived unscathed were already in the basement setting up cots. I tossed down his gear. "Have a good day!" he shouted.

I crossed the street and went into the office. The plastic bags of paper had tripled since the night before, and Sergeant Edwards was still typing on the green machine. The roster of missing and killed in action he was working on was a little shorter than the first list of names, but not by much.

I turned on the transister radio Mudfart and I had listened to so frequently. The programming sounded the same, but when ten o'clock came there wasn't any news. With the BLT's destruction, our link to the outside world was gone, and I wondered how the networks were reporting the story. The intelligence section had gotten hold of an English language newspaper published in Beirut, and I read the headline with dismay: Marine Headquarters Destroyed.

"Can't the press get anything right?" I angrily demanded. "This is Marine Headquarters. It was the BLT that was destroyed, not us." The difference was an important one. My parents knew I worked in Marine Headquarters. They must think I'm dead, I thought. They won't find out I'm alive for a week or more. I deeply regretted the pain and worry I knew I was causing them.

Replacements for the men killed began arriving by air from Camp Lejeune, North Carolina early Monday evening. Accusations and recriminations began immediately. The troops from the arriving Second Battalion, Sixth Marines insisted they were our saviors. Many of them had served with the 22d MAU on the previous float and had lived inside the BLT. After their float, they had been placed on air alert, ready to respond to any emergency. "This would never have happened if we were still here," a lance corporal from the new battalion stated flatly in Branigan's. "The Marines in 24 MAU couldn't hack it. Colonel Geraghty's a lousy commander, and it's his fault so many got killed."

Space Chase smashed his fist into the lance corporal's mouth. "Bastard," Chase yelled. "I'll show you who can't hack it." Nels and Archie grabbed Chase's arms and held him back.

The lance corporal picked himself up off the floor. "You'll pay for that," he threatened. Spitting blood, he slowly retreated from the bar.

"Better not show your face in here, asshole," someone called after him.

Chase was declared the hero of the hour, and everyone rushed to buy him a beer. Chase was toasting himself for the third or fourth time when a BLT Marine who had survived the explosion went berserk. One moment he was quietly drinking a beer, the next he was thrashing around on the floor screaming.

"All my buddies are dead," he sobbed. "They're dead!" The Marine had been sleeping inside an armored amphibious tractor parked outside the chow hall the morning of the bombing. His friends were sleeping inside the building, and he must have felt tremendous guilt because he alone had survived. Chase and some of the other guys tried to hold him down, but the Marine had superhuman strength. Two or three others grabbed his kicking legs, and Silone sat on his head to keep him from battering it against the floor.

"He's insane!" someone shouted. The Marine was frothing at the mouth and his body convulsed like an epileptic's.

"Don't let him swallow his tongue."

"Get a corpsman!" Someone rushed out of Branigan's to bring back medical help from MSSG. A corpsman arrived within a few minutes and injected the Marine with a sedative. The men who had been holding him down carried his limp body to a jeep, and the corpsman drove him to LZ Brown for evacuation to the ship.

"Poor guy," Nels said.

"He just snapped," someone else commented.

"I've never seen anything like it."

"What could make a man do that?"

I went back to the office to help Sergeant Edwards. We took turns typing most of the night. The adjutant and the legal officer sat at a table behind us updating the lists of dead and missing. The task was monumental. Each roster had to be reconstructed from partial listings, and maintining accuracy was of paramount importance. We checked and double-checked our work. Identifying a live Marine as dead was something we desperately wanted to avoid.

Gunny Thorn strode into the administration office sometime after dawn. He'd been digging, and soot covered his face. "I don't know how they'll ever identify some of the bodies," he said. "We lifted a slab off one. He was crushed and burned. There wasn't much more than a blackened shadow left, a handful of teeth and bone."

"There's so many gone," I said. "The roster of missing and dead is over 250 names long."

"While you've been typing names I've been digging bodies." I didn't say anything. "Where in the hell's Mudfart?" Gunny demanded. "Is he goofing off again?"

"Mudfart's dead, Gunny." Gunny stared at me unbelieving. I don't think the death he'd witnessed hit him until that moment.

"Dead? How?"

"I don't know. He's on the missing roster."

"Goddamn fool kid. Why did he have to go and die?" Gunny turned abruptly and fled the office.

Major Converse returned at ten that night. Ross and I were in the supply tent talking when Tolbert sashayed in. "Your dad's back," he announced.

I hurried to the COC. George was being briefed by Captain Kettering. I wanted to give George a big hug and tell him how happy I was that he was back. I made do with a half-squeeze of his arm. "I understand you've had a bit of a rough time," he said.

"Yes, sir," I answered, trying to keep my voice steady. I didn't want Major Converse to know I was on the verge of crying. "Have you been to the BLT yet, sir?"

"I haven't had a chance."

"It's devastating."

"We'll pull through okay. Marines always do."

"Yes, sir. Welcome back, sir." Feeling better, I went to the basement. I tried to sleep, but each time I closed my eyes I saw the wreckage. I didn't understand why the building drew me, but I couldn't stay away. I slipped on my boots and walked to the site. Nothing had changed: workers still dug with shovels and jackhammers under the glare of floodlights, the cranes slowly lifted slabs of concrete from the pile, more bodies were gently removed. Yet, the frantic pace had slowed. The workers moved a little more lethargically as they went about their grim task. Common sense dictated that there couldn't be any more survivors.

I don't know how long I stood there staring at the building. They found another Marine as I watched. Father Pucciarelli was standing in the morgue, and he crossed himself before anointing the Marine's forehead with oil. "In the name of the Father, the Son, and the Holy Ghost," I heard his voice waver. The corpsman sprinkled a preserving agent on the body before he zipped it into a bag. Father Pucciarelli looked tired and lost, and like the rest of us, I don't think he understood why such a monstrous thing had happened.

I went back to the command post. Lieutenant Davis had updated the roster with more confirmed dead, and I typed names into the computer until I could no longer focus my eyes. "Get some sleep," Sergeant Edwards insisted.

I walked toward the basement like a zombie. The green glow of the computer screen still swam before me, staring like a great baleful eye. The names I had typed clicked through my memory one by one: Hudson, Walker, Plymel, Hue.

I needed to talk with someone. Nels was sitting at his table in the basement, staring at the wall. His rack was in a dead-end corridor, and the end wall was dark red earth. Pictures of home littered his makeshift desk, and a fifties' pinup girl on a calender shyly smiled at me.

"I have trouble accepting it," I said. "I keep finding myself down there, staring at the building, thinking somehow it's going to be made whole again. That sickly sweet smell permeates everything. I was down there a little while ago, watching as they pulled out another body. He had turned dark brown, and his arms flopped as they carried him. The corpsman sprinkled on a white powder, and Zip! he was inside a body bag, neat and clean."

Nels directed his stare toward me. He handed me one of the beers he kept on his desk. I popped the top and took a sip of the heavy, bitter brew.

"I was in the chow hall, near the corner," he said. "The far corner where the wooden tables were. The wall had collapsed, and I was digging."

My body sank on Nels' rack. I tossed my helmet to the side and loosened the Velcro strips of my flak jacket. I couldn't remember the last time I'd taken it off.

"I found an envelope," Nels said. "It was addressed to Reynolds." Nels' left cheek trembled a bit. "I must have dug down a foot or so when I first heard that sound." Nels made a guttural noise, a gasping, horrid sound deep in his throat. "The sound was just like that," he said. "It can't be, I thought. I dug some more. I uncovered a hand and somehow knew it was him.

" 'Don't let it be!' I pleaded. But of course it was. He must have been drinking his morning coffee while reading letters from home. I kept digging and digging. Then his face was looking up at me, and he made that sound again.

" 'You're going to be okay,' I said. I knew I was lying, and I know he knew it too. I held his hand real tight. He was under a huge slab from the waist down and there wasn't any way I could get him out.

"I took a poncho liner and covered him so he wouldn't have to look at what had happened. The corpsman came and gave him a shot. I tried to get him out but I couldn't. There wasn't any way unless I could move the whole damn wall.

"He lived a long time. I held him as best I could. He kept making that sound. After a while he didn't make it any more, and he was dead. I just sat there, rocking him and holding his hand. I kept saying, 'It's going to be okay. It's going to be okay.'

"I know there's got to be a soul. There has to be. Otherwise it's so worthless."

I didn't say anything for a long time. "Did you feel him go?" I finally asked. "Did you feel the precise moment when his soul left his body?"

Nels didn't answer. I thought he might not want to, then he began to cry. "I didn't feel anything," he whispered. "He just died. He's dead. There isn't any soul. I tried to help him, but there wasn't anything I could do."

"I feel so empty," I said. "So worthless. I've learned something about myself that no one should ever have to face. I wasn't any good down there. I didn't help anyone. I saw all those dead men, and I fell apart. Maybe I could have saved someone if I would have been in control of my emotions, if I would have dug a little harder. Mudfart needed me, and I let him down. I let myself down."

Nels and I embraced. We didn't say anything; there wasn't anything more to be said.

I put on my helmet and tightened my flak jacket. The distant sound of jackhammers summoned me like a seductive siren's song, and I wearily climbed the basement stairs, drawn once again to the building.

       ❦   ❦   ❦

Ross thought he was being clever. Sitting outside the command post, he started singing the Alan Sherman parody at the top of his lungs as I walked by. I heard a faint "Muddah" and "Faddah," and then his voice crescendoed with "They're 'at Camp Grenada!'"

"What are you talking about?" I asked. It was early Wednesday morning, and I was coming from the basement.

"Guess you haven't heard the latest," he said. "Our fearless replacements aren't on their way to relieve us."

"Very funny."

"Funny but true. The U.S. has invaded Grenada. Some little island in the middle of the Caribbean was stormed by 22 MAU yesterday morning."

"You can't be serious."

"I wish I weren't."

"When are we going home?"

"We've been extended indefinitely. Maybe we'll never go home. Welcome to Beirut, Lebanon, the capital of the fifty-first state of the United States of America."

Ross' news didn't make any sense. I went into the Combat Operations Center and read the daily message board. Unfortunately, Ross was right. One of the messages explained that Grenada, some speck of land in the Caribbean I'd never heard of, was becoming a Soviet-Cuban base that threatened U.S. strategic interests in the area. Apparently, we had invaded on the pretext of rescuing American medical students at St. George's University. The message gave no indication of when the USS *Guam* and 22 MAU would leave the island to relieve us. I felt bewildered. Didn't anyone care how badly we wanted to go home?

The bad news spread quickly. Soon everyone was walking around the command post singing Ross' little ditty.

"This is probably the beginning of World War III," Nels said. "First Lebanon and now Grenada."

"Destroying the BLT wasn't a terrorist bombing," I commented. "It was an act of war. I wonder if it's going to end with a mushroom cloud over Moscow."

The commandant arrived from Washington later in the day. He had flown via Wiesbaden, Germany, to visit and award Purple Hearts to the wounded Marines who were recovering in the Air Force hospital there. Colonel Geraghty escorted the commandant to the BLT immediately after his helicopter touched down. There were swarms of press covering the visit. Cav later told me the commandant was very moved and watched silently as two more bodies were dragged from the rubble.

In the afternoon, the commandant announced that he wanted to speak with the enlisted troops. I went into the Officers and Staff Club with Ross. The small room was packed, and General Kelley had already started his speech. The news media were barred, but one crew had snaked a boom microphone over our heads to record the commandant's words.

The commandant had tears in his eyes as he told us a poignant story about a wounded Marine he'd met in Wiesbaden. "He had more tubes going in and out of his body than I have ever seen in one body," Kelley said. "When he heard me say who I was, he grabbed my camouflage coat, went up to the collar and counted the stars. He squeezed my hand and motioned for a piece of paper. One of the nurses handed me a note pad and a pen, and I gave them to him. On the paper he wrote the words Semper Fi."

Semper Fi is a shortening of the Marine Corps' Latin motto *Semper Fidelis*—always faithful.

"When I left the hospital," the commandant continued, "I realized I had met a great human being, and I took off those stars because at the time I felt they belonged more to him than to me.

"No other example I can give could ever hope to show the gallantry and heroism of you men standing here. I want you to know I'm proud of each and every one of you. You've done an admirable job under arduous circumstances, and your exceptionally fine performance personifies the highest traditions of the Marine Corps. I have no doubt that when historians look back upon your service in Lebanon, they'll remark 'Uncommon valor was a common virtue.'"

The commandant strode from the room. I wasn't sure if I was supposed to feel inspired. I felt too empty for that. Ross and I went into the operations office. The huge stack of paper recovered from the BLT confronted me. I had been given two privates from the new battalion to help, and the three of us began sifting through each piece of paper. I cried a lot. It didn't take much to cause my emotions to spill over: a photograph, a glimpse of a letter, part of a birthday card.

Marines from the companies on the perimeter began to line up outside the command post early in the evening. American Telephone and Telegraph had donated their overseas phone lines to allow each Marine a two-minute call home. The Marines who lived in the BLT had first priority, and by the time my turn came, it was almost 2:00 A.M.

The calls were made from the telephone in Father Pucciarelli's office, and two minutes was barely long enough to say, "Hey, I'm alive. Don't worry." But that two minutes made all the difference in the world. Some of the Marines emerged from the office with tears in their eyes, but all were smiling broadly, relieved that their loved ones in the States knew they were okay.

As the line inched closer to the door, I could hear the Marines ahead of me speak a few words of reassurance to their families.

"I'm all right. Honest, Ma. Please don't cry."

"No, I'm not in Granada, Grandmother. I'm in Beirut, Lebanon. Beirut, Grandmother, Beirut!"

"I don't want you to worry. I'm stubborn as hell and there's no way I'm going to get myself killed. You take care of Laura for me. I love you all."

Finally it was my turn. I stepped into the office and sat in the chair in front of Father Pucciarelli's desk. He handed me the receiver. "Don't hang up when you're done," he cautioned. "We don't want to lose the overseas operator."

I put the receiver to my ear and heard the operator ask for my number. I gave it to her, and a few seconds later my parent's telephone was ringing.

"Hello?"

"Mom, it's me."

There was a sigh of relief. "Are you all right?"

"Yes, but I can only talk a minute. I just want you to know I'm alive."

"We saw you on the news Monday night."

"Good. Everything's okay now. It's pretty scary, but don't worry. I love you. Always remember that, no matter what happens."

"We love you too. Here's your father."

"I'm okay, Dad," I said when I heard his voice.

"Come home, Son."

"I will." The line went dead. I handed the receiver to Father Pucciarelli and gave my seat to the next Marine in line.

My parents know I'm alive, I rejoiced. What I didn't know was that they had spent two sleepless days watching every television newscast, searching for my face on the screen with a magnifying glass. The vigil of so many others did not end as happily.

        ♘   ♘   ♘

Ben staggered back to the command post from LZ Brown on Thursday. He'd been working nonstop since the bombing and was exhausted. We almost collided head-on in the parking lot.

"How was everything at LZ Brown?" I asked.

"I saw Mudfart."

"Are you sure it was him?"

Ben nodded. "He had on his striped basketball shorts. Bradley and I put him in a body bag."

"I don't think I could have handled seeing him."

"It wasn't easy. None of it was. We filled four transfer cases with nothing but arms and legs. You should see the stacks of aluminum cases in the hangar. There's pallet after pallet. A C-130 cargo plane took some out, but there's still a lot left."

"The total count's close to two hundred and they're still digging them out. I didn't believe Mudfart's name belonged on that list until now. I still can't believe he's gone."

"Remember Red in the chow hall?" Ben asked. "He was always getting into trouble. I put him in a body bag too."

"This is all so senseless. Those men died for nothing."

"I know."

Word was passed a short time later that Vice President Bush was going to be inspecting the BLT. He had flown to Cyprus from Washington and was taking a helicopter to the *Iwo Jima*. Security was to be extraordinarily tight. Plans were made to stop traffic on the boulevard outside the compound, and a cordon of Marines, in addition to Bush's nine secret service agents, was to surround the vice president at all times. Staff Sergeant Summers made the rounds to find "volunteers" to act as security, and Ben was assigned as one of Bush's bodyguards.

"I'm too tired for this," Ben protested, but Summers wouldn't let him out of the duty.

Bush's jeep convoy roared into the compound later in the day. Colonel Geraghty showed him around the command post, and everyone was excited that the Vice President of the United States had arrived. Bush was a lot taller than I expected. He was wearing a flak jacket and helmet, and Colonel Geraghty introduced everyone in the operations office to him. The vice president was very personable, and after a few rounds of hand shaking, he left with his entourage for the BLT.

"Who was that anyway?" a lieutenant from the new battalion asked.

I assumed he was joking. "Anwar Sadat," I gibed.

"Oh."

"You mean you really don't know who that was?"

"No. Should I?"

"That was the Vice President of the United States!"

"Oh."

Poor Bush, I thought. It must be tough being number two. I stepped outside and watched as Bush, surrounded by bodyguards and a dozen cameras, strolled down the street toward the BLT. Bush surveyed the damage for fifteen minutes or so before flying to the Presidential Palace to meet with Amin Gemayel. He flew back to the *Iwo Jima* after the meeting and left Lebanon.

A lot of rumors floated around the compound after Bush's visit. That evening Ben and I walked to the shower tent at MSSG to wash the stink off our bodies. It was the first time since the bombing that the showers had been turned on, and the tent was crowded. I let the soothing water pour over my head as I listened to the conversations around me.

"They found someone alive today," one Marine said.

I knew that couldn't be true. A lot of the rubble had been cleared away, and it was unthinkable that someone could have survived five days trapped between the crushed floors.

"I heard they found a woman in there," someone else said.

"In one of the officer's quarters no less."

"Shuffles was killed too." Shuffles was the old Lebanese man who had sold candy and sodas. I knew he was dead. The old man's son had come to collect the body.

"Did you hear one of the Lebanese rescue workers was stoned to death?" someone asked.

"No."

"I heard they caught him wearing a bunch of wrist watches he'd been stealing off the bodies. Six or seven Marines grabbed him and beat him to death."

"I heard they caught one guy picking money out of the rubble. He had almost two thousand dollars."

I didn't know which stories to believe. I thought most were probably the results of wild speculation, but in Branigan's that night Space Chase insisted the rumor about the girl was true.

"I found her buried in the rubble," he said. "She had long, black hair, and some gunnery sergeant covered her with a poncho. He told me to forget what I'd seen."

"That sounds like bullshit," Hadley said.

"You can believe what you want. I think it was Liliane, that girl who worked in the Hey Joe."

"I heard she was a spy and took off for Syria," Hadley said. "But that's probably bullshit too."

Whether or not the rumors were true didn't matter. The reality was much more frightening. The intelligence section confirmed reports that three vehicles laden with explosives were cruising the neighborhood waiting to crash through another Marine barricade. There were other so-called martyrs out to get us as well. Some members of the Islamic Jihad had strapped explosives to their chests and planned to take us out individually if they could get close enough. One message I read said that a pro-Iranian group called Hizballah (Party of God) had a single-engine Cessna airplane full of explosives. As soon as a pilot was trained, the group was going to crash it into the command post.

Security around the compound intensified. The main entrance to the compound was closed and completely blocked with dirt-filled barrels and sandbags. A school bus and a shot up Chevrolet kept anyone from using the dirt road behind the Hey Joe, and all but the most essential Lebanese nationals were kicked out. The only way in and out of the compound was across the parking lot outside the BLT, and that route was heavily guarded by an amphibious tractor and a .50 caliber machine gun.

We were placed in an indefinite Condition I status. An additional rifle company, Echo Company, was sent from Camp Lejeune to provide extra security.

The French were no longer playing around either. Their death toll stood at fifty-eight. Moments after the BLT went up, a van bomb exploded outside a French barracks in the Ramlet al Bayda quarter of West Beirut. The eight-story building housed ninety-seven soldiers, and it toppled over like a house of cards. The French closed off several main roads around their outposts, ignoring the traffic jams and Lebanese protests.

The MAU's intelligence section appraised the Joint Chiefs of Staff in Washington of the situation with a brief. "To prevent suicide attacks, commando raids, suicide sappers [mines], and other terrorist threats," the brief stated, "all Multinational Force contingent positions have become virtual fortresses isolated from the mainsteam of the Lebanese population. [This is] the only recourse available to peacekeepers at this time."

Security is a nebulous thing, however. No matter how well prepared we were, it seemed there were always chinks in our armor that someone might be able to squeeze through. "The threat from everything stemming from infiltration commando actions to snipers to airborne kamikaze attacks," the brief warned, "make absolute, airtight security impossible."

My fear changed to anger as I read the second part of the intelligence section's report. It clearly explained that we were being used by the Lebanese: "The Lebanese Army has recently positioned itself between British Headquarters and Alpha Company for the purpose of firing into Hey es Sellom while initiating the engagement. The response has been for the militia to fire on Alpha Company, which is in front of the Lebanese Armed Forces' position. The Lebanese are using Alpha Company as a shield to fight the war in Hey es Sellom."

Marine lives were in jeopardy, and I felt heartened that our intelligence section had the courage to tell those back in Washington what was really going on. "This country is at war," the brief unequivocally stated.

> There is no cease-fire. Tactics have changed, but the artillery in
> the mountains continues. The Multinational Force is not the
> target of an Iranian madman suicide commando. The Multi-
> national Force is the target of a collective group of Syrian

surrogates and Syrian-dependent militias who are conducting a war, a terrorist war, against the French 11th Division paratroopers and the U.S. Marines. Negotiations will not advance peace because it is contrary to Syrian interests. The Multinational Forces will face a constant terrorist threat, and unless the military capability is increased, control of Beirut will soon be lost.

Fighting in the city resumed the next day. Alpha Company was hit by rocket-propelled grenades, and two Marines were wounded. By week's end, the wreckage of the BLT was almost completely dismantled. The death toll stood at 233, and only the bodies of those in the collapsed portions of the basement remained.

Sad stories circulated around the compound. The parents of Doctor Hudson, the BLT's medical officer, insisted they had seen their son tending to the wounded on television the morning of the bombing. When a navy chaplain in uniform knocked on their door to say, "The secretary of the Navy has asked that I inform you..." the family refused to believe it. Lieutenant Davis wrote a heartfelt letter in Colonel Geraghty's name expressing sympathy.

The mother of one Marine had sent her son a box of cookies a few days before the blast. The administration section received a message from Headquarters Marine Corps asking that the cookies be distributed to surviving Marines. "Ensure that the box is not returned to the Marine's family. The mother is adamant that she does not wish to see it again."

A pretty Lebanese girl dressed in black came to the administration office several times to make arrangements for her trip to the States. She had just married a BLT corpsman, and they had returned from a brief honeymoon the day before the bombing. I couldn't imagine how the corpsman had had time to meet—let alone fall in love and marry—someone, but the girl's grief seemed genuine. Each time she arrived, her eyes were red from tears.

Not all the stories that circulated around the compound were sad. Those of some of the survivors were recounted. One Marine who lived on the fourth floor was hurled from his window as he slept. He regained consciousness on the stairs behind the building with a broken ankle. Another Marine had gone outside for a drink of water seconds before the blast and was spared. The four Marines assigned to guard duty on the roof managed to ride the collapsing building down, escaping serious injury. Each one that survived could count himself among the lucky few.

I spent the latter part of the week sorting through the remaining paper recovered from the building. After the secret documents were accounted for, we built a huge bonfire behind the command post and burned everything.

I still found myself haunting the BLT at all hours. Only the first-floor superstructure and the columns that supported it remained; all the other rubble had been cleared away. A rope with a KEEP OUT sign hanging from it encircled the bomb crater. The FBI had arrived and was sifting through the debris at the bottom with a fine mesh screen, looking for any remaining pieces of the truck.

The last body was dug out of the basement on 31 October, exactly a week and a day after the blast. It was number two hundred and forty-one. The sun was setting when they found him. I watched as a backhoe carefully dug in the section of the basement where the Battalion Aid Station had been.

"Ho!" someone shouted. I saw a hand sticking out of the dirt.

The backhoe stopped, and two Marines with shovels jumped into the pit. They dug slowly. The body was in a fetal position, and it took them a long time to uncover the legs. The smell of putrefied flesh was nauseating, and I wanted to leave. But I was unable to tear myself away; my body was riveted to the spot.

Occasionally, one of the Marines would tug on one of the dead man's legs to see if the rest of him was free. The Marines finally resorted to digging underneath the body with their hands, but the body refused to budge from the packed soil. Eventually, they used a shovel as a lever and managed to pry him lose.

I waited until they gently placed him into a body bag before I slowly walked to the command post.

VI
Aftermath

15

CONGRESS WAS IN an uproar. "Our Marines have been placed in an untenable situation, and I think it's criminal," Texas Democrat Sam Hall was quoted as saying in *Time* magazine. Senator Robert Byrd of West Virginia insisted, "A nation cannot wear two hats, one being that of a peacekeeping force and the other being that of taking sides with one of the warring factions." Pennsylvania Republican Joe McCade stated, "There's a real need to clarify our policy and to explain exactly what the administration's goals are." Suddenly everyone was an expert on what had gone wrong in Lebanon.

"I can tell you exactly what went wrong," Nels said in Branigan's. "We were put in a lousy position right from the start."

"Everyone in Washington is screaming about the lack of security and how vulnerable the BLT was," Chase said. "Funny how none of the dozens of congressmen here on 'fact-finding missions' mentioned it before now."

"Everyone's got 20/20 vision in hindsight," I commented. "It's so easy to profess wisdom after the fact, but where were all these self-proclaimed experts before the BLT was blown up?"

"I wonder what's going to happen to Colonel Geraghty," Chase said.

"That's easy," Nels answered. "His career is over. There'll be a lot of investigations and reports. Then someone will pronounce official judgment on the colonel. They've always got to find a scapegoat for things like this, and Colonel Geraghty's going to be it."

"It's not his fault the BLT was destroyed," Chase insisted. "It's almost impossible to stop a determined suicide attack. If the BLT hadn't been blown up, then some other Marine position would have been."

"That may be true," Nels said, "but they still need a scapegoat."

One thing was certain; the Marines were going to remain in Lebanon. In a press conference, President Reagan told the American people, "These deeds make so evident the bestial nature of those who would assume power if they could have their way and drive us out of [Lebanon]. We must be more determined than ever that they cannot take over that vital and strategic area of the earth or for that matter any other part of the earth." Even Tip O'Neill, the Democratic Speaker of the House, supported the president's position. "This is not the time," O'Neill said, "to cut and run."

The consensus in Branigan's was the same. "We can't let the terrorists push us out of Lebanon now," Nels said. "If we do, the death of the men in the BLT will have been in vain."

"I say we should nuke Damascus," Chase said. "The Syrians had to be behind the bombing."

"Nuke Teheran too," Hadley chimed in. "The Iranians have blood on their hands. The terrorists were too well equipped. You don't go to a local drug store and buy a couple of tons of TNT. That takes the support of a government."

Beckford agreed. "As long as there's a possibility of making an overall peace plan work," he said, "we've got to stay."

"Fuck peace," Chase argued. "We should be in the Chouf burying the bastards that blew up the BLT. We've got one choice—retaliate!"

"We don't know who's responsible," Beckford said. "Who do you want to retaliate against?"

"Don't give me that 'we don't want to hurt any civilians' shit," Chase said sarcastically. "There aren't any civilians in Lebanon."

"No matter what the U.S. does," Nels said, "we'll be accused of imperialism. I think we should show the rest of the world just how imperialistic the United States can be. The only way this country is ever going to have peace is if we shove it down their throats."

"Yeah!" Chase exclaimed. "And I'd like to start shoving right now with a couple of M-60 tank rounds."

I didn't know which course the United States should follow. It was clear that sending the Marines home would be a victory for the terrorists; that was exactly what they wanted. But sending more Marines ashore with vengeful retaliation on their minds would only further draw the U.S. into Lebanon's chaotic civil war. I agreed that our role had to be changed. We needed a clear-cut mission, not one of mere symbolic presence, and unless we were given something useful to do we would continue to founder in Lebanon's quagmire. The longer we stayed, the more inevitable it became that other Marines would die.

The American people stood firmly behind us, no matter how they perceived our mission. Within a week after the destruction of the BLT, the MAU began receiving thousands of letters from concerned people in the U.S. I was surprised by the outpouring. Entire classes of school children sent poems and cards they had made. Someone started "Operation Cookie," and the Marines began receiving hundreds of boxes of homemade baked goods.

The mail clerks were no longer bombarded with questions about the low volume of mail. Instead we were swamped, and each Marine was given a handful of letters to open at every mail call. Most of the letters were addressed to "A Marine. Beirut, Lebanon," and almost all were supportive. One I opened was from a ten-year-old fifth grader named Corina. "Hope you get well soon," she wrote, "and that you come home. I know what you are going through. I hope the violence stops soon. Be careful please. I [am] sorry to hear that a lot of people died."

Another letter was signed simply, "Just a guy in California." His letter warned of the threat of communism. "I can't imagine what kind of life you must have there being surrounded by religious fanatics who have been brainwashed since birth with anti-American propaganda. Though we are criticized for our military interventions, if we didn't respond when asked, the world would surely be lost to communism. Democracy will prevail with the aid of your efforts and those of your fallen comrades. They will never be forgotten."

I found one letter buried at the bottom of a box of cookies mailed from Hampton, Virginia:

Young American,

These few cookies are small payment for the sacrifices you are making for the cause of freedom in Lebanon, in the Middle East, and ultimately in the entire world. They were made with the loving hands of an American mother much like your own who shares her anxieties about your safety.

Our hearts are saddened as we grieve with you over the senseless loss of your comrades. It is to your credit that you remain steadfast in your resolve to successfully complete your mission. We want you to know that you have earned our unending gratitude and respect and that you are in our prayers.

Our Love, The Hill Family

Security around the compound continued to be tightened. The boulevard to the airport was reduced to one lane of traffic, and anti-tank ditches were dug at strategic points around the compound. An obstacle course of earthen dams was built across the BLT's parking lot, preventing direct access to Marine positions. To leave the compound, all jeeps had to drive down the twisting, one-lane roadway between the piles of dirt.

Colonel Geraghty ordered that all headquarters personnel be dispersed. Captain Kettering and some of the other officers moved out of their quarters in the command post and into an unused maintenance building next to the ruins of the BLT. All nonessential personnel were ordered back to the *Iwo*. I laughed at Gunny Thorn's scowl when Major Converse informed him he was no longer needed ashore.

Most of the supply clerks and a third of the communicators were declared nonessential. They piled into the back of a flatbed truck one morning with their gear, and Ben and I waved goodbye as Wheebles, Lieutenant Block, Gunny Thorn, Scaly, and some of the others left.

"I'm sorry to see them go," Ben said. "We won't have Lieutenant Block to make fun of anymore."

"I hope our turn comes soon," I said. "I'm beginning to wonder if I'll ever leave Lebanon."

"22 MAU's got to pull out of Grenada eventually. I heard that the relief-in-place has been scheduled for the seventeenth."

"I'll believe it when it happens."

While the Marines were beefing up security, the commandant was testifying before the Senate and House Armed Services Committees. "Was security adequate?" the commandant was asked.

"It was adequate to meet what any reasonable and prudent commander would have expected prior to dawn on Sunday, 23 October 1983," the commandant said in his opening remarks to the joint committee. "If you were to ask me whether the security around the [BLT] headquarters building was adequate to protect the occupants against a five-ton Mercedes truck carrying five thousand pounds of explosives at high speed—my answer would be No!

"If you were to ask me, on the other hand, would a reasonable and prudent commander have sufficient cause to suspect such a threat from intelligence sources available to him—again, the answer would be No!"

I admired the commandant for supporting Colonel Geraghty, but I wondered why our intelligence gathering system had failed so catastrophically. The news media reported that Colonel Geraghty had received a warning of the truck bomb a few days before the BLT was destroyed. That wasn't quite true. At Colonel Geraghty's weekly military coordination meeting on 19 October, a list of suspected vehicles loaded with explosives, complete with descriptions of the cars and license plate numbers, was disseminated. Since the Marines' arrival in Beirut, however, over one hundred potential car bombs had been identified. No special action was taken other than to pass a copy of the list to the sentries on duty. Kamikaze attacks or the possiblity of a large truck bomb were not discussed. The need to do so simply never occurred to anyone.

The commandant reached a bitter conclusion during his testimony. "I do not believe," he said, "that we can ever create an effective passive capability that can counter all forms of terrorism in Lebanon or anywhere else."

The House Armed Services Committee sent an investigative subcommittee of five congressmen to Beirut to probe into the circumstances that led to the truck bombing. The Pentagon also began an inquiry, and a day after the subcommitee arrived, the Long Commission—three generals from the U.S. Air Force, Army, and Marine Corps headed by a retired Navy admiral—flew in to question Colonel Geraghty. Other high-ranking officers were interviewed, and Major Converse prepared a lengthy report on security procedures for both teams of investigators.

Three months later, after eight days of hearings in Washington during November and December, the House subcommittee issued a 654-page report highly critical of military officials for failing to protect the Marines. The Long Commission eventually recommended that disciplinary action be administered to the top commanders. That meant official blame was to be placed on Colonel Geraghty; Captain France, the Navy officer in command of the ships; and Lieutenant Colonel Larry Gerlach, the surviving commander of the Battalion Landing Team. President Reagan rejected the Long Commission's recommendation, however, stating that the officers "have already suffered quite enough." Nevertheless, on 9 February 1983, Secretary of Defense Caspar Weinberger issued "nonpunitive letters of instruction" to Geraghty and Gerlach.

Colonel Geraghty was stoic throughout the investigation. The few times I saw him in the command post, he wore a mask of composure. Colonel Geraghty always struck me as being too hard on himself, and I knew that deep down he would never forgive himself for the deaths of the men in the BLT. The enlisted troops still highly respected him. They realized that as commander of the Marines ashore Colonel Geraghty was ultimately responsible for every action, good or bad. "That's why he gets paid the big bucks," Nels reminded us. But at the same time, the troops couldn't help but feel the colonel was getting the shaft.

The attitude of some of the investigators didn't help. Silone picked up one of the armed services subcommittee members at LZ Brown. "You'll never believe how stupid that congressman was," Silone said later in Branigan's. "When I drove past the wreckage of the BLT, he asked me if it was part of an overpass from an old highway. I wanted to slap him. 'No, sir,' I said, giving him the most hateful look I could muster. 'That's a monument to the 241 men killed.'"

"What did he say?" Hadley asked.

"Nothing. He was in his own world. What we've gone through here doesn't mean a damn thing to him."

          ॐ   ॐ   ॐ

The weather changed in November. The rainy season had started, and the clear, hot days of October were replaced for the most part by overcast skies and drizzle. The fighting in the hills continued as the factions attempted to improve their positions and resupply. It was common for small groups of militiamen to patrol along the perimeter at night and attack Marine positions with sniper fire and rocket-propelled grenades. Echo Company, the new Marines on the block, got their first taste of combat when they were hit with machine gun fire on the evening of 4 November.

The Israelis were hit hard that same day. An outpost in southern Lebanon near Tyre was leveled by a car bomb, killing several Israeli soldiers. It was another suicide attack, and the driver of the bomb went up with the outpost. The Israelis immediately retaliated, and we could see their planes as they made bombing runs on Muslim positions in the Chouf.

"That's what we should have done," Chase commented. "The Israelis don't care if they get those responsible or not, but at least they take action."

Echo Company got hit by snipers the next night. The Marines returned fire, but the militiamen in Hey es Sellom were unconcerned. The pot shots directed at Echo Company continued until dawn.

On the morning of the sixth, 22 MAU's advance party flew into Beirut International. Ben and I celebrated by dancing a jig in the office. 22 MAU's combat role in Grenada was over, and USS *Guam* had set sail for the Middle East. The relief-in-place schedule was confirmed; I'd be leaving Lebanon on 17 November.

The arrival of the 22d MAU aboard a U.S. C-141 airplane provided the militias with another chance to attack. The intelligence section obtained information that one of the Muslim factions had a SA-7 surface-to-air missile and planned to destroy the C-141. A missile-firing team was moving into position at the southern end of the airport to fire on the plane, but with the advance warning, the plane quickly reloaded and took off to the north. Subsequent intelligence reports confirmed that the action had foiled the attack, and as a result all U.S. planes were prohibited from landing at Beirut International.

I had my first hot meal in over two weeks that night. I was working at my desk in the office when Ben poked his head around the door. "There's hot food behind the CP," he announced.

"Great! Just in time to avert an MRE overdose." I grabbed my flak jacket and helmet and followed Ben behind the command post. Staff Sergeant Farley, a wireman who worked in the communications section, had appointed himself chief cook. He had mixed several miscellaneous cans of food sent ashore by *Iwo Jima* into a large pot and was heating it over a fire.

Ben and I grabbed a paper plate and plastic spoon, and Farley gave each of us a scoop of something he called his "secret recipe." It looked pretty unappetizing. I thought I recognized corn and lima beans somewhere in the mixture, but I couldn't be positive.

"Does this stuff have a name?" I asked.

"It's called mulligan stew," Farley answered. "It's easy to make. Whatever you can find goes into the pot."

I took a tentative bite. Farley must have poured in two bottles of Tabasco sauce. The stuff was hot.

"Not bad," I said, "but I think I'm going to need to wash this down with about a gallon of water."

Ben and I went back to the office and mixed a package of MRE crackers into our stew. "I wonder what's on the menu for tomorrow night," Ben said.

"Want to bet it's mulligan stew?"

The following night the stew was wildly different. There didn't seem to be any reasoning behind the types of foodstuffs the ship sent us. That day we had received two cans of beef stew and an assortment of succotash, pork and beans, and boiled potatoes. Farley had mixed everything together, and as the mulligan stew bubbled in the pot, it looked like it might make a good varnish remover.

"Maybe you weren't supposed to mix this stuff together," I suggested to Farley.

"Nonsense," he said. "This stew is better than anything you'd find in a restaurant. Trust me." Farley dished out Ben and me a huge ladle.

"I hope it doesn't eat a hole through the paper plate," Ben said.

I took a handful of cookies from the box next to the eating utensils. With Operation Cookie in full swing, there were always plenty of sweets to load up on. I shoved the cookies into my right front pocket.

The Marine positions had been hit with scattered small arms fire most of the day. The intensity of the fighting had grown throughout the afternoon, and by the time Ben and I were being served dinner it sounded like a small war had started. A sniper began firing on the command post from a nearby rooftop, and I could hear rounds zinging by overhead. Farley decided to cut short his experiment in cooking and bolted for the foxhole next to the communicator's tent.

"Think we can make it to the basement?" Ben asked.

"Discretion's supposed to be the better part of valor," I said. "We better get in a hole."

Ben and I ran for a foxhole fifty feet away, carefully balancing our plates in one hand while carrying our M-16s in the other. Ben scrambled in first. The foxhole wasn't bad. Fairly comfortable, it had a plywood floor and two bench seats someone had removed from the back of a jeep. The hole was big enough to hold four or five, but Ben and I were the only ones who had jumped in.

There wasn't anything to do but wait. Ben and I started eating our mulligan stew. Staff Sergeant Farley had outdone himself with the

Tabasco sauce. The stew was like eating fire. "I wish I had a drink of water," I said. I began to hear the pitter-patter of raindrops striking the sandbag roof of the foxhole.

"Now you've done it," Ben said.

I tossed my empty paper plate out of the foxhole's entrance and started eating the cookie crumbs in my pocket. It began to rain harder, and the fighting increased in intensity. The machine gun fire sounded particularly close, and after a few minutes artillery shells started falling. The explosions were close and shook the ground.

It was dark in the foxhole, but I could see Ben flinch at every explosion. I knew I was doing it too. Ducking at loud noises had become second nature over the months, and on more than one occasion I had found myself automatically diving for the ground when I heard the whine of an artillery shell passing overhead.

"I've had as much of this as I can stand," Ben said. The intensity of Ben's voice surprised me. Normally he was very collected, even during the heaviest of fighting.

A particularly close explosion shook the hole, and a light dusting of sand fell from the roof. "Damn, that was close," Ben said. "Look outside and see if the command post is still there."

"The explosion wasn't that close, Ben."

"Just look for heaven's sake. I have this awful feeling we're going to be picking bodies out of rubble again."

I peeked out of the entrance of the foxhole. The command post was still intact, and I could see light coming from the Combat Operations Center. "Don't worry. It's still there, Ben. It's starting to rain harder now."

"I hate the Marine Corps," Ben said. "I hate my life."

Ben's tone scared me. I always looked to him for solace. His calm had comforted me more than once when I thought the end had come, but I had never seen him so frightened. "Don't freak out on me now," I cautioned. "We'll pull through this okay. We're going home soon."

"That's what they thought down at the BLT. Now they're all dead."

"We will go home. We will."

"I don't think we are."

"We've only got ten days left. Nothing's going to happen in the next ten days."

"I have this visual image of Dan Rather. He's sitting behind his news desk with a solemn expression on his face saying, 'For the second time in two weeks the Marines in Lebanon were wiped out by a truck bomb.' "

"There's no way anyone can get through our security now."

"They'll be pulling my body out of the wreckage next."

"Don't think about that. Just think about home."

The incoming shells continued to explode around us for another half hour. After a while I heard the thump-whine of outgoing artillery rounds. "We're firing back," Ben said.

"Sounds like it's coming from the west. It must be Lebanese Army artillery."

"I don't care who it is as long as they aren't aiming at me."

Ten minutes later it started to hail. The guns that had been firing on us for the past hour fell silent first. The outgoing artillery stopped soon after, and the only sound was that of the driving rain as it hit the roof of the foxhole. Ben and I crawled out of the hole.

"We made it," I said. Ben draped his arm around my shoulder, and the two of us trudged through the mud and rain to the basement.

Alpha Company pulled back from its position at the Lebanese University library the next morning. The operation had actually started the previous day with the positioning of empty five-ton trucks at the American Embassy and other points in the city. The truck convoys were kept small to avoid calling attention to the Marine exodus, and at 0135 on the morning of the eighth, the operation began when the previously staged vehicles converged on Alpha Company. The Marines loaded all their equipment and supplies into the trucks, and the strategic position that had been the site of so much fighting was returned to the Lebanese Army's control.

By 0600, the Marines from Alpha Company had arrived at the airport without incident. They were a motley crew, tired and filthy. With the exception of the BLT headquarters, Alpha Company had been hit the hardest. All the Marines killed before the bombing had been assigned to Alpha, and death seemed to follow the company each time it was redeployed along the perimeter. At ten o'clock the men of Alpha saw Beirut for the last time. They boarded a landing craft docked at the beach and were taken to their ship, the USS *Harlan County*.

I spent my last week in Lebanon packing. Cleaning the mount-out boxes and field desks alone was a big job, but Ben helped me carry everything outside to the parking lot. The boxes and desks were secured to pallets with steel bands, and a forklift loaded the gear onto a five-ton truck. CH-53 helicopters would fly the pallets to the ship. The two remaining supply clerks were busy conducting an inventory to insure that a proper accounting of equipment and vehicles was made. The office was curiously empty afterwards. All that remained were a single mount-out box for last-minute items and a few chairs.

We celebrated the Marine Corps' birthday on the tenth. No matter where in the world Marines serve, they always mark the anniversary of the Corps' founding and have done so since 1775. The MAU headquarters held a cake-cutting ceremony in front of the command post, and as is custom, the youngest and oldest Marine in the unit were served the first slice. The press was out in full force, and Colonel Geraghty read a congratulatory message from the commandant. The message was about pride.

"Pride is an eighteen-year-old recruit when he is called Marine for the first time," Colonel Geraghty read. "Pride is our predecessors at Belleau Wood, Iwo Jima, Inchon, Hue City, or any other battle where uncommon valor was a common virtue. Pride is standing in harm's way in Lebanon so that others less fortunate can find peace. And, finally, pride is what draws together those of us who have earned the title 'Marine' to celebrate our 208th birthday."

Sporadic small arms fire against the Marines continued. The engagements were usually brief, and no serious attacks were launched against us. It rained off and on all week, and there was no doubt that the bad weather had at least slowed the fighting. The final incident of violence directed against the Marines of 24 MAU occured near midnight on the fifteenth. A car stopped on the highway near Bravo Company's position, and a man jumped out and threw a hand grenade at the Marine sentry on duty. The Marine fired eight rounds at the car as it sped away; the grenade exploded harmlessly.

The five-ship flotilla of the 22d Marine Amphibious Unit arrived on the morning of the seventeenth, and the relief-in-place began in earnest. The men of Battalion Landing Team 2/8 assumed responsibility as the ground combat element from BLT 1/8 at two o'clock in the afternoon. By eleven that night, all elements of the 24th Marine Amphibious Unit had boarded their ships.

Silone was the driver of the jeep I took to LZ Brown for my helicopter ride to the *Iwo Jima*. Only a handful of enlisted troops remained on shore, a few communicators, and Colonel Geraghty's personal driver. Archie was taking care of last-minute details for Staff Sergeant Summers. As I tossed my sea bag and ALICE pack into the back of the jeep, I noticed Archie had a can of yellow spray paint. He was writing something on the parking lot's pavement.

"What are you doing, Archie?" I asked.

"I'm painting a giant bull's-eye. I hope this hellhole takes a direct hit."

Ben came out of the command post and tossed his gear into the jeep. I got into the passenger seat next to Silone, and Ben climbed in back. "Let's go," I said.

Silone took a right out of the parking lot, and we drove down the hill and past the wreckage of the BLT. A stretcher left by the Red Cross had been placed upright on its end near the corner of the building to serve as a gravestone. Flowers were arrayed around its base.

"Goodbye, Mudfart," I whispered. "Goodbye."

Silone drove out of the compound, and we raced down the boulevard to LZ Brown. Marines from 22 MAU were still flying in by helicopter. Fresh from their triumph in Grenada, they seemed very sure of themselves, almost cocky. But Lebanon wasn't like Grenada. Halfway across the Atlantic, we would learn that eight Marines were killed when a single artillery shell landed directly on top of their rooftop bunker. Another four would die in combat before the 22d Marine Amphibious Unit was withdrawn from Lebanon.

22 MAU assumed full responsibility as the U.S. Contingent of the Multinational Force at twelve noon, 19 November. I was standing in the lunch line on the hangar deck of the *Iwo Jima* when the official announcement was made. There was a short whistle blast, and the captain of the ship came over the intercom. "Gentlemen," he said. "It gives me great pleasure to announce the following order. Ensign, set a course for 270 degrees west. Full speed ahead!"

Everyone began to cheer, and the Navy's song blasted over the intercom, "Anchors aweigh, my boys, anchors aweigh!" Everyone started singing and pounding one another on the back.

Home. We were going home.

Epilogue

A LITTLE OVER A year later I got out of the Marine Corps. For a brief moment I considered reenlisting. I knew I would miss the camaraderie and feeling of belonging to something bigger than myself, but I also realized another chapter of my life had ended, and that it was time to move on. My departure from Camp Lejeune was quiet; there was no celebration, no pomp, or ceremony, such as what had occasioned the return of the MAU from Beirut a year before.

After eighteeen days at sea, the 24th Marine Amphibious Unit had sailed into Morehead City amid the fanfare of brass bands and cheering crowds. We were heros. The mayor presented Colonel Geraghty with the key to the city. People standing along our bus route to Camp Lejeune waved American flags as we passed, and yellow ribbons tied around street lamps and trees fluttered in the breeze. Dozens of marquees and billboards proclaimed, WELCOME HOME 24 MAU! It was probably the first time since the end of World War II that the American people had publicly cheered a group of returning combat veterans.

A special parade and ceremony was held in our honor on Camp Lejeune. The entire MAU stood at attention in the middle of the parade field while the commandant marched by and inspected the troops. There had been some speculation that President Reagan might attend the ceremony, but with the presidential election less than a year away the campaign was already heating up. The United States' foreign policy in Lebanon had not been an overwhelming success, and I suppose Reagan wanted to call as little attention to it as possible.

I stood at parade rest while the commandant made a few prepared remarks. He reiterated the president's words: "Let us close ranks in tribute to our fallen heros. They are now part of the soul of this great country and will live as long as our liberty shines as a beacon of hope to all those who long for freedom and a better world." The commandant ended his speech with a surprising announcement. By direction of the secretary of the Navy, the men of 24 MAU were being awarded the

Combat Action Ribbon. After so many denials that the Marines were engaged in combat, it was a relief that the truth had finally been publicly admitted. Later the MAU was awarded the Navy Unit Commendation. The citation stated that we had "displayed exceptional courage, resolve, and flexibility in providing. . . conditions in which the duly constituted Government of Lebanon could survive."

"That's funny," Nels said. "I thought all we did was get shot at."

I flew home to see my parents the weekend after our return. I finally achieved fame—at least for the fifteen minutes I was allotted before the press moved on to new stories. A crowd greeted me at the airport, and my mother rushed into my arms, tears in her eyes.

Several reporters questioned me, and a camera crew followed me home for an interview. I didn't discuss my bitterness. I didn't protest that I wasn't a hero and didn't deserve to be treated like one. I didn't say that the Marines had accomplished nothing in Lebanon but the senseless loss of life. I simply said I was happy to be home. I was treated gingerly, as though I might suddenly go berserk if reminded of Lebanon. Returning to Camp Lejeune and my Marine buddies was a relief.

Colonel Geraghty was under a great deal of pressure. He received threatening phone calls and spent the first few weeks after our return in seclusion with his wife and son. The executive officer had warned us about saying anything to the press. "I know you want to help Colonel Geraghty," he told us, "but it's best if you say nothing. Wait until the Long Commission delivers its report."

MAU headquarters began gearing up for another float. I was going back to Lebanon. The second trip was completely different from the first, however. Half of the MAU headquarters' personnel had been assigned to new units. Gunny Thorn left for his new post with the Tenth Marine Regiment, and another lance corporal was assigned to take Mudfart's place. We no longer had Wheebles or Lieutenant Block to laugh at, and with Nels and Beckford gone our political discussions stopped. Colonel Geraghty was needed for testimony in Washington, and Colonel Myron Harrington became our new commanding officer.

I never set foot in Beirut again. Bowing to political pressure, President Reagan ended the United States' commitment to the Multinational Peacekeeping Force on 27 February 1984, and Beirut International Airport was returned to the control of the Lebanese

Armed Forces. The British withdrew their troops on 8 February, and the Italians left twelve days later. The Lebanese Army was in ruin. Down to 40 percent of its authorized strength, most of the soldiers had gone home or had deserted to the Muslim militias.

A single rifle company remained in Beirut to provide security at the American Embassy. The company was withdrawn in August, and less than a month later, on 20 September, Muslim extremists drove a truck full of explosives into the newly built embassy annex, killing eight people. I was on board USS *Nassau* as it sailed up and down the coast of Lebanon.

My second return to the United States was much less triumphant than the first. Lebanon was becoming old news, and although the fighting among the militias continued, the Marines were no longer involved. U.S. policy in Lebanon had been a catastrophic failure. We were eventually driven out, and those who had fought so hard to see us leave emerged the victors. The civil war continued, and civilian Americans still in the country were kidnapped one by one by the Islamic Jihad. Their fate remains unknown. The tactics of the war had changed again, and the United States remained completely powerless to stop the conflict in Lebanon.

I left Camp Lejeune in January 1985. My last official act as a Marine was to pay a visit to the Beirut Memorial. A brass and marble monument had been built on a grass slope overlooking New River. The names of all those killed were inscribed on it, and I ran my finger down the etched list, saying goodbye.

My trial by fire was complete, and it was time to move on to new engagements with life. The Marines had died in vain, but I hoped there was some purpose, some meaningful and enduring reason for their sacrifice. I could think of none.

I got into my car and headed west.

In Memory

Marines

Cpl Terry Hudson
Prichard

PFC James Price
Attala

PFC Bill Stelpflug
Auburn

Cpl Henry Townsend
Montgomery

LCpl Leonard Walker
Dothan

LCpl David Randolph
Siloam Springs

Cpl John Wolfe
Phoenix

LCpl Randall Garcia
Modesto

LCpl Luis Nava
Gardena

PFC Donald Vallone, Jr.
Palmdale

LCpl R. Dibenedetto
Mansfield Center

SSgt Thomas Smith
Middletown

LCpl Devon Sundar
Stanford

PFC Stephen Tingley
Ellington

LCpl Dwayne Wigglesworth
Naugatuck

PFC Michael Hastings
Seaford

DISTRICT OF COLUMBIA
Sgt Gilbert Hanton
Washington

FLORIDA

LCpl Clemon Alexander
Monticello

PFC John Blocker
Yulee

PFC Juan Comas
Hialeah

Sgt Robert Conley
Orlando

LCpl Brett Croft
Lakeland

Cpl William Gaines, Jr.
Port Charlotte

LCpl Ferrandy Henderson
Tampa

LCpl Nathaniel Jenkins
Daytona Beach

LCpl F. H. Kreischer III
Indialantic

Sgt Michael Lariviere
Perry

LCpl Paul Lyon, Jr.
Milton

PFC Jack Martin
Oveido

1stLt Clyde Plymel
Merritt

SSgt Patrick Prindeville
Gainesville

Sgt Juan Rodriquez
Miami

LCpl B. Sanpedro
Hialeah

LCpl Kirk Smith
Miami

LCpl Rodney Williams
Opa Locka

GEORGIA

LCpl Benjamin Fuller
Duluth

Sgt Val Lewis
Atlanta

Cpl Victor Prevatt
Columbus

PFC Jerryl Shropshire
Macon

LCpl Jeffrey Stokes
Waynesboro

ILLINOIS

PFC Melvin Holmes
Chicago

Sgt John Phillips, Jr.
Wilmette

PFC Eric Pulliam
East St. Louis

Cpl Gary Scott
Rankin

(ILLINOIS, cont'd.)

1stLt William Sommerhof
Springfield

LCpl Eric Sturghill
Chicago

LCpl Eric Walker
Chicago

INDIANA

PFC Danny Estes
Gary

SSgt Thomas Thorstad
Chesterton

IOWA

GySgt E. Kimm
Atlantic

KENTUCKY

PFC Sidney Decker
Clarkston

LCpl Virgil Hamilton
McDowell

Sgt Thomas Keown
Louisville

LOUISIANA

LCpl Lyndon Hue
Des Allemands

Pvt L. D. Trahan
Lafayette

MAINE

Cpl Bruce Howard
Strong

MARYLAND

PFC Charles Bailey
Berlin

Pvt Nathaniel Dorsey
Baltimore

LCpl D. M. Green
Baltimore

LCpl Jeffrey James
Baltimore

LCpl Ulysses Parker
Baltimore

PFC Horace Stephens
Capitol Heights

MASSACHUSETTS

PFC Bradley Campus
Lynn

PFC Michael Devlin
Westwood

(MASSACHUSETTS, cont'd.)

SgtMaj F. B. Douglass
Cataumet

LCpl Sean Gallagher
North Andover

LCpl Richard Gordon
Somerville

Cpl Steven Lariviere
Chicopee

PFC Thomas Perron
Whitinsville

MICHIGAN

LCpl Johansen Banks
Detroit

Cpl David Bousum
Fife Lake

Cpl Anthony Brown
Detroit

1stLt William Zimmerman
Grand Haven

MINNESOTA

LCpl Kevin Custard
Virginia

LCpl Thomas Lamb
Coon Rapids

Cpl John Olson
Sabin

LCpl John Tishmack
Minneapolis

MISSOURI
Cpl Joseph Moore
St. Louis

NEBRASKA
PFC Mark Helms
Dwight

NEW HAMPSHIRE
Sgt Alan Solfert
Nashua

NEW JERSEY

PFC William Burley
Linden

PFC Sean Estler
Kendall Park

WO1 Paul Innocenzi
Trenton

LCpl J. J. Langon
Lakehurst

Cpl Jeffrey Young
Morristown

PFC John Allman
Carlsbad

Cpl Alex Munoz
Bloomfield

Capt Joseph Boccia, Jr.
Northport

LCpl Jeffrey Boulos
Islip

Cpl Bret Corcoran
Katonah

Sgt Kevin Coulman
Seminary

LCpl Harold Gratton
Conoes

PFC John Ingalls
Interlaken

LCpl James Jackowski
S. Salem

LCpl Steven Johnes
Brooklyn

LCpl John McCall
Rochester

Capt Michael J. Ohler
Huntington

PFC Robert Olson
Lawtons

SSgt Alexander M. Ortega
Rochester

LCpl Mark Payne
Binghamton

PFC Terrence Rich
Brooklyn

LCpl Warren Richardson
Brooklyn

Cpl Paul Rivers
Brooklyn

PFC Scott Schultz
Keeseville

Cpl Ronald Shallo
Hudson

PFC Craig Stockton
Rochester

Cpl Dennis Thompson
Bronx

Cpl Obrian Weekes
Brooklyn

PFC Craig Wyche
Jamaica

1stSgt D. L. Battle
Hubert

GySgt Alvin Belmer
Jacksonville

PFC Stephen Bland
Midway Park

Cpl Richard Blankenship
Hubert

Cpl Leon Bohannon
Jacksonville

1stLt John Boyett
Camp Lejeune

(NORTH CAROLINA, cont'd.)

LCpl Bobby Buchanan, Jr.
Midway Park

Cpl M.E. Camara
Jacksonville

Cpl Charles Cook
Advance

LCpl Johnny Copeland
Burlington

Maj Andrew Davis
Jacksonville

MSgt Roy Edwards
Camp Lejeune

Cpl Steven Forrester
Jacksonville

SSgt Leland Gann
Camp Lejeune

SSgt Ronald Garcia
Jacksonville

LCpl David Gay
Jacksonville

SSgt Harold Ghumm
Jacksonville

LCpl William Hart
Jacksonville

Capt Michael Haskell
Camp Lejeune

Capt Paul Hein
Camp Lejeune

LCpl Douglas Held
Jacksonville

GySgt Matilde Hernandez, Jr.
Midway Park

Cpl Stanley Hester
Raleigh

GySgt D. W. Hildreth
Sneads Ferry

2ndLt Maurice Hukill
Jacksonville

MSgt Richard Lemnah
Camp Lejeune

2ndLt Donald Losey
Winston-Salem

LCpl Timothy McNeely
Mooresville

Maj John Macroglou
Jacksonville

Cpl Samuel Maitland
Jacksonville

SSgt Charlie Martin
Camp Lejeune

Pvt Joseph Mattacchione
Sanford

Cpl M. Mercer
Vale

LCpl Ronald Meurer
Jacksonville

Cpl Harry Myers
Whittler

1stLt David Nairn
Jacksonville

Cpl Ray Page
Erwin

GySgt John Pearson
Jacksonville

Sgt William Pollard
Jacksonville

GySgt Charles Ray
Camp Lejeune

(NORTH CAROLINA, cont'd.)

1stLt Charles Schnorf
Camp Lejeune

Capt Peter Scialabba
Morehead City

LCpl Thomas Shipp
Jacksonville

Capt Vincent Smith
Jacksonville

LCpl Thomas Stowe
Jacksonville

1stSgt Tandy Wells
Jacksonville

SSgt John Weyl
Jacksonville

GySgt Lloyd West
Jacksonville

Cpl Burton Wherland
Jacksonville

LCpl Johnny A. Williamson
Asheboro

OHIO

Cpl Terry Abbott
New Richmond

Cpl John Buckmaster
Vandalia

Cpl Paul Callahan
Lorain

PFC Marc Cole
Ludlow Falls

LCpl George Gangur
Cleveland

LCpl Bruce Hollingshead
Fairborne

Cpl Edward Johnston
Struthers

Cpl David Lewis
Garfield Heights

LCpl Stanley Sliwinski
Niles

LCpl Michael Spaulding
Akron

OKLAHOMA

CWO3 Richard Ortiz
Ft. Sill

1stLt Donald Woollett
Barthesville

PENNSYLVANIA

Cpl M. Arnold
Philadelphia

Cpl John Bonk, Jr.
Philadelphia

LCpl Curtis Cooper
North Wales

PFC Richard Fluegel
Erie

Sgt Robert Greaser
Lansdale

LCpl Thomas Hairston
Philadelphia

Cpl James McDonough
Newcastle

LCpl Richard Morrow
Clairton

(PENNSYLVANIA, cont'd.)

LCpl John Muffler
Philadelphia

Sgt Rafael Pomalestorres
Philadelphia

PFC R. A. Relvas
Philadelphia

LCpl Louis Rotondo
Philadelphia

LCpl John Spearing
Lancaster

LCpl Steven Wentworth
Reading

Sgt Allen Wesley
Philadelphia

Capt Walter Wint, Jr.
Wilkes-Barre

PUERTO RICO

PFC Louis Melendez
Puerto Rico

Cpl Pedro J. Valle
San Juan

RHODE ISLAND

LCpl Rick Crudale
Warwick

Cpl Timothy Giblin
N. Providence

LCpl Edward Iacovino, Jr.
Warwick

PFC Thomas Julian
Middletown

Cpl David Massa
Warren

LCpl James Silvia
Portsmouth

LCpl Edward Soares
Tiverton

LCpl Stephen Spencer
Portsmouth

SOUTH CAROLINA

Sgt Freddie Haltiwanger, Jr.
Little Mountain

SSgt Richard Holberton
Beaufort

LCpl Michael Sauls
Waterboro

GySgt Scipio Williams
Charleston

Capt William Winter
Fripp Island

TENNESSEE
SSgt John Bohnet
Memphis

TEXAS

LCpl David Brown
Conroe

LCpl Johnnie Ceasar
El Campo

LCpl Michael Fulton
Ft. Worth

PFC Timothy McMahon
Austin

VIRGINIA

LCpl Nicholas Baker
Alexandria

LCpl Richard Barrett
Tappahanock

LCpl James Baynard
Richmond

Cpl Michael Fulcher
Madison Heights

LCpl Warner Gibbs
Portsmouth

LCpl James Knipple
Alexandria

Cpl Robert McMaugh
Manassas

PFC J. B. Owen
Virginia Beach

Cpl Joseph Owens
Chesterfield

Cpl David L. Reagan
Virginia Beach

Cpl Eric Washington
Alexandria

WEST VIRGINIA

LCpl David Cosner
Elkins

LCpl Russell Cyzick
Star City

Cpl Timothy Dunnigan
Princeton

WISCONSIN

LCpl Randy Clark
Minong

LCpl Jesse Ellison
Soldiers Grove

LCpl David Gander
Milwaukee

LCpl Walter Kingsley
Wisconsin Dells

Marine
Name withheld at next
of kin's request

Marine
Name withheld at next
of kin's request

Navy

HM1 Ronny K. Bates
Aiken, SC

HN Jimmy R. Cain
Birmingham, AL

HM3 William D. Elliot, Jr.
Lancaster, PA

HM3 William B. Foster
Richmond, VA

HM3 Robert S. Holland
Gilbertsville, KY

HM2 Michael H. Johnson
Detroit, MI

HM2 George N. McVicker II
Wabash, IN

HMC George W. Piercy
Mt. Savage, MD

Lt James F. Surch, Jr.
Lompoc, CA

HN Jesse W. Beamon
Haines City, FL

HN Bryan L. Earle
Painesville, OH

HM3 James E. Faulk
Panama City, FL

ETC Michael W. Gorchinski
Evansville, IN

Lt John R. Hudson
Riverdale, GA

HM2 Marlon E. Kees
Martinsburg, WV

HM3 Joseph Milano
Farmington, NY

HM3 Diomeded J. Quirante
Calcoocan City, PR

HM3 David E. Worley
Baltimore, MD

Army

SP4 Marcus E. Coleman
Dallas, TX

Sgt Daniel S. Kluck
Owensboro, KY

SFC James G. Yarber
Vacaville, CA

Glossary of Military Terms and Acronyms

AH-1T	Sea Cobra Helicopter (Bell), specialized Marine gunship
AK-47	Soviet-made Kalashnikov submachine gun
ALICE pack	All-purpose Lightweight Individual Carrying Equipment pack
Alpha	Phonetic A
Amal	Shiite militia
BLT	Battalion Landing Team, Battalion Headquarters Building
Bravo	Phonetic B
CH-53	Sea Stallion Helicopter (Sikorsky), heavy assault helicopter
CH-46	Sea Knight Helicopter (Boeing Vertol), principal assault helicopter of the Marine Corps
Charlie	Phonetic C
CINCUSNAVEUR	Commander in Chief, U.S. Naval Forces Europe (pronounced sink-us-NAV-yur)
COC	Combat Operations Center
Cover	Marine Corps hat
CP	Command Post
CTF	Commander Task Force
Delta	Phonetic D
DIA	Defense Intelligence Agency
Druze	Muslim sect
Echo	Phonetic E
FA MAS	French 5.56mm Automatic Rifle
FASTAB	Field Artillery School's Target Acquisition Battery (U.S. Army)

Float	Deployment
FMFlant	Fleet Marine Force, Atlantic
Foxtrot	Phonetic F
Golf	Phonetic G
Green machine	IBM field computer
Grunt	Marine infantryman
Gunny	Gunnery sergeant
Head	Toilet
High-and-tight	Short haircut
HMM	Marine Medium Helicopter Squadron
Hotel	Phonetic H
IDF	Israeli Defense Force
India	Phonetic I
Juliet	Phonetic J
Kilo	Phonetic K
LAF	Lebanese Armed Forces
LF	Lebanese Forces (Phalange Militia)
Lima	Phonetic L
LPH	Landing Platform, Helicopter (Amphibious Assault Ship)
LZ	Landing Zone
MAC	Military Airlift Command
MAGTF	Marine Air Ground Task Force (pronounced MAG-taf)
MARG	Mediterranean Amphibious Ready Group
MAU	Marine Amphibious Unit
Mau-maus	Marines who complete a deployment or float
Medevac	Medical Evacuation
Mike	Phonetic M
M-198	U.S. 155mm howitzer cannon

MOS	Military Occupational Speciality
MRE	Meal, Ready-to-Eat
M-16	U.S. 5.56mm service rifle
M-60	U.S. 7.62mm machine gun
M-60A1	U.S. battle tank
MSSG	MAU Service Support Group
NCO	Noncommissioned Officer
Net	Communication Network
NLP	National Liberal Party (Christian faction)
November	Phonetic N
1-MC	Ship's intercom
OPSEC	Operational Security
Oscar	Phonetic O
Papa	Phonetic P
PFT	Physical Fitness Test
Phalange	Christian faction
PLO	Palestine Liberation Organization
Pos	Position
PSP	Progressive Socialist Party (Druze militia)
PT	Physical Training
Quebec	Phonetic Q
Rack	Marine Corps bed
ROE	Rules of Engagement
Romeo	Phonetic R
The 'Root	Marine name for the city of Beirut
S-4	Logistics and Supply Section
S-1	Personnel and Administration Section
S-3	Operations Section
S-2	Intelligence Section
SA-7	Surface-to-Air missile

Shiite	Muslim sect
Sierra	Phonetic S
Smaj	Sergeant major
SPIE rigging	Special Patrol Insertion Extraction rigging (pronounced spy)
Tango	Phonetic T
TARPs mission	Tactical Air Reconnaissance Photo mission
TOW	Tube-launched, Optically guided, Wire-controlled missile (pronounced toe)
Uniform	Phonetic U
Victor	Phonetic V
Whiskey	Phonetic W
X-ray	Phonetic X
Yankee	Phonetic Y
Zulu	Phonetic Z